America's Best Recipes

☆ ★ ☆

A 1992 HOMETOWN COLLECTION

America's Best Recipes

©1992 by Oxmoor House, Inc.
Book Division of Southern Progress Corporation
P.O. Box 2463, Birmingham, Alabama 35201

ISBN: 0-8487-1085-1
ISSN: 0898-9982

Manufactured in the United States of America
Second Printing 1992

Executive Editor: Ann H. Harvey
Director of Manufacturing: Jerry R. Higdon
Art Director: James Boone

America's Best Recipes: A 1992 Hometown Collection

Editor: Janice L. Krahn
Senior Foods Editor: Susan Carlisle Payne
Copy Editor: Donna Baldone
Editorial Coordinator: Kay Hicks
Editorial Assistant: Kelly E. Hooper
Director, Test Kitchen: Vanessa Taylor Johnson
Assistant Director, Test Kitchen: Gayle Hays Sadler
Test Kitchen Home Economists: L. Michele Brown,
    Elizabeth Tyler Luckett, Christina A. Pieroni, Kathleen
    Royal, Angie Neskaug Sinclair, Jan A. Smith
Senior Photographer: Jim Bathie
Senior Photo Stylist: Kay E. Clarke
Designer: Melissa Jones Clark
Layout Artist: Larry Hunter
Indexer: Mary Ann Laurens
Production Manager: Rick Litton
Associate Production Manager: Theresa L. Beste
Production Assistant: Pam Beasley Bullock

Project Consultants: Meryle Evans, Audrey P. Stehle

Illustrations by Dana Moore

Cover: *My Favorite Pound Cake (page 37), Cinnamon-Apple Jelly
(page 282), Clinton Pecan Classics (page 114), and Double
Chocolate Rebels (page 46).*

Frontispiece: *Meticulously carved into the granite cliffs of Mount
Rushmore in the Black Hills of South Dakota, the Shrine of
Democracy depicts four great presidents—George Washington,
Thomas Jefferson, Theodore Roosevelt, and Abraham Lincoln.*

Contents

Introduction

America's Best Recipes is a collection of the very best recipes contained in charitable cookbooks from communities across the country. The recipes have been donated by your friends, families, and neighbors to support a wide variety of worthwhile causes. Whether the goal is to provide student scholarships, build a Little League ballpark, put a new roof on a church, keep an opera company's piano tuned, or purchase new equipment for a hospital, each community cookbook sold helps organizations raise the funds to meet the needs of their communities.

To create *America's Best Recipes*, experienced food writers collected hundreds of community cookbooks from across the country. Then over 600 recipes were chosen to be tested in our test kitchen by home economists. Each recipe was carefully judged and rated, and only those receiving the highest ratings were included. Also, in an effort to use natural ingredients, we eliminated any recipes containing canned soups or packaged mixes.

Each year, *America's Best Recipes* devotes one chapter to a special subject. This year, we provide delicious answers to the question "What should I bring to the potluck?" We offer outstanding recipes for everything from hearty casseroles to feed-a-crowd sheet cakes in "America's Favorite Potluck Recipes." We hope this chapter will give you some fresh ideas and dependable new favorites to take along next time you are asked to a "bring-a-dish" gathering.

Whether polished and hardbound or handwritten and homespun, all of the cookbooks featured in *America's Best Recipes* were created with the same heartfelt purpose, yet each book has its own charm. We encourage you to review the Acknowledgments beginning on page 322 and order the cookbooks that catch your eye. You will experience the satisfaction that comes from knowing you have played a part in the fund-raising efforts of the organizations responsible for creating the unique community cookbooks that are a part of *America's Best Recipes*.

The Editors

America's Favorite Potluck Recipes

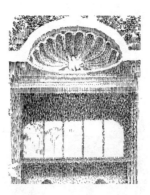

An inviting doorway welcomes passersby through the portals of a bygone era. Through the efforts of the Lincoln Park Conservation Association, houses such as this one located in the Mid-North district of Chicago, Illinois, are being authentically restored to preserve our architectural past. The high stairway from the front door to the sidewalk evolved as a result of flooding and the street level constantly being raised.

America's Favorite Potluck Recipes

Whether you call it a pitch-in dinner, a covered-dish supper, or a potluck party, the social practice of bringing along a favorite dish to combine with food from others has been popular for a long while. The covered-dish community supper dates back in American history to the days of barn-raisings and quilting bees when people worked together to produce a nourishing meal for the participants. Another form of potluck dining, the church supper, evolved as a means of raising funds for church repairs and expansion.

In today's world, you may be asked to B.Y.O.F. (bring your own food) to an office party, a neighborhood block party, a progressive supper, or a family reunion. Sooner or later you will probably contribute a dish to a wiener roast or other cookout. You may be inspired to build an entire meal around portable fare for a picnic in the park, an evening of casual entertaining, or a dinner for new neighbors. Whatever the occasion, the guidelines for creating the perfect potluck dish remain the same: the food should be flavorful and attractive as well as fairly economical to prepare, easy to transport, simple to serve, and stable at room temperature; if you can make the dish ahead of time, all the better.

As you plan your potluck meal, you will probably wonder where your friends and neighbors find the recipes for the delicious food they contribute to potluck suppers. Even the best cooks tend to second-guess themselves when asked to contribute to mealtime-get-togethers. In an effort to allay any panic and to raise your cooking confidence to new levels, we offer a collection of America's favorite potluck recipes. Here you will find the cherished, family-style recipes your friends and neighbors bring to P.T.A. meetings and church suppers. We have scoured the country's best community cookbooks to discover the most reliable and tasty potluck dishes from America's best cooks. Some recipes are simple and some a little more involved, but all are sure to be a hit at any function. All of the food will hold well, and can be easily transported and served. We have purposefully avoided the familiar dishes which call for canned soup and packaged mixes, and decided instead to offer recipes that use more natural ingredients and are a little more special. In addition, we have included some timely tips on how to transport and serve your favorite potluck fare.

People have potluck meals for a variety of reasons. Whatever your occasion, we hope you will find just what you are looking for in the special recipe section that follows.

Potluck Tips

- Appoint one person to coordinate the food selections so that everyone does not prepare the same type of dish. One creative group has its members bring a dish that starts with the first letter of their last name to ensure variety.

- Remember to provide the serving utensils that are appropriate for the food you are bringing.

- Write your name and phone number on a piece of masking tape, and place the label on the bottom of your casserole dish or the handle of your utensil; this will ensure that it can be easily identified if it becomes lost in the shuffle.

- Keep hot foods hot and cold foods cold to avoid the risk of food poisoning. The U.S. Department of Agriculture recommends keeping hot foods above 140° F and cold foods below 40° F. Do not allow perishable foods to remain at room temperature for more than two hours.

- Take advantage of items such as casserole quilts, lightweight insulated coolers, and baking dish baskets to help transport food and keep it at the proper temperature.

- Stabilize serving dishes for transport by placing them in a box or basket lined with a towel. Tape the lids onto the dishes, if necessary, to make sure they stay in place.

- Bring along oven mitts or hot pads if your food will need reheating at your final destination.

- If you will need to reheat your food, plan ahead of time to use a microwave oven if one is available at the site. Be sure to place the food in a microwave-able dish.

Mississippi Sin

2 cups (8 ounces) shredded
  Cheddar cheese
1 (8-ounce) package cream
  cheese, softened
1½ cups sour cream
½ cup chopped cooked ham

⅓ cup chopped green chiles
⅓ cup chopped green onions
⅛ teaspoon Worcestershire
  sauce
1 (1-pound) round loaf French
  bread

Combine first 7 ingredients in a medium bowl, stirring well. Set dip aside.

Cut a thin slice from top of bread loaf; set slice aside. Using a gently sawing motion, cut vertically to, but not through, bottom of loaf, ½ inch from edge. Lift out center of loaf; cut into 1-inch cubes, and set aside. Fill hollowed bread loaf with dip; cover with reserved top slice of bread loaf. Wrap reserved loaf with aluminum foil. Bake at 350° for 1 hour. Serve dip with reserved bread cubes, crackers, or potato chips. Yield: about 4 cups.

Favorite Recipes from Union Baptist Church Cooks
Union Baptist Church
Tylertown, Mississippi

Cheese Ball

4 cups (16 ounces) shredded
  sharp Cheddar cheese
1 (8-ounce) package cream
  cheese, softened
1 (2-ounce) jar diced pimiento,
  drained
1 tablespoon chopped onion

1 tablespoon chopped green
  pepper
1 tablespoon Worcestershire
  sauce
1 teaspoon lemon juice
Dash of salt
1 cup chopped pecans

Position knife blade in food processor bowl; add first 8 ingredients, and process until blended. Shape mixture into a ball; roll in chopped pecans. Cover and chill at least 1 hour. Serve with crackers. Yield: one 5-inch cheese ball.   Pam Phillips

Come and Get It!
The Junior Welfare League of Talladega, Alabama

Deviled Eggs

8 hard-cooked eggs
½ (3-ounce) package cream
  cheese, softened
2 tablespoons mayonnaise
2 teaspoons sweet pickle relish
1 teaspoon white vinegar
1 teaspoon lemon juice
1 teaspoon prepared mustard
⅛ teaspoon sugar
Dash of garlic salt
Dash of curry powder
Paprika (optional)

Slice eggs in half lengthwise, and carefully remove yolks. Mash yolks with a fork. Add cream cheese, stirring until smooth. Stir in mayonnaise and next 7 ingredients. Spoon yolk mixture into egg whites. Cover and chill. Sprinkle with paprika just before serving, if desired. Yield: 8 servings.   Bessie P. Failes

Musical Tastes
Chancel and Bell Choir, First United Methodist Church
Charlottesville, Virginia

Cranberry Waldorf Gelatin Salad

1 (3-ounce) package raspberry-
  flavored gelatin
1 envelope unflavored gelatin
1 teaspoon ground cinnamon
¼ teaspoon salt
¼ teaspoon ground ginger
2 cups boiling water
1 cup cold water
2 large Red Delicious apples,
  peeled and chopped
1 cup chopped pecans or
  walnuts
⅔ cup whole-berry cranberry
  sauce

Combine first 5 ingredients in a large bowl. Add boiling water, and stir until gelatin dissolves. Stir in cold water. Cover and chill 1 hour and 15 minutes or until mixture is the consistency of unbeaten egg white.

Add apple, pecans, and cranberry sauce to chilled gelatin mixture; stir well. Pour into a lightly oiled 13- x 9- x 2-inch dish. Cover and chill until firm. Cut into squares. Yield: 15 servings.

Savor the Flavor of Oregon
The Junior League of Eugene, Oregon

Red, White, and Blueberry Party Salad

2 (3-ounce) packages
  raspberry-flavored gelatin,
  divided
3 cups boiling water, divided
1 envelope unflavored gelatin
½ cup cold water
1 cup half-and-half
1 cup sugar
1 teaspoon vanilla extract
1 (8-ounce) package cream
  cheese, softened
½ cup chopped pecans or
  walnuts (optional)
1 (21-ounce) can blueberry pie
  filling

Dissolve 1 package raspberry-flavored gelatin in 2 cups boiling water. Pour into a 13- x 9- x 2-inch dish; cover and chill until firm.

Sprinkle unflavored gelatin over ½ cup cold water in a medium saucepan; let stand 1 minute. Cook over low heat, stirring until gelatin dissolves.

Combine half-and-half and sugar in a small saucepan; cook over low heat, stirring until sugar dissolves.

Combine gelatin mixture, half-and-half mixture, vanilla, and cream cheese in a large mixing bowl. Beat at medium speed of an electric mixer until smooth. Stir in chopped pecans, if desired. Gently pour cream cheese mixture over first layer of salad. Cover and chill until firm.

Dissolve remaining package raspberry-flavored gelatin in remaining 1 cup boiling water; stir in blueberry pie filling. Gently pour pie filling mixture over first two layers of salad. Cover and chill at least 8 hours or until firm. To serve, cut salad into squares. Yield: 15 servings.

Carol Hefner

First Gentleman's Cookbook
Governor's Mansion Restoration Foundation
Lincoln, Nebraska

Rainbow Bean Salad

2 cups finely chopped celery
1 medium cucumber, chopped
1 medium onion, chopped
1 green pepper, chopped
1 medium-size sweet red
   pepper, chopped
2 teaspoons salt
4 tomatoes, coarsely chopped
1 (8-ounce) can green beans,
   drained
1 (8-ounce) can English peas,
   drained
½ (16-ounce) can wax beans,
   drained
1½ cups sugar
½ cup white vinegar
½ cup vegetable oil
2 cups water

Combine first 6 ingredients in a large bowl; add water to cover. Cover and let stand 4 hours. Drain; rinse well, and drain. Add tomato, green beans, peas, and wax beans; stir gently to combine.

Combine sugar, vinegar, oil, and water in a medium bowl; stir well with a wire whisk. Pour sugar mixture over vegetable mixture. Cover and chill at least 8 hours, stirring occasionally. Serve with a slotted spoon. Yield: 12 servings.

Prairie Potpourri
North Iowa Girl Scout Council
Mason City, Iowa

Classic Potato Salad

3 pounds baking potatoes
1 large green pepper, diced
1 large carrot, scraped and
   grated
2 sweet pickles or small dill
   pickles, diced
2 green onions, chopped
⅔ cup mayonnaise
2 tablespoons lemon juice
1 teaspoon salt
½ teaspoon garlic powder
¼ teaspoon pepper
½ teaspoon dry mustard
   (optional)

Cook potatoes in boiling water to cover 30 minutes or until potatoes are tender. Drain well, and let cool slightly. Peel and cube potatoes. Combine potato, green pepper, carrot, pickle, and green onions in a large bowl; toss gently, and set aside.

Combine mayonnaise, lemon juice, salt, garlic powder, pepper, and, if desired, dry mustard in a small bowl; stir well. Pour mayonnaise mixture over potato mixture, tossing gently to combine. Serve warm or chilled. Yield: 8 servings.

Spice and Spirit: The Complete Kosher Jewish Cookbook
Lubavitch Women's Organization
Brooklyn, New York

Bacon, Lettuce, and Tomato Salad

1 pound bacon, cooked and crumbled	1 small purple onion, thinly sliced
1 medium head romaine lettuce, torn	1 cup mayonnaise
1 pint cherry tomatoes, halved	½ cup grated Romano cheese
6 cups fresh broccoli flowerets	1 tablespoon sugar

Layer bacon, lettuce, tomato, broccoli, and onion in order listed in a large glass salad bowl.

Combine mayonnaise, cheese, and sugar; stir well. Spread mixture over top of salad. Cover and chill 8 hours. Toss salad lightly just before serving. Yield: 10 servings.   Jack Ferguson

The Western Gentlemen's Cookbook
The Men's Culinary Cup
Cheyenne, Wyoming

Cheyenne, Wyoming, businessmen share their secrets about campfire cooking, barbecuing, and preparing wild game in The Western Gentlemen's Cookbook. *Proceeds will benefit the STRIDE Learning Center, a preschool serving developmentally delayed children.*

Macaroni Salad

1 (16-ounce) package macaroni
4 to 5 large carrots, scraped
  and grated
1 large onion, chopped
1 large green pepper, chopped
2 cups mayonnaise

1 (14-ounce) can sweetened
  condensed milk
½ cup sugar
½ cup white vinegar
Salt and pepper to taste

Cook macaroni according to package directions; drain. Rinse with cold water; drain well. Combine macaroni, carrot, onion, and green pepper in a large bowl; toss gently, and set aside.

Combine mayonnaise and remaining ingredients in a small bowl; stir well. Pour dressing over macaroni mixture; toss gently to combine. Cover and chill 8 hours (mixture will thicken as it chills). Yield: 16 to 18 servings.   Marie Ewert

Palate Pleasers II
Redeemer Women's Guild
Elmhurst, Illinois

Italian Picnic Salad

1 (14-ounce) can quartered
  artichoke hearts, drained
1 large green pepper, chopped
1 cup (4 ounces) coarsely
  shredded Cheddar cheese
1 cup (4 ounces) coarsely
  shredded Monterey Jack
  cheese
¼ pound thinly sliced cooked
  ham, cut into strips

¼ pound thinly sliced salami,
  cut into strips
⅓ cup grated Parmesan cheese
¼ cup grated onion
Salt and pepper to taste
Hot sauce to taste
8 ounces thin spaghetti,
  uncooked
Dressing (recipe follows)

Combine first 10 ingredients in a large bowl; toss gently. Set artichoke heart mixture aside.

Break spaghetti into pieces. Cook spaghetti according to package directions; drain well. Add spaghetti and dressing to artichoke heart mixture, tossing gently to combine. Cover and chill thoroughly. Yield: 10 servings.

Dressing

1 cup vegetable oil
⅓ cup white vinegar
1 clove garlic, crushed
½ teaspoon sugar
½ teaspoon salt

½ teaspoon dried whole basil
½ teaspoon dried whole
  oregano
¼ teaspoon pepper

Combine all ingredients in a jar. Cover tightly, and shake vigorously. Yield: about 1½ cups.   Harvey Fiser

Family Secrets . . . the Best of the Delta
Lee Academy
Clarksdale, Mississippi

Annual Meeting Chicken Salad

18 chicken breast halves,
  skinned and boned
1½ heads iceberg lettuce, torn
3 cups thinly sliced celery
2 cups thinly sliced green
  onions
1½ cups olive oil
¼ cup red wine vinegar

3 cloves garlic, crushed
2 to 3 teaspoons salt
1½ teaspoons pepper
3 (3-ounce) cans chow mein
  noodles
¼ cup plus 2 tablespoons
  sesame seeds, toasted

Place chicken in a large Dutch oven; add water to cover. Bring to a boil over medium heat; cover and simmer 30 minutes or until chicken is done. Drain well, and let chicken cool to the touch. Cut chicken into strips. Combine chicken, lettuce, celery, and green onions in a large bowl; toss well.

Combine oil, vinegar, garlic, salt, and pepper; beat with a wire whisk until blended. Pour dressing over chicken mixture; toss gently to combine. Sprinkle with chow mein noodles and sesame seeds. Serve immediately. Yield: 24 servings.

The Fine Art of Cooking
The Women's Committee of the Philadelphia Museum of Art
Philadelphia, Pennsylvania

Walker's Baked Beans

1 (31-ounce) can pork and
  beans
2 (15-ounce) cans kidney
  beans, drained
¼ pound bacon, chopped
1 cup firmly packed brown
  sugar

1 cup catsup
1 medium onion, chopped
½ cup chopped green pepper
  (optional)
1 teaspoon prepared mustard

Combine all ingredients in a large bowl; stir well. Spoon bean mixture into a lightly greased 3-quart casserole. Bake, uncovered, at 300° for 2 hours or until hot and bubbly, stirring occasionally. Yield: 12 servings.   Bruce Walker

South Dakota Centennial Cookbook
The South Dakota Historical Society
Pierre, South Dakota

String Bean Casserole

¼ cup butter or margarine,
  divided
2 tablespoons all-purpose flour
½ cup milk
½ teaspoon sugar
½ teaspoon salt
Dash of pepper

½ teaspoon grated onion
½ cup sour cream
2 (9-ounce) packages frozen
  French-style green beans
1 cup (4 ounces) shredded
  Cheddar cheese
½ cup fine, dry breadcrumbs

Melt 2 tablespoons butter in a heavy saucepan over low heat; add flour, and stir until smooth. Cook 1 minute, stirring constantly. Gradually add milk; cook over medium heat, stirring constantly, until mixture is thickened and bubbly. Stir in sugar, salt, and pepper. Remove from heat; stir in onion and sour cream. Set aside.

Cook green beans according to package directions; drain well. Combine green beans and reserved sour cream mixture in a medium bowl. Spoon half the bean mixture into the bottom of a 1-quart casserole; top with half the cheese. Repeat with remaining half of bean mixture and cheese.

Melt remaining 2 tablespoons butter in a small saucepan over low heat; stir in breadcrumbs. Sprinkle breadcrumb mixture evenly over casserole. Bake at 400° for 20 to 30 minutes or until thoroughly heated. Yield: 8 servings.   Liz Cooper

Liberal Portions
The Unitarian Universalist Church of Nashua, New Hampshire

Penny's Broccoli Casserole

2 (10-ounce) packages frozen chopped broccoli
¼ cup butter or margarine, divided
2 tablespoons all-purpose flour
1 cup milk
¼ to ½ teaspoon salt

⅛ teaspoon pepper
1 (3-ounce) package cream cheese, softened
½ cup (2 ounces) shredded Cheddar cheese
½ cup fine, dry breadcrumbs

Cook broccoli according to package directions; drain well. Place broccoli in a lightly greased 1-quart casserole; set aside.

Melt 2 tablespoons butter in a heavy saucepan over low heat; add flour, stirring until smooth. Cook 1 minute, stirring constantly. Gradually add milk; cook over medium heat, stirring constantly, until mixture is thickened and bubbly. Add salt and pepper; stir well. Add cream cheese, stirring until smooth.

Pour cream cheese sauce over broccoli in casserole; stir gently to combine. Sprinkle with Cheddar cheese. Melt remaining 2 tablespoons butter in a small saucepan over low heat; remove from heat, and stir in breadcrumbs. Sprinkle breadcrumb mixture evenly over casserole. Bake at 350° for 40 minutes or until thoroughly heated. Yield: 6 servings.   Laura Harms

Best Friends
Terranova West Women's Club
Spring, Texas

Jalapeño-Corn Casserole

1 cup long-grain rice,
  uncooked
1 medium onion, chopped
1 medium-size green pepper,
  chopped
1 cup chopped celery
½ cup butter or margarine,
  melted
1 to 2 large jalapeño peppers,
  seeded and chopped

2 (16½-ounce) cans cream-style
  corn
1½ cups (6 ounces) shredded
  mild Cheddar cheese
1 tablespoon sugar
Garnishes: green pepper rings,
  cherry tomatoes, and
  chopped fresh parsley

Cook rice according to package directions; set rice aside.

Sauté onion, green pepper, and celery in melted butter in a large skillet until vegetables are tender. Combine reserved rice and sautéed vegetable mixture in a large bowl. Add jalapeño peppers, corn, cheese, and sugar; stir well. Spoon corn mixture into a lightly greased, shallow 2-quart casserole. Bake at 350° for 40 to 45 minutes or until thoroughly heated. Garnish, if desired. Yield: 8 to 10 servings.   Mary Jane Sanders

Feeding Your Neighbor
Neighbor to Neighbor
Pine Bluff, Arkansas

Zucchini-Cheese Casserole

4 cups diced zucchini (about 3
  medium)
½ cup chopped onion
1 clove garlic, crushed
2 tablespoons butter or
  margarine, melted
2 tablespoons all-purpose flour

1 teaspoon salt
1 (5-ounce) can evaporated
  milk
½ cup sour cream
½ cup (2 ounces) shredded
  Cheddar cheese

Sauté zucchini, onion, and garlic in melted butter in a large skillet 5 minutes or until vegetables are crisp-tender; remove from heat. Sprinkle flour and salt over sautéed vegetables, tossing gently to combine. Stir in evaporated milk, sour cream, and cheese.

Spoon zucchini mixture into a 1-quart casserole. Bake at 375° for 20 minutes or until cheese melts and mixture is hot and bubbly. Serve immediately. Yield: 6 servings.   Debbie Lukasik

View Beyond the Park
The Junior Women's Club of Fairview Park, Ohio

Mixed Vegetable Casserole

1 (20-ounce) package frozen
  mixed vegetables
1 cup chopped onion
1 cup chopped celery
1 cup (4 ounces) shredded
  Cheddar cheese

1 cup mayonnaise
1½ cups round buttery cracker
  crumbs
½ cup butter or margarine,
  melted

Cook frozen vegetables according to package directions; drain well. Combine cooked vegetables, onion, celery, cheese, and mayonnaise in a large bowl, stirring well.

Spoon mixture into a greased 11- x 7- x 1½-inch baking dish. Combine cracker crumbs and butter; stir well. Sprinkle crumb mixture evenly over casserole. Bake at 350° for 30 to 35 minutes or until thoroughly heated. Yield: 8 to 10 servings.   Evelyn Alfonso

Camellia Delights
The Altrusa Club of Gulfport, Mississippi

Altrusa is an international organization comprised of executives and professionals whose purpose is to strive for the best in character, business, and citizenship. Funds raised from the sale of the organization's cookbook, Camellia Delights, *will support a fund which provides one scholarship each year to a deserving college student.*

Golden Potato Casserole

6 medium baking potatoes
1 (16-ounce) carton sour cream
2½ cups (10 ounces) shredded
  sharp Cheddar cheese
1¾ cups chopped green onions
3 tablespoons milk

1 teaspoon salt
⅛ teaspoon pepper
⅓ cup fine, dry breadcrumbs
2 tablespoons butter or
  margarine, melted

Cook potatoes in boiling salted water to cover 20 minutes or until tender; drain and let cool. Peel and coarsely grate potatoes. Combine grated potato, sour cream, and next 5 ingredients in a large bowl; stir well. Spoon potato mixture into a greased 13- x 9- x 2-inch baking dish. Combine breadcrumbs and melted butter in a small bowl; stir well. Sprinkle breadcrumb mixture evenly over casserole. Bake at 350° for 50 minutes or until thoroughly heated. Yield: 10 to 12 servings.   Sue Iacobucci

Bakers' Secrets
Edison Women's Club
Akron, Ohio

Mushroom-Rice Bake

2 cups water
1 teaspoon salt
1 cup long-grain rice,
  uncooked
2 cups chopped fresh
  mushrooms
¼ cup chopped onion
2 tablespoons butter or
  margarine, melted

2 (3-ounce) packages cream
  cheese, softened
2 eggs
1 (12-ounce) can evaporated
  milk
¼ cup chopped fresh parsley
1 teaspoon salt
Garnishes: fresh mushrooms
  and parsley sprigs

Bring water and 1 teaspoon salt to a boil in a medium saucepan; gradually add rice, stirring constantly. Cover, reduce heat, and simmer 20 to 25 minutes or until rice is tender and liquid is absorbed. Set aside.

Sauté mushrooms and onion in melted butter in a small skillet until vegetables are tender; remove from heat, and set aside.

Beat cream cheese in a small bowl at high speed of an electric mixer until light and fluffy. Add eggs, one at a time, beating well after each addition. Add reserved cooked rice, mushroom mixture, evaporated milk, chopped parsley, and 1 teaspoon salt; stir well to combine. Spoon rice mixture into an 11- x 7- x 1½-inch baking dish. Bake, uncovered, at 350° for 30 to 35 minutes or until a knife inserted in center comes out clean. Garnish, if desired. Yield: 8 to 10 servings.   Tricia Esposito

What's Cooking in Chagrin Falls
Chagrin Falls Parent Teacher Organization
Chagrin Falls, Ohio

Banana, Sour Cream, and Walnut Loaf

⅔ cup butter or margarine,
  softened
1⅓ cups sugar
2¾ cups all-purpose flour
1 teaspoon baking powder
1 teaspoon baking soda

½ teaspoon salt
2 eggs, lightly beaten
1½ cups mashed bananas
½ cup sour cream
1 cup chopped walnuts

Cream butter; gradually add sugar, beating at medium speed of an electric mixer.

Combine flour and next 3 ingredients in a medium bowl; stir well. Combine eggs, banana, and sour cream; stir well. Add flour mixture to creamed mixture, alternately with banana mixture, beginning and ending with flour mixture. Mix until blended after each addition; stir in walnuts.

Pour batter into a greased and floured 9- x 5- x 3-inch loafpan. Bake at 350° for 1 hour and 15 minutes or until a wooden pick inserted in center comes out clean. (Shield with aluminum foil to prevent excessive browning, if necessary.) Let cool in pan 10 minutes; remove from pan, and let cool completely on a wire rack. Yield: 1 loaf.   Mrs. Charles T. Donley

Flenniken's Favorites
The Flenniken Public Library
Carmichaels, Pennsylvania

Lemon Ribbon Bread

½ cup butter, softened
1 cup sugar
1 egg
2 teaspoons grated lemon rind
1½ cups all-purpose flour
1 teaspoon baking powder
½ teaspoon salt
½ cup milk
1 cup chopped pecans or
    walnuts

2 (3-ounce) packages cream
    cheese, softened
⅓ cup sugar
1 egg
1 tablespoon all-purpose flour
1 teaspoon vanilla extract
1 teaspoon powdered sugar

Cream butter; gradually add 1 cup sugar, beating well at medium speed of an electric mixer. Add egg and lemon rind, beating until blended.

Combine 1½ cups flour, baking powder, and salt; add to creamed mixture alternately with milk, beginning and ending with flour mixture. Mix just until blended after each addition. Stir in pecans, and set aside.

Beat cream cheese at medium speed until smooth; gradually add ⅓ cup sugar, beating well. Add egg, beating well. Stir in 1 tablespoon flour and vanilla.

Pour half of batter into a greased 9- x 5- x 3-inch loafpan. Gently spread cream cheese mixture over batter. Spoon remaining half of batter over cream cheese mixture. Bake at 350° for 1 hour and 10 minutes or until a wooden pick inserted in center comes out clean. Let cool in pan 10 minutes; remove from pan, and place on a wire rack. Sprinkle with powdered sugar; let cool completely. Yield: 1 loaf.

Gateways
Auxiliary-Twigs . . . Friends of St. Louis Children's Hospital
St. Louis, Missouri

Zucchini Molasses-Raisin Bread

4 eggs	1 teaspoon baking soda
2 cups firmly packed brown sugar	¼ teaspoon baking powder
1 cup vegetable oil	1 teaspoon salt
3 cups coarsely grated zucchini	2 teaspoons ground cinnamon
2 tablespoons molasses	½ teaspoon ground ginger
2 teaspoons vanilla extract	½ teaspoon ground cloves
4 cups all-purpose flour	⅛ teaspoon ground nutmeg
	1 cup raisins

Beat eggs in a large mixing bowl at medium speed of an electric mixer until foamy; gradually add sugar, beating well. Add oil; beat until blended. Add zucchini, molasses, and vanilla; stir well.

Combine flour and next 7 ingredients; stir well. Add flour mixture to zucchini mixture, stirring well to combine. Add raisins; stir well. Pour batter into 2 greased and floured 9- x 5- x 3-inch loafpans. Bake at 350° for 55 to 60 minutes. Let cool in pans 10 minutes; remove from pans, and let cool on wire racks. Yield: 2 loaves.   Terry Schenkenberger

The Best Recipes of Green Valley United Methodist Women
Green Valley United Methodist Women
Akron, Ohio

St. Louis, known as the Gateway City, has long enjoyed a rich blend of diverse cultures. Today's St. Louis cuisine reflects influences of early French, German, and Italian settlers, as well as later regional influences from the Old South, the East Coast, and the Southwest. Gateways offers an eclectic blend of recipes from members of St. Louis Children's Hospital Auxiliary-Twigs. Proceeds will support the vital work of the St. Louis Children's Hospital.

Overnight Crunch Coffee Cake

⅔ cup butter or margarine,
   softened
1 cup sugar
½ cup firmly packed brown
   sugar
2 eggs
2 cups all-purpose flour

1 teaspoon baking powder
1 teaspoon baking soda
½ teaspoon salt
1 teaspoon ground cinnamon
1 cup buttermilk
Topping (recipe follows)

Cream butter; gradually add sugars, beating well at medium speed of an electric mixer. Add eggs, one at a time, beating after each addition.

Combine flour, baking powder, soda, salt, and cinnamon; stir well. Add flour mixture to creamed mixture alternately with buttermilk, beginning and ending with flour mixture.

Pour batter into a greased and floured 13- x 9- x 2-inch baking pan. Sprinkle topping evenly over batter. Cover and chill 8 hours. Bake at 350° for 40 to 45 minutes or until lightly browned. Cut coffee cake into squares. Yield: 16 servings.

Topping

½ cup firmly packed brown
   sugar
½ cup chopped walnuts

½ teaspoon ground nutmeg
½ teaspoon ground cinnamon

Combine brown sugar, walnuts, nutmeg, and cinnamon in a small bowl, stirring well. Yield: 1 cup.   Delores Frederick

"R" Little Red School Cookbook
Cedar Falls Historical Society
Cedar Falls, Iowa

Parker House Rolls

6½ to 7½ cups all-purpose
  flour, divided
½ cup sugar
2 packages dry yeast
2 teaspoons salt

2 cups water
½ cup butter or margarine
1 egg, lightly beaten
½ cup butter or margarine,
  melted

Combine 2¼ cups flour, sugar, yeast, and salt in a large mixing bowl; stir well.

Combine water and ½ cup butter in a saucepan; heat until butter melts, stirring occasionally. Let cool to 120° to 130°.

Gradually add liquid mixture and egg to flour mixture, beating well at high speed of an electric mixer. Beat an additional 2 minutes at medium speed. Gradually add ¾ cup flour, beating 2 minutes at medium speed. Gradually stir in enough remaining 4½ cups flour to make a soft dough.

Turn dough out onto a floured surface, and knead until smooth and elastic (about 10 minutes). Place in a well-greased bowl, turning to grease top. Cover and let rise in a warm place (85°), free from drafts, 1 hour or until doubled in bulk.

Punch dough down; turn out onto a lightly floured surface, and knead lightly 4 or 5 times. Cover and let rest 15 minutes.

Roll dough to ½-inch thickness. Cut dough with a 2-inch biscuit cutter. With the dull edge of knife, make a crease across each round of dough. Brush tops of rounds with ½ cup melted butter. Fold rounds in half, gently pressing edges to seal.

Arrange rolls in 3 ungreased 8-inch round cakepans. Cover and let rise in a warm place, free from drafts, 45 minutes or until doubled in bulk. Bake at 350° for 18 to 20 minutes or until golden. Yield: 5 dozen.   Susan Young House

You Make the Best Better
The Macoupin County 4-H Foundation
Carlinville, Illinois

Creamy Deluxe Macaroni and Cheese

1¾ cups elbow macaroni,
  uncooked
2 cups small-curd cottage
  cheese
2 cups (8 ounces) shredded
  Cheddar cheese
1 (8-ounce) carton sour cream

3 tablespoons finely chopped
  onion
1 egg, beaten
¾ teaspoon salt
¼ cup soft breadcrumbs
1½ tablespoons butter or
  margarine, melted

Cook macaroni according to package directions; drain. Combine macaroni and next 6 ingredients, stirring well. Spoon mixture into a greased 2-quart casserole. Combine breadcrumbs and butter, stirring well. Sprinkle breadcrumb mixture evenly over casserole. Bake, uncovered, at 350° for 45 minutes or until thoroughly heated. Yield: 6 servings.   Chris Hixon

25 Years of Cooking at Green Valley Baptist Church
Green Valley Baptist Church
Birmingham, Alabama

Salmon-Macaroni Casserole

1 cup elbow macaroni,
  uncooked
¼ cup butter or margarine
3 tablespoons all-purpose flour
1¾ cups milk
½ teaspoon salt
¼ teaspoon garlic salt
⅛ teaspoon pepper
1 (12-ounce) carton cottage
  cheese

1 cup (4 ounces) shredded
  process American cheese
1 (16-ounce) can salmon,
  drained and flaked
2 eggs, beaten
1½ cups soft breadcrumbs
2 tablespoons butter or
  margarine, melted

Cook macaroni according to package directions. Drain well, and set aside.

Melt ¼ cup butter in a heavy saucepan over low heat; add flour, stirring until smooth. Cook 1 minute, stirring constantly. Gradually add milk; cook over medium heat, stirring constantly, until mixture is thickened and bubbly. Add salt, garlic salt, and pepper, stirring well.

Combine sauce, reserved macaroni, cheeses, salmon, and eggs in a large bowl; stir well. Spoon salmon mixture into a greased 11- x 7- x 1½-inch baking dish. Combine breadcrumbs and 2 tablespoons melted butter; stir well. Sprinkle breadcrumb mixture evenly over casserole. Bake at 350° for 1 hour or until set. Yield: 8 servings.   Helen Rodgers

Favorite Recipes of the Episcopal Churches on the Kenai
The Episcopal Churches on the Kenai
Nikiski, Alaska

Noodle Casserole with Ground Pork

1 pound ground pork
¼ cup chopped onion
4 ounces medium egg noodles, uncooked
1 (16-ounce) can stewed tomatoes, undrained
1 (11-ounce) can whole kernel corn, drained

1 (6-ounce) can tomato paste
1 teaspoon chili powder
1 teaspoon salt
¼ teaspoon garlic powder
Dash of pepper
1 cup (4 ounces) shredded Cheddar cheese

Cook pork and onion in a skillet until meat is browned and onion is tender, stirring to crumble meat; drain well, and set aside.

Cook noodles according to package directions; drain well. Combine noodles, reserved meat mixture, tomatoes, and next 6 ingredients; stir well. Spoon noodle mixture into an 11- x 7- x 1½-inch baking dish. Cover and bake at 350° for 30 minutes. Remove from oven; sprinkle cheese evenly over casserole. Bake an additional 3 to 5 minutes or until cheese melts. Yield: 6 to 8 servings.   Carol Cunneff

Kitchen Keys
The Episcopal Church Women Organization of St. Peter's Parish Church
New Kent, Virginia

Wonderful Lasagna

1 pound hot Italian sausage
½ pound ground chuck
½ cup minced green onions
2 to 3 cloves garlic, crushed
3 to 4 tablespoons olive oil
1 (29-ounce) can tomato sauce
1 (6-ounce) can tomato paste
¼ teaspoon dried whole oregano
Dash of dried whole basil
½ teaspoon salt
¼ teaspoon freshly ground pepper
2 cups (4 ounces) shredded Monterey Jack cheese, divided
1 cup ricotta cheese
1 cup cottage cheese
½ cup minced green onions
½ cup minced fresh parsley
1 egg, beaten
½ teaspoon dried whole basil, crushed
½ teaspoon dried whole marjoram, crushed
6 to 8 slices bacon
1 (10-ounce) package frozen chopped spinach, thawed and drained
½ cup freshly grated Parmesan cheese
½ cup soft breadcrumbs
1 egg yolk
2 tablespoons olive oil (optional)
5 cooked lasagna noodles
1 (8-ounce) package sliced Swiss cheese

Cook sausage, ground chuck, ½ cup green onions, and garlic in 3 to 4 tablespoons olive oil in a large skillet until meat is browned, stirring to crumble meat; drain. Add tomato sauce, tomato paste, ¼ teaspoon oregano, dash of basil, salt, and pepper; stir well. Bring to a boil; cover, reduce heat, and simmer 20 to 30 minutes, stirring frequently. Cover and chill 8 hours.

Combine 1 cup Monterey Jack cheese and next 7 ingredients in a medium bowl; stir well, and set aside.

Cook bacon in a large skillet until crisp; remove bacon and crumble. Combine bacon, spinach, Parmesan cheese, breadcrumbs, egg yolk, and, if desired, 2 tablespoons olive oil.

Spoon half of reserved meat sauce in a lightly greased 13- x 9- x 2-inch baking dish. Layer half of reserved ricotta cheese mixture over meat sauce; top with half of spinach mixture. Arrange noodles evenly over spinach mixture. Repeat layers with remaining half of meat sauce, ricotta cheese mixture, and spinach mixture.

Sprinkle remaining 1 cup Monterey Jack cheese evenly over lasagna mixture; top evenly with Swiss cheese slices. Bake at 350°

for 40 to 45 minutes or until cheese melts and mixture is hot and bubbly. Yield: 8 to 10 servings.   Donna Burch

Cooks and Company
The Muscle Shoals District Service League
Sheffield, Alabama

Spaghetti Supreme

2 pounds ground round
2 large onions, chopped
3 large cloves garlic, minced
1 tablespoon vegetable oil
1 (28-ounce) can whole
  tomatoes, drained and
  chopped
2 (8-ounce) cans tomato sauce
½ teaspoon creole seasoning
1 (4-ounce) can sliced
  mushrooms, drained

½ cup chopped celery
½ cup chopped green pepper
1 (4-ounce) jar diced pimiento,
  drained
1 tablespoon butter or
  margarine, melted
1 (12-ounce) package spaghetti
6 cups (24 ounces) shredded
  process American cheese,
  divided

Cook meat, onion, and garlic in oil in a large Dutch oven over medium heat until meat is browned, stirring to crumble meat; drain. Add tomatoes, tomato sauce, and seasoning; stir well. Bring to a boil; cover, reduce heat, and simmer 20 minutes. Set aside.

Sauté mushrooms, celery, green pepper, and pimiento in melted butter in a skillet until vegetables are tender. Add to reserved meat mixture; cover and simmer 30 minutes.

Cook spaghetti according to package directions; drain well. Combine spaghetti, meat mixture, and 5 cups cheese, stirring well. Pour mixture into a 4-quart casserole. Bake at 350° for 20 minutes. Remove from oven; sprinkle remaining 1 cup cheese evenly over casserole. Bake an additional 5 minutes or until cheese melts. Yield: 12 servings.   Claudette Bonin

The Cajun Connection Cookbook
Trinity Catholic School Booster Club
St. Martinville, Louisiana

Sour Cream and Hamburger Layered Casserole

2 pounds lean ground beef	1 (8-ounce) carton sour cream
2 tablespoons butter or margarine, melted	¾ cup thinly sliced green onions
1 (15-ounce) can tomato sauce	3 cups cooked fine egg noodles
2 cloves garlic, crushed	
1 teaspoon sugar	2 cups (8 ounces) shredded Cheddar cheese
1 teaspoon salt	
1 teaspoon pepper	⅛ teaspoon paprika
1 (8-ounce) package cream cheese, softened	

Cook ground beef in melted butter in a large skillet over medium heat until meat is browned, stirring to crumble meat; drain well. Add tomato sauce and next 4 ingredients; stir well. Bring to a boil; cover, reduce heat, and simmer 20 minutes, stirring occasionally. Transfer meat mixture to a buttered 13- x 9- x 2-inch baking dish. Set aside.

Beat cream cheese and sour cream at low speed of an electric mixer until smooth. Add green onions, stirring gently to combine. Spread cream cheese mixture evenly over meat mixture. Top with noodles. Sprinkle Cheddar cheese over casserole. Sprinkle with paprika. Bake at 350° for 25 to 30 minutes or until hot and bubbly. Yield: 8 servings.   Joan Dowsett Osborne

Dining with the Daughters
The Daughters of Hawaii
Honolulu, Hawaii

Sloppy Joes

1 pound ground beef	2 tablespoons water
2 tablespoons chopped onion	2 tablespoons lemon juice
2 tablespoons chopped green pepper	2 tablespoons white vinegar
½ cup catsup	1 tablespoon Worcestershire sauce
1½ tablespoons brown sugar	6 hamburger buns

Cook ground beef in a large skillet until meat is browned, stirring to crumble meat; drain, reserving 2 tablespoons drippings in skillet. Set meat aside.

Sauté onion and pepper in drippings in skillet until tender. Add catsup and next 5 ingredients. Bring to a boil; reduce heat, and simmer, uncovered, 10 minutes. Add meat; simmer an additional 10 minutes. Serve on hamburger buns. Yield: 6 servings.

"One Lump or Two?"
All Children's Hospital Foundation
St. Petersburg, Florida

Chili con Carne

1 pound dried pinto beans
6 cups water
1½ pounds ground chuck
1 cup chopped onion
1 cup chopped green pepper
2 cloves garlic, minced
1 (28-ounce) can whole
   tomatoes, undrained and
   chopped

1 (10½-ounce) can beef broth,
   undiluted
1 (6-ounce) can tomato paste
3 tablespoons chili powder
2 tablespoons dried whole
   oregano, crushed
1 tablespoon ground cumin
2 to 3 teaspoons salt

Sort and wash beans; place in a large Dutch oven. Cover with water 2 inches above beans; let soak 8 hours.

Drain beans; add 6 cups water. Bring to a boil; cover, reduce heat, and simmer 1 hour. Drain beans, reserving 2½ cups liquid. Set beans and liquid aside.

Cook ground chuck, onion, green pepper, and garlic in a skillet until meat is browned, stirring to crumble meat; drain well. Stir in tomatoes and remaining ingredients. Bring to a boil; cover, reduce heat, and simmer 1 hour, stirring occasionally. Stir in reserved beans and liquid. Cover and simmer an additional 1 to 2 hours, stirring occasionally. Yield: 12 to 14 servings.   Sue Feldman

Friends Come in All Flavors
Buckingham Friends School
Lahaska, Pennsylvania

Chicken and Artichoke Casserole Mobile

12 chicken breast halves
1 (12-ounce) package medium
   seashell macaroni
1 cup butter or margarine
1 cup all-purpose flour
7 cups milk
1½ cups (6 ounces) shredded
   Swiss cheese
1½ cups (6 ounces) shredded
   Cheddar cheese

3 cloves garlic, minced
1 tablespoon plus 1 teaspoon
   salt
1½ teaspoons crushed red
   pepper
4 (14-ounce) cans quartered
   artichoke hearts, drained
3 (8-ounce) cans mushroom
   stems and pieces, drained

Cook chicken in boiling water to cover 15 minutes or until tender; drain well. Let chicken cool. Remove skin, bone chicken, and chop meat; set aside.

Cook macaroni according to package directions. Drain well, and set aside.

Melt butter in a heavy saucepan over low heat; add flour, stirring until smooth. Cook 1 minute, stirring constantly. Gradually add milk; cook over medium heat, stirring constantly, until mixture is thickened and bubbly. Add cheeses, garlic, salt, and pepper; stir until cheeses melt.

Combine reserved chicken, macaroni, cheese sauce, artichokes, and mushrooms; stir well. Spoon into two 13- x 9- x 2-inch baking dishes. Bake, uncovered, at 350° for 30 minutes or until thoroughly heated. Yield: 16 servings.   Carol Voellger

Not So Secret Recipes
4450th Tactical Group, Nellis Air Force Base
Las Vegas, Nevada

Chicken and Cornbread Casserole

6 cups crumbled cornbread
½ cup butter or margarine,
  melted
¼ cup minced onion
3 tablespoons minced fresh
  parsley
1 teaspoon celery seeds
¾ teaspoon salt
½ teaspoon poultry seasoning
⅛ teaspoon pepper

5 cups chopped cooked
  chicken
¼ cup butter or margarine
¼ cup all-purpose flour
1½ teaspoons salt
2 cups canned diluted chicken
  broth
4 cups milk
2 eggs, beaten

Combine first 8 ingredients in a large bowl; toss gently with a fork. Spoon cornbread mixture into a greased 13- x 9- x 2-inch baking dish. Arrange chopped chicken evenly over cornbread mixture, and set aside.

Melt ¼ cup butter in a heavy saucepan over low heat; add flour and salt, stirring until smooth. Cook 1 minute, stirring constantly. Gradually add chicken broth; cook over medium heat, stirring constantly, until mixture is thoroughly heated.

Combine milk and beaten eggs, stirring well. Gradually add milk mixture to chicken broth mixture; cook over low heat, stirring constantly, until mixture is thickened and bubbly. Spoon sauce over chicken. Bake, uncovered, at 375° for 45 minutes or until mixture is thoroughly heated. Yield: 8 to 10 servings.

Angel Fare
Ladies Benevolent Association, Christ Episcopal Church
Manlius, New York

Turkey-Cheddar Casserole

1 (8-ounce) package medium egg noodles	1 teaspoon salt
1 (10-ounce) package frozen broccoli spears	¼ teaspoon pepper
3 tablespoons butter or margarine	¼ teaspoon prepared mustard
3 tablespoons all-purpose flour	1½ cups (6 ounces) shredded Cheddar cheese
2 cups milk	2 cups cubed cooked turkey
	½ cup slivered almonds, toasted

Cook noodles according to package directions; drain well, and set noodles aside.

Cook broccoli spears according to package directions; drain broccoli well. Cut broccoli into flowerets, and coarsely chop stalks. Set aside.

Melt butter in a heavy saucepan over low heat; add flour, stirring until smooth. Cook 1 minute, stirring constantly. Gradually add milk; cook over medium heat, stirring constantly, until mixture is thickened and bubbly. Add salt, pepper, and mustard; stir well. Remove from heat; add cheese, stirring until cheese melts.

Place half of reserved noodles in a greased 11- x 7- x 1½-inch baking dish. Top with reserved broccoli and turkey; place remaining half of noodles over turkey. Pour cheese sauce over noodles; arrange reserved broccoli flowerets on top of casserole, gently pressing them into the cheese sauce. Sprinkle almonds evenly over casserole. Cover and bake at 350° for 30 minutes or until hot and bubbly. Yield: 6 servings.   Ruth Pinckard

Sharing Recipes
St. John's Lutheran Church
Springfield, Illinois

My Favorite Pound Cake

1 cup butter, softened	**¼ teaspoon salt**
½ cup shortening	**¼ teaspoon ground mace**
3 cups sugar	**1 cup milk**
5 eggs	**1 teaspoon vanilla extract**
3 cups all-purpose flour	**½ teaspoon lemon extract**
½ teaspoon baking powder	

Cream butter and shortening; gradually add sugar, beating well at medium speed of an electric mixer. Add eggs, one at a time, beating after each addition.

Combine flour, baking powder, salt, and mace; stir well. Add flour mixture to creamed mixture alternately with milk, beginning and ending with flour mixture. Mix just until blended after each addition. Stir in flavorings.

Pour batter into a greased and floured 12-cup Bundt or 10-inch tube pan. Bake at 325° for 1 hour and 35 minutes or until a wooden pick inserted in center comes out clean. Let cool in pan 10 minutes; remove from pan, and let cool completely on a wire rack. Yield: one 10-inch cake.   Doris Newton

Delaware DAR Historical Cookbook
The Delaware State Society of the Daughters of the American
Revolution
Newark, Delaware

Delawareans are very proud of their colonial history. Their state voted for independence from the Crown in 1776 and was the first to ratify the Constitution in 1787. Pride in Delaware's heritage is recorded in the Delaware DAR Historical Cookbook *compiled by the Delaware State Society of the Daughters of the American Revolution. Proceeds generated from the sale of the cookbook will benefit the State Society Endowment Fund.*

Banana Cake

¾ cup butter or margarine, softened
1 (16-ounce) package brown sugar
4 eggs
4 cups sifted cake flour
2 teaspoons baking soda
2 cups mashed ripe bananas (about 4 large)
½ cup sour cream
2 teaspoons vanilla extract
1 cup chopped pecans or walnuts (optional)
Frosting (recipe follows)

Cream butter; gradually add brown sugar, beating well at medium speed of an electric mixer. Add eggs, one at a time, beating well after each addition.

Combine flour and soda; stir well. Combine mashed banana and sour cream; stir well. Add flour mixture to creamed mixture alternately with banana mixture, beginning and ending with flour mixture. Mix after each addition. Stir in vanilla and, if desired, pecans.

Pour batter into a greased and floured 15- x 10- x 1-inch jellyroll pan. Bake at 325° for 40 to 45 minutes or until a wooden pick inserted in center comes out clean. Let cool completely in pan on a wire rack. Spread frosting over cake. Yield: 15 servings.

Frosting

2 to 2½ cups sifted powdered sugar
¼ cup butter or margarine, softened
¼ cup sour cream
½ teaspoon vanilla extract

Combine all ingredients in a medium mixing bowl; beat at medium speed of an electric mixer until smooth and spreading consistency. Yield: 1 cup.   Debbie Slotnick

The Best Specialties of the House . . . and More
North Suburban Guild of Children's Memorial Medical Center
Chicago, Illinois

Lemon-Coconut Sheet Cake

1 cup butter, softened
2 cups sugar
5 eggs
2½ cups all-purpose flour
1 teaspoon baking powder
1 teaspoon baking soda
¼ teaspoon salt

1 cup buttermilk
1 cup grated coconut
½ teaspoon lemon extract
½ teaspoon coconut flavoring
Lemon Buttercream Frosting
Garnish: lemon slices

Cream butter; gradually add sugar, beating well at medium speed of an electric mixer. Add eggs, one at a time, beating well after each addition.

Combine flour, baking powder, soda, and salt; add to creamed mixture alternately with buttermilk, beginning and ending with flour mixture. Mix after each addition. Stir in coconut and flavorings.

Pour batter into a greased and floured 13- x 9- x 2-inch baking pan. Bake at 350° for 35 to 40 minutes or until a wooden pick inserted in center comes out clean. Let cool in pan 10 minutes; remove from pan, and let cool completely on a wire rack. Spread Lemon Buttercream Frosting on top and sides of cake. Garnish, if desired. Yield: 15 servings.

Lemon Buttercream Frosting

½ cup butter, softened
4 cups sifted powdered sugar
3 tablespoons milk
1 teaspoon grated lemon rind

2 tablespoons lemon juice
½ teaspoon vanilla extract
½ teaspoon butter flavoring

Cream butter; gradually add sugar, beating well at medium speed of an electric mixer. Add milk and remaining ingredients, beating until smooth. Yield: 3 cups.   Nancy Henschel

Treasured Recipes from Wellington Christian School
Parent Teacher Fellowship of Wellington Christian School
West Palm Beach, Florida

Ribbon Fudge Cake

1 (8-ounce) package cream
  cheese, softened
1 egg
¼ cup sugar
3 tablespoons milk
2 tablespoons butter or
  margarine, softened
1 tablespoon cornstarch
½ teaspoon vanilla extract
4 (1-ounce) squares
  unsweetened chocolate

½ cup butter or margarine,
  softened
2 cups sugar
2 eggs
2 cups all-purpose flour
1 teaspoon baking powder
½ teaspoon baking soda
¼ teaspoon salt
1⅓ cups milk
1 teaspoon vanilla extract
Fudge Frosting

Combine cream cheese, egg, and ¼ cup sugar in a medium mixing bowl; beat at high speed of an electric mixer until smooth. Gradually add milk and next 3 ingredients. Set aside.

Place chocolate squares in top of a double boiler; bring water to a boil. Reduce heat to low; cook until chocolate melts, stirring occasionally. Remove from heat, and let cool.

Cream ½ cup butter; gradually add 2 cups sugar, beating well at medium speed. Add 2 eggs, one at a time, beating well after each addition. Combine flour, baking powder, soda, and salt; stir well. Add flour mixture to creamed mixture alternately with 1⅓ cups milk, beginning and ending with flour mixture. Mix after each addition. Stir in melted chocolate and 1 teaspoon vanilla.

Spread half of chocolate batter in a greased and floured 13- x 9- x 2-inch baking pan. Spoon reserved cream cheese mixture evenly over chocolate batter; top with remaining half of chocolate batter. Bake at 350° for 60 to 70 minutes or until a wooden pick inserted in center comes out clean. Let cool completely in pan on a wire rack. Spread frosting over cake. Yield: 15 servings.

Fudge Frosting

2 (1-ounce) squares
  unsweetened chocolate
¼ cup butter or margarine

1½ cups sifted powdered sugar
⅓ cup milk
1 teaspoon vanilla extract

Combine chocolate and butter in top of a double boiler; bring water to a boil. Reduce heat to low; cook until chocolate and butter melt, stirring occasionally. Remove mixture from heat, and let cool. Add powdered sugar and milk to chocolate mixture, beating at low speed of an electric mixer until smooth. Stir in vanilla. Yield: 1⅓ cups.

North Dakota Family Favorites . . . a Collection of Recipes
The Division of Continuing Studies, North Dakota State
University
Fargo, North Dakota

Buttermilk Cupcakes

2½ cups all-purpose flour
2 teaspoons baking soda
¼ teaspoon salt
2 cups sugar
¼ cup plus 1 tablespoon cocoa
2 eggs

1 cup vegetable oil
1 cup buttermilk
1 cup hot water
1 teaspoon vanilla extract
Frosting (recipe follows)

Combine first 10 ingredients in a large mixing bowl; beat at low speed of an electric mixer just until blended. Beat at high speed 2 minutes.

Spoon batter into paper-lined muffin pans, filling two-thirds full. Bake at 350° for 15 to 18 minutes or until a wooden pick inserted in center comes out clean. Remove from pans, and let cool completely on wire racks. Spread frosting on top of each cupcake. Yield: 33 cupcakes.

Frosting

1 (16-ounce) package
  powdered sugar, sifted
¼ cup cocoa
½ cup butter or margarine,
  melted

⅓ cup buttermilk
1 teaspoon vanilla extract

Combine all ingredients in a mixing bowl; beat at low speed of an electric mixer until smooth. Yield: 2½ cups.   Steve Campbell

Note-Worthy Recipes
Iowa Falls High School
Iowa Falls, Iowa

Rocky Road Brownies

½ cup butter or margarine,
  softened
1 cup sugar
1 (1-ounce) square
  unsweetened chocolate,
  melted
2 eggs, beaten
½ cup all-purpose flour
¾ cup chopped pecans,
  divided
2 (3-ounce) packages cream
  cheese, softened

¼ cup butter or margarine,
  softened
¼ cup sugar
1 egg, beaten
1 tablespoon all-purpose flour
¼ teaspoon vanilla extract
½ cup semisweet chocolate
  mini-morsels
2 cups miniature marshmallows
Frosting (recipe follows)

Cream ½ cup butter; gradually add 1 cup sugar, beating at medium speed of an electric mixer until light and fluffy. Add melted chocolate, 2 eggs, and ½ cup flour; mix well. Stir in ½ cup chopped pecans. Spread batter in a greased and floured 13- x 9- x 2-inch baking pan. Set aside.

Combine cream cheese and ¼ cup butter; beat at medium speed until smooth. Gradually add ¼ cup sugar, beating until light and fluffy. Add 1 egg, 1 tablespoon flour, and vanilla; mix well. Stir in remaining ¼ cup pecans.

Spread cream cheese mixture over chocolate layer in pan (do not mix layers together). Sprinkle chocolate morsels evenly over cream cheese layer. Bake at 350° for 35 to 40 minutes. Remove from oven; let cool in pan 5 minutes. Sprinkle evenly with marshmallows. Let cool completely in pan on a wire rack. Spread frosting over top of brownies. Cover and chill thoroughly. Cut into bars. Yield: 3 dozen.

Frosting

2 (1-ounce) squares
  unsweetened chocolate
½ cup milk

½ cup butter or margarine
4 cups sifted powdered sugar
¼ teaspoon vanilla extract

Combine chocolate, milk, and butter in top of a double boiler; bring water to a boil. Reduce heat to low; cook until chocolate and butter melt, stirring occasionally. Remove from heat; stir in powdered sugar and vanilla. Beat at medium speed of an electric mixer until smooth. Yield: 2 cups.   Sarah Brennan

For Crying Out Loud . . . Let's Eat!
The Service League of Hammond, Indiana

Very Best Blonde Brownies

1 (16-ounce) package brown
  sugar
¾ cup butter or margarine,
  melted
3 eggs, beaten
2¾ cups all-purpose flour

2½ teaspoons baking powder
½ teaspoon salt
1 (12-ounce) package
  semisweet chocolate morsels
1 teaspoon vanilla extract

Combine sugar and butter in a bowl; stir well. Add eggs; stir well. Combine flour, baking powder, and salt. Add flour mixture to sugar mixture, stirring well to combine. Stir in chocolate morsels and vanilla. Pour batter into a greased and floured 13- x 9- x 2-inch baking pan. Bake at 350° for 35 to 40 minutes. Let cool in pan on a wire rack. Cut into bars. Yield: 2 dozen.

Thymes Remembered
The Junior League of Tallahassee, Florida

In existence since 1935, The Service League of Hammond is a philanthropic organization which currently serves over thirty charities in Hammond and surrounding areas. Monies earned from the sale of the league's cookbook, For Crying Out Loud . . . Let's Eat!, *support organizations such as Boy Scouts and Girl Scouts of America; Humane Society of Calumet Area, Inc.; Meals on Wheels; Northern Indiana Arts Association, Inc.; and YMCA and YWCA of Hammond.*

Zucchini Bars

1 cup vegetable oil
1½ cups sugar
4 eggs
2 cups all-purpose flour
2 teaspoons baking powder
1 teaspoon baking soda

¼ teaspoon salt
2 teaspoons ground cinnamon
¼ teaspoon ground cloves
3 cups coarsely shredded
    zucchini
Cream Cheese Frosting

Combine oil, sugar, and eggs in a large mixing bowl; beat at medium speed of an electric mixer until well blended.

Combine flour and next 5 ingredients; stir well. Add flour mixture to creamed mixture, beating until well blended. Stir in zucchini.

Pour batter into an ungreased 15- x 10- x 1-inch jellyroll pan. Bake at 350° for 25 minutes or until a wooden pick inserted in center comes out clean. Let cool in pan on a wire rack. Spread Cream Cheese Frosting evenly over top; cut into bars. Yield: 2 dozen.

Cream Cheese Frosting

1 (3-ounce) package cream
    cheese, softened
2 tablespoons butter, softened

1 teaspoon vanilla extract
2 cups sifted powdered sugar

Combine cream cheese, butter, and vanilla in a small mixing bowl; beat at medium speed of an electric mixer until light and fluffy. Add powdered sugar, beating until frosting is smooth. Yield: 1 cup.   Mrs. Frederick N. Brass

The Center of Attention Cookbook
The Medical Center Foundation
Beaver, Pennsylvania

Mae Mortensen's Butter Pecan Cookies

½ cup butter, softened
½ cup margarine, softened
¼ cup plus 2 tablespoons sugar
1 tablespoon cold water

1 teaspoon vanilla extract
2 cups all-purpose flour
1 cup ground pecans
Additional sugar

Cream butter and margarine; gradually add ¼ cup plus 2 tablespoons sugar, beating well at medium speed of an electric mixer. Add water and vanilla, beating well. Gradually add flour to creamed mixture, beating well. Stir in pecans.

Shape dough into 1-inch balls; place 2 inches apart on greased cookie sheets. Flatten balls to ¼-inch thickness with palm of hand. Bake at 350° for 10 to 12 minutes. Let cool slightly on cookie sheets. Roll cookies in additional sugar to coat. Let cool completely on wire racks. Yield: 4 dozen.   Barbara Smith

Fellowship Favorites from First Presbyterian
First Presbyterian Church
Downers Grove, Illinois

Crunch Drops

1 cup butter or margarine, softened
1 cup sugar
1 cup firmly packed brown sugar
2 eggs
1 teaspoon vanilla extract

2 cups all-purpose flour
1 teaspoon baking soda
½ teaspoon salt
2 cups quick-cooking oats, uncooked
2 cups crisp rice cereal
1 cup flaked coconut

Cream butter; gradually add sugars, beating well at medium speed of an electric mixer. Add eggs and vanilla, beating well.

Combine flour, soda, and salt; add to creamed mixture, mixing well. Stir in oats, cereal, and coconut.

Drop dough by rounded teaspoonfuls onto greased cookie sheets. Bake at 350° for 12 to 14 minutes. Let cool completely on wire racks. Yield: 9 dozen.   Inita Segura

Methodist Blessings
The United Methodist Women, First United Methodist Church
New Iberia, Louisiana

Double Chocolate Rebels

1 cup butter or margarine,
   softened
1½ cups sugar
1 egg
1½ cups all-purpose flour
½ teaspoon baking soda
½ teaspoon salt

¼ cup plus 2 tablespoons
   cocoa
¼ cup water
1 teaspoon vanilla extract
3 cups regular oats, uncooked
1 (6-ounce) package semisweet
   chocolate morsels

Cream butter; gradually add sugar, beating well at medium speed of an electric mixer. Add egg, beating well. Combine flour, soda, salt, and cocoa; stir well. Add flour mixture to creamed mixture alternately with water, beginning and ending with flour mixture. Mix well after each addition. Stir in vanilla. Add oats and chocolate morsels, stirring well to combine.

Drop dough by heaping teaspoonfuls onto ungreased cookie sheets. Bake at 350° for 10 minutes. Let cool slightly on cookie sheets; transfer cookies to wire racks, and let cool completely. Yield: 7 dozen.   Carol Dumond

The Galloping Chef
The Combined Training Equestrian Team Alliance
Woodside, California

Appetizers & Beverages

General merchandisers were once the mainstay of the American population. Customers could purchase a variety of foods and household supplies within walking distance of their homes at the neighborhood grocery store.

Different Dip for Fruit

½ cup butter or margarine
⅔ cup firmly packed brown
   sugar

½ cup sour cream
1 teaspoon vanilla extract

Melt butter in a small saucepan over low heat. Add brown sugar; cook until sugar melts, stirring constantly. Remove from heat; stir in sour cream and vanilla. Serve dip with an assortment of fresh fruit. Yield: 1⅓ cups.   Marilyn Elliott

cook and love it more
Lovett Parent Association, The Lovett School
Atlanta, Georgia

Kahlúa Dip

1 (8-ounce) package cream
   cheese, softened
2 tablespoons sugar
¼ cup Kahlúa or other coffee-
   flavored liqueur

2 tablespoons evaporated milk
2 tablespoons chopped
   blanched almonds, toasted

Combine cream cheese and sugar in a small mixing bowl; beat at medium speed of an electric mixer until smooth. Gradually add Kahlúa and evaporated milk, beating well. Cover and chill thoroughly. Sprinkle with chopped almonds just before serving. Serve with an assortment of fresh fruit. Yield: 1 cup.

Second Round, Tea-Time at the Masters®
The Junior League of Augusta, Georgia

Peanut Butter Fruit Dip

1 (8-ounce) carton low-fat sour
  cream
½ cup creamy peanut butter

¼ cup milk
2 tablespoons honey
1 teaspoon ground cinnamon

Combine all ingredients in a small bowl, stirring well. Cover and chill thoroughly. Serve dip with an assortment of fresh fruit. Yield: 1⅔ cups.   Agnes Nasner

Wolf Point, Montana, 75th Jubilee Cookbook
Wolf Point Chamber of Commerce & Agriculture
Wolf Point, Montana

Mushroom Dip

4 slices bacon
½ pound sliced fresh
  mushrooms
1 medium onion, finely
  chopped
1 clove garlic, minced
2 tablespoons all-purpose flour
¼ teaspoon salt

⅛ teaspoon pepper
1 (8-ounce) package cream
  cheese, cubed and softened
2 teaspoons Worcestershire
  sauce
2 teaspoons soy sauce
½ cup sour cream

Cook bacon in a large skillet until crisp; remove bacon, reserving 1 tablespoon drippings in skillet. Crumble bacon, and set aside.

Sauté mushrooms, onion, and garlic in drippings 6 to 8 minutes or until vegetables are tender and mixture is almost dry. Add flour, salt, and pepper, stirring well. Add cream cheese, Worcestershire sauce, and soy sauce; reduce heat, and cook, stirring constantly, until cheese melts. Remove from heat. Stir in sour cream and reserved bacon. Serve warm with an assortment of crackers and breadsticks. Yield: 3 cups.   Gael Romoser

Palate Pleasers II
Redeemer Women's Guild
Elmhurst, Illinois

Baked Vidalia Onion Dip

2 cups (8 ounces) finely
  shredded Swiss cheese
2 cups chopped Vidalia onions
  or other sweet onions

2 cups mayonnaise
2 tablespoons grated Parmesan
  cheese

Combine Swiss cheese, onion, and mayonnaise in a medium bowl, stirring well. Spoon mixture into a lightly greased, deep 1-quart baking dish; sprinkle with Parmesan cheese. Bake at 325° for 40 to 45 minutes or until onion is tender and mixture is thoroughly heated. Serve dip with an assortment of crackers or French bread cubes. Yield: 4 cups. Teresa Joel

The Broker's Cookbook, Second Edition
The Robinson-Humphrey Company, Inc.
Atlanta, Georgia

Three-Cheese Ball

1 (8-ounce) package cream
  cheese, softened
2 cups (8 ounces) shredded
  Cheddar cheese
8 ounces crumbled blue cheese
1 cup chopped walnuts
1 (8-ounce) can crushed
  pineapple, drained

½ cup chopped fresh parsley
¼ cup minced green onions
1 teaspoon Worcestershire
  sauce
¼ teaspoon garlic powder
¼ teaspoon curry powder
¼ cup toasted sesame seeds

Combine cream cheese, Cheddar cheese, and blue cheese in a medium mixing bowl; stir until well blended. Add walnuts and next 6 ingredients; stir well to combine.

Shape cheese mixture into a ball; cover and chill at least 1 hour. Roll in toasted sesame seeds. Serve with an assortment of crackers. Yield: one 6-inch cheese ball. Eva McBride

25 Years of Cooking at Green Valley Baptist Church
Green Valley Baptist Church
Birmingham, Alabama

Pineapple Cheese Ball

1 (8-ounce) package cream
  cheese, softened
½ cup crushed pineapple,
  drained
1 cup chopped pecans, divided

2 tablespoons finely chopped
  green pepper
1 tablespoon minced purple
  onion
1½ teaspoons seasoned salt

Combine cream cheese and pineapple in a mixing bowl; beat at medium speed of an electric mixer until well blended. Add ¾ cup pecans, green pepper, onion, and salt; stir well.

Shape cheese mixture into a ball. Roll in remaining ¼ cup pecans. Cover and chill at least 1 hour. Serve with an assortment of crackers. Yield: one 4-inch cheese ball.   Marsha Pollock

Chef's EscORT
Women's American ORT, Southeast District
Hallandale, Florida

Basil-Cheese Torte

2 to 3 cups loosely packed
  fresh basil leaves
1 cup loosely packed fresh
  parsley sprigs
¾ cup freshly grated Parmesan
  cheese
1½ tablespoons olive oil
3 tablespoons pine nuts
  (optional)

1 (8-ounce) package cream
  cheese, softened
1 (3-ounce) package cream
  cheese, softened
½ cup butter or margarine,
  softened
1½ teaspoons lemon juice
⅛ teaspoon hot sauce
Dash of salt

Position knife blade in food processor bowl; add basil and parsley, and process until finely chopped. Add Parmesan cheese; process until blended. Pour olive oil through food chute in a slow, steady stream with processor running, processing until combined. Transfer to a small bowl; stir in pine nuts, if desired. Set aside.

Combine cream cheese and remaining ingredients in a medium mixing bowl; beat at medium speed of an electric mixer until smooth. Dampen enough cheesecloth to line an empty ice-cube tray or 3-cup mold. Alternately layer half the reserved herb mixture and half the cream cheese mixture, beginning with herb mixture and ending with cheese mixture. Fold cheesecloth over layers, and gently press to smooth top. Chill at least 1 hour.

Unmold onto a serving platter; carefully peel off cheesecloth. Serve with an assortment of crackers. Yield: 3 cups.   Dee Delaney

Three Rivers Cookbook, Volume III
Child Health Association of Sewickley, Pennsylvania

Pepper Cheesecake

2 (8-ounce) packages cream cheese, softened
2 cups (8 ounces) shredded sharp Cheddar cheese
1 (1¼-ounce) package taco seasoning
3 eggs
1 (16-ounce) carton sour cream, divided
1 (4-ounce) can chopped green chiles, drained
½ cup diced sweet red pepper
½ cup hot salsa
2 (8-ounce) containers frozen guacamole, thawed
Garnishes: chopped fresh tomatoes, sliced ripe olives, and shredded sharp Cheddar cheese

Combine cream cheese, Cheddar cheese, and taco seasoning; beat well at high speed of an electric mixer. Add eggs, one at a time, beating well after each addition. Stir in half of sour cream. Fold in chiles and red pepper. Pour mixture into a greased 10-inch springform pan. Bake at 350° for 35 minutes or until set.

Combine remaining half of sour cream and salsa. Spread mixture evenly over cheesecake. Bake an additional 5 minutes. Let cool in pan on a wire rack; cover and chill at least 8 hours.

To serve, carefully remove sides of springform pan. Spread with guacamole. Garnish, if desired. Serve with tortilla chips. Yield: one 10-inch cheesecake.   Sue Blackall

Return Engagement
The Junior Board of the Quad City Symphony Orchestra Association
Davenport, Iowa

Smoked Salmon-Cheese Pâté

½ cup soft breadcrumbs
1 large onion, chopped
3 tablespoons butter or
   margarine, melted
3 (8-ounce) packages cream
   cheese, softened
8 ounces smoked salmon,
   chopped

1 tablespoon minced fresh
   dillweed
1 tablespoon lemon juice
4 eggs
Garnishes: rolled strips of
   smoked salmon, fresh
   dillweed sprigs, and thin
   lemon slices

Place breadcrumbs in a greased 8-inch springform pan. Rotate pan to coat bottom and halfway up sides of pan; chill.

Sauté onion in melted butter in a medium skillet until tender; remove from heat, and set aside.

Place knife blade in food processor bowl; add cream cheese, and process until smooth. Add reserved onion, salmon, dillweed, and lemon juice; process until smooth. Add eggs, one at a time, through food chute with processor running, processing just until mixture is smooth.

Pour salmon mixture into prepared pan; place pan in a large shallow baking dish. Pour hot water to a depth of 1 inch into dish. Bake at 325° for 1 hour. Turn oven off. Partially open oven door, and let pâté cool in oven 1 hour. Let cool to room temperature in pan on a wire rack. Cover and chill at least 8 hours. To serve, carefully remove sides of springform pan, and let come to room temperature. Garnish, if desired, and cut into thin wedges. Yield: one 8-inch pâté.   Peggy Sharpe

The Best Specialties of the House . . . and More
North Suburban Guild of Children's Memorial Medical Center
Chicago, Illinois

Garlicky Stuffed Mushrooms

12 large fresh mushrooms
1 tablespoon butter or
  margarine
½ (8-ounce) package cream
  cheese, softened
1 to 2 cloves garlic,
  crushed
2 tablespoons Chablis or other
  dry white wine
1 tablespoon chopped fresh
  parsley

1 tablespoon butter or
  margarine, melted
¼ teaspoon dried whole
  dillweed
⅛ teaspoon salt
⅛ teaspoon dried whole basil
⅛ teaspoon freeze-dried chives
⅛ teaspoon dried whole
  marjoram
Dash of dried whole thyme
Dash of pepper

Clean mushrooms with damp paper towels. Remove and chop stems; set caps aside. Sauté stems in 1 tablespoon butter in a skillet until tender; set aside.

Combine cream cheese and remaining ingredients in a small mixing bowl; beat at medium speed of an electric mixer until smooth. Stir in chopped mushroom stems. Spoon mixture evenly into reserved mushroom caps. Place mushrooms on an ungreased baking sheet; broil 6 inches from heat 1 minute or until lightly browned. Yield: 1 dozen.   Genevieve Freeman

The When You Live in Hawaii You Get Very Creative During Passover
Cookbook
Congregation Sof Ma'arav
Honolulu, Hawaii

Living in Hawaii creates a food challenge for the Jewish
community during Passover. In response, the Congregation Sof
Ma'arav offers a variety of kosher recipes in The When You
Live in Hawaii You Get Very Creative During Passover
Cookbook.

Zucchini-Cheese Appetizer Squares

1 small onion, chopped
1 clove garlic, minced
¼ cup vegetable oil
2½ cups shredded zucchini
6 eggs, beaten
3 cups (12 ounces) shredded
  Cheddar cheese
⅓ cup fine, dry breadcrumbs

½ teaspoon salt
½ teaspoon dried whole basil
½ teaspoon dried whole
  oregano
¼ teaspoon pepper
½ cup grated Parmesan cheese
¼ cup sesame seeds, toasted

Sauté onion and garlic in oil in a large skillet until tender. Add zucchini, and sauté just until zucchini is crisp-tender. Remove from heat, and let cool.

Combine zucchini mixture, eggs, and next 6 ingredients in a large bowl; stir well. Spoon into a greased 13- x 9- x 2-inch baking dish. Sprinkle with Parmesan cheese and sesame seeds. Bake at 325° for 30 minutes or until set and lightly browned. Remove from oven, and let stand 15 minutes. Cut into squares, and serve warm. Yield: 3 dozen.   Linda Christensen

The Galloping Chef
The Combined Training Equestrian Team Alliance
Woodside, California

Petite Broccoli Quiches

1 (3-ounce) package cream
  cheese, softened
½ cup butter or margarine,
  softened
1 cup all-purpose flour
¾ cup frozen chopped
  broccoli, thawed and
  drained

¾ cup (3 ounces) shredded
  Swiss cheese
2 eggs, beaten
¼ cup plus 2 tablespoons
  half-and-half
¾ teaspoon salt

Combine softened cream cheese and butter in a medium mixing bowl; beat at medium speed of an electric mixer until smooth. Add flour, and beat at medium speed until mixture is smooth.

Shape pastry into 24 (1-inch) balls. Place each ball into an ungreased miniature (1¾-inch) muffin pan; press dough onto bottom and sides to form shells. Set aside.

Combine chopped broccoli and remaining ingredients in a medium bowl, stirring well. Spoon broccoli mixture evenly into shells. Bake at 400° for 25 minutes or until set and lightly browned. Yield: 2 dozen.   Anne Page

Home Cookin' "AT&T's Right Choices"
Western Electric Council Telephone Pioneers of America
Ballwin, Missouri

Cheese Capers

**2 cups (8 ounces) shredded
  Cheddar cheese**
½ cup mayonnaise
**¼ cup finely sliced green
  onions**
**¼ cup finely chopped salad
  olives**

**1 tablespoon finely chopped
  pimiento**
1 tablespoon chopped capers
4 English muffins, split
Grated Parmesan cheese

Combine first 6 ingredients in a large bowl, stirring until blended.

Spread about ¼ cup cheese mixture evenly over each muffin half; place on an ungreased baking sheet. Sprinkle lightly with Parmesan cheese; cut into quarters. Bake at 350° for 15 minutes, or broil 3 inches from heat 2 minutes or until cheese melts. Yield: 32 appetizers.

Only in California
The Children's Home Society of California
Los Angeles, California

Cheese Tasters

1 cup butter or margarine,
  softened
2 cups all-purpose flour
1 cup (4 ounces) shredded
  sharp Cheddar cheese

½ teaspoon salt
¼ teaspoon ground red pepper
2 cups crisp rice cereal

Cream butter; add flour and next 3 ingredients, mixing until well blended. Stir in cereal. Shape mixture into 1-inch balls. Place balls about 1 inch apart on ungreased baking sheets. Flatten each ball with a fork dipped in flour. Bake at 325° for 20 to 22 minutes or until lightly browned. Let cool completely on wire racks. Yield: 5½ dozen.   Elizabeth White

Methodist Blessings
The United Methodist Women, First United Methodist Church
New Iberia, Louisiana

Crisp Savory Almonds

2 egg whites
1½ teaspoons Dijon mustard
⅛ teaspoon ground red pepper
⅛ teaspoon paprika

4 cups blanched whole
  almonds
⅔ cup grated Parmesan cheese
½ teaspoon salt

Beat egg whites in a large bowl at high speed of an electric mixer until foamy. Add mustard, red pepper, and paprika; beat at low speed until well blended. Stir in almonds; toss to coat evenly.

Combine Parmesan cheese and salt on a sheet of wax paper. Pour almond mixture over cheese mixture; toss gently to coat evenly. Spread almonds on a baking sheet lined with parchment paper. Bake at 300° for 25 minutes, stirring occasionally. Turn oven off; let almonds stand 30 minutes. Remove almonds from oven, and let cool completely. Store almonds in an airtight container. Yield: 4½ cups.   Elisabeth B. Davis

World Heritage of Cooking
Friends of the World Heritage Museum
Urbana, Illinois

Prosciutto and Parmesan Palmiers

1 sheet commercial frozen puff
  pastry, thawed
3 tablespoons honey mustard
4 ounces thinly sliced
  prosciutto

1 cup freshly grated Parmesan
  cheese
1 egg
2 teaspoons water

Place pastry sheet on a work surface; spread mustard evenly over pastry. Arrange prosciutto slices evenly over mustard; sprinkle with cheese. Lightly press cheese into prosciutto with a rolling pin.

Roll up pastry, jellyroll fashion, starting at long side and ending at middle of pastry sheet. Roll up remaining pastry, jellyroll fashion, starting at remaining long side until both rolls meet. Cover and chill 30 minutes or until firm.

Cut roll crosswise into ½-inch slices. (Slices will resemble a figure "8".) Place slices on baking sheet lined with parchment paper.

Combine egg and water in a small bowl; beat lightly. Brush top of each palmier with egg mixture. Bake at 350° for 20 to 25 minutes or until puffed and golden. Serve warm or at room temperature. Yield: 1½ dozen.

Sound Seasonings
The Junior League of Westchester on the Sound
Larchmont, New York

The Junior League of Westchester on the Sound traces its roots back to 1933 when its social gatherings involved sewing layettes and rolling bandages for New York hospitals. Today, through funds raised from the sale of the organization's cookbook, Sound Seasonings, *the league is able to provide food and clothing to needy persons, sponsor a haven for runaway youths, and organize a holiday gift drive for children with AIDS and their siblings.*

Chicken Wings with Jalapeño Pepper Sauce

1 (12-ounce) bottle chili sauce
½ cup firmly packed dark
  brown sugar
½ cup vegetable oil
½ cup white vinegar
¼ cup catsup
1 medium onion, sliced

5 jalapeño peppers, seeded
2 tablespoons Worcestershire
  sauce
2 teaspoons salt
32 chicken wings (about 5½
  pounds)

Combine first 9 ingredients in container of an electric blender, and process 30 seconds or until mixture is well blended. Set sauce mixture aside.

Remove and discard chicken wing tips. Cut wings in half at joint; place in a greased roasting pan. Pour half of sauce over wings. Bake at 375° for 30 minutes. Turn wings, and top with remaining half of sauce. Bake an additional 30 minutes or until done. Serve warm. Yield: 8 appetizer servings.   Shawn Ebbling

What the Winners Eat
Sugar Creek Swim Club
St. Louis, Missouri

Chicken Nuggets with Pineapple Sauce

1¼ cups all-purpose flour,
  divided
2 eggs, beaten
2 tablespoons water
1 teaspoon salt

6 chicken breast halves,
  skinned, boned, and cut into
  1-inch pieces
¾ cup peanut oil
Pineapple Sauce

Combine ¼ cup flour, eggs, water, and salt in a small bowl; stir well. Cover and chill batter 1 hour.

Dip chicken in chilled batter; dredge in remaining 1 cup flour. Fry 4 to 5 pieces of chicken at a time in hot peanut oil (375°) in a large skillet or wok until golden. Drain well on paper towels. Serve warm with Pineapple Sauce. Yield: 9 appetizer servings.

Pineapple Sauce

1¼ cups pineapple juice, divided
1 tablespoon sugar
1 tablespoon cornstarch

1 (8-ounce) can crushed pineapple, drained
2 tablespoons cider vinegar
2 teaspoons prepared mustard

Combine 1 cup juice and sugar in a saucepan; cook over medium heat, stirring constantly, until sugar dissolves. Combine cornstarch and remaining ¼ cup juice; add to saucepan. Bring to a boil; cook 1 minute, stirring constantly. Stir in pineapple, vinegar, and mustard. Serve warm. Yield: 1½ cups.   Pat Brozinski

Our Pet Recipes
The Humane Society Calumet Area, Inc.
Hammond, Indiana

Glazed Meatballs

3 slices white bread
⅔ cup milk
2 eggs, lightly beaten
1 tablespoon prepared horseradish
¼ teaspoon salt
¼ teaspoon pepper

1½ pounds ground beef
½ cup catsup
¼ cup water
¼ cup soy sauce
¼ cup maple-flavored syrup
1 teaspoon ground allspice
½ teaspoon dry mustard

Soak bread in milk. Combine bread, eggs, horseradish, salt, and pepper in a mixing bowl; beat well at medium speed of an electric mixer. Add beef; mix well. Shape mixture into 1-inch balls. Place on a rack in a shallow roasting pan. Bake at 450° for 10 to 15 minutes.

Combine catsup and remaining ingredients in a saucepan; cook over medium heat until bubbly, stirring occasionally. Add meatballs to sauce, and cook until thoroughly heated. Serve warm. Yield: 6 dozen.   Cindy Pate

Cooking Elementary Style
Ridgedale Elementary School PTA
Knoxville, Tennessee

Jungle Juice Punch

1½ quarts water
4 cups sugar
1 (46-ounce) can pineapple
  juice
1 (46-ounce) can orange juice

¼ cup lemon juice
6 ripe bananas, mashed
2 (32-ounce) bottles ginger ale,
  chilled

Combine water and sugar in a large Dutch oven. Bring to a boil; cook 5 minutes or until sugar dissolves, stirring frequently. Let mixture cool slightly. Add juices and mashed banana, stirring well. Transfer juice mixture to a freezer container; cover and freeze at least 8 hours.

To serve, let stand at room temperature 4 to 5 hours or until slushy. Gently stir in ginger ale just before serving. Yield: about 2¼ gallons.   Jane D. Melancon

The Cajun Connection Cookbook
Trinity Catholic School Booster Club
St. Martinville, Louisiana

Jackson House Hot Spiced Cider

1 gallon apple cider
½ to 1 cup firmly packed
  brown sugar
1 (3-inch) stick cinnamon,
  broken into pieces

1 tablespoon whole allspice
1 tablespoon whole cloves

Combine apple cider and brown sugar in a large Dutch oven; stir well. Tie cinnamon, allspice, and cloves in a cheesecloth bag; add spice bag to cider mixture. Bring to a boil; reduce heat, and simmer 10 minutes. Remove and discard spice bag. Serve warm. Yield: 1 gallon.   Edna Pickral

Historic Lexington Cooks: Rockbridge Regional Recipes
Historic Lexington Foundation
Lexington, Virginia

OJ Special

⅓ cup frozen orange juice
concentrate, thawed and
undiluted
½ cup milk

½ cup water
¼ cup sugar
½ teaspoon vanilla extract
6 ice cubes

Combine juice concentrate, milk, water, sugar, vanilla, and ice cubes in container of an electric blender; process until frothy. Serve immediately. Yield: 2 cups.   Karen Wingate Campbell

East Cooper Cuisine
Christ Our King Ladies Club
Mt. Pleasant, South Carolina

Citrus Frappé

½ cup orange juice
½ teaspoon grated lemon rind
¼ cup lemon juice

1 cup lemon sherbet
10 ice cubes
2 tablespoons dry sherry

Combine orange juice, lemon rind, and lemon juice in container of an electric blender; process at high speed 5 seconds.

Add sherbet and ice cubes; process at high speed 1 minute or until frothy. Add sherry; process until smooth. Serve immediately. Yield: 2 cups.   Irene Rudolph

Kettle's On, Cooking with Leaders
Burlington County Girl Scout Council
Rancocas, New Jersey

Spiced Grape Tea

2½ quarts water
2½ tablespoons loose tea
1 teaspoon whole allspice
2 cups sugar

2 cups grape juice
⅔ cup orange juice
½ cup lemon juice

Bring water to a boil in a large Dutch oven; add tea and allspice. Remove from heat; cover and let stand 5 minutes. Strain tea mixture; return to Dutch oven. Add sugar and remaining ingredients; cook over low heat, stirring until sugar dissolves. Serve warm. Yield: 3 quarts.

"One Lump or Two?"
All Children's Hospital Foundation
St. Petersburg, Florida

New Mexican Chocolate

1 (4-ounce) package sweet
  baking chocolate
1 cup hot water
5½ cups milk
½ cup half-and-half

1 teaspoon ground cinnamon
⅛ teaspoon ground nutmeg
1 teaspoon vanilla extract
8 (4-inch) sticks cinnamon

Combine chocolate and 1 cup hot water in top of a double boiler; bring water in bottom of double boiler to a boil. Reduce heat to low; cook until chocolate melts, stirring occasionally. Remove from heat, and set aside.

Combine milk, half-and-half, cinnamon, and nutmeg in a saucepan; cook over medium heat, stirring occasionally, until thoroughly heated. Remove from heat; add chocolate mixture and vanilla. Beat with a wire whisk until blended. Pour into mugs; add cinnamon sticks. Serve warm. Yield: 7 cups.   Felix Lopez

Bless This Food, Man Does Not Live by Art Alone
The New Mexico Alliance for Arts Education
Los Alamos, New Mexico

Breads

A picturesque gristmill stands at the Wayside Inn in Sudbury, Massachusetts. Gristmills were once used for grinding grains that were processed into flour and meal.

Spiced Pumpkin Loaf

1¾ cups all-purpose flour
1 teaspoon baking powder
1 teaspoon baking soda
½ teaspoon salt
1 cup cooked, mashed
  pumpkin
⅔ cup sugar
⅓ cup sour cream
⅓ cup vegetable oil
3 tablespoons orange
  marmalade

1 egg, beaten
1 teaspoon ground cinnamon
½ teaspoon ground ginger
¼ teaspoon freshly grated
  nutmeg
⅛ teaspoon ground cloves
⅔ cup chopped walnuts
Cream Cheese Spread

Grease and flour a 9- x 5- x 3-inch loafpan; line with wax paper. Grease and flour wax paper. Set aside.

Combine flour, baking powder, soda, and salt; stir well. Combine pumpkin and next 9 ingredients in a medium mixing bowl; beat well at medium speed of an electric mixer. Add flour mixture to pumpkin mixture, beating well. Stir in walnuts.

Pour batter into prepared pan. Bake at 350° for 45 to 50 minutes or until a wooden pick inserted in center comes out clean. Let cool in pan 10 minutes. Remove from pan; remove wax paper, and let cool completely on a wire rack. Serve with Cream Cheese Spread. Yield: 1 loaf.

Cream Cheese Spread

1 (8-ounce) package cream
  cheese, softened

½ cup orange marmalade

Beat cream cheese at medium speed of an electric mixer until smooth. Add orange marmalade, beating mixture until well blended. Yield: 1⅓ cups.
                                          Cathryn Dubow

The Broker's Cookbook, Second Edition
The Robinson-Humphrey Company, Inc.
Atlanta, Georgia

Alaska Cranberry-Nut Bread

¾ cup orange juice
½ cup mayonnaise
2 eggs, lightly beaten
2½ cups all-purpose flour
2 teaspoons baking powder
½ teaspoon baking soda
¼ teaspoon salt

1 cup sugar
½ cup chopped pecans or
   walnuts
2 teaspoons grated orange rind
1½ cups fresh cranberries
2 tablespoons sugar
1 teaspoon grated orange rind

Combine orange juice, mayonnaise, and eggs in a small bowl; stir well.

Combine flour and next 6 ingredients in a large bowl; stir well. Add orange juice mixture to flour mixture, stirring until blended. Gently fold in cranberries.

Pour batter into a greased and floured 9- x 5- x 3-inch loafpan. Combine 2 tablespoons sugar and 1 teaspoon orange rind; sprinkle evenly over batter. Bake at 350° for 1 hour to 1 hour and 10 minutes or until a wooden pick inserted in center comes out clean. Let cool in pan 10 minutes; remove from pan, and let cool completely on a wire rack. Yield: 1 loaf.   Jean Pearce

Alaska's Cooking, Volume II
The Woman's Club of Anchorage, Alaska

Cheddar-Apple Bread

2½ cups all-purpose flour
2 teaspoons baking powder
½ teaspoon salt
¾ cup sugar
½ teaspoon ground cinnamon
¾ cup milk
⅓ cup butter or margarine,
   melted

2 eggs, beaten
2 cups (8 ounces) shredded
   sharp Cheddar cheese
1½ cups peeled, chopped
   cooking apples
¾ cup chopped pecans or
   walnuts

Combine first 5 ingredients in a medium bowl; stir well. Combine milk, butter, and eggs; stir well. Add to dry ingredients, stirring until blended. Stir in cheese, apple, and pecans. Pour batter into a greased and floured 9- x 5- x 3-inch loafpan. Bake at

350° for 1 hour or until a wooden pick inserted in center comes out clean. Let cool in pan 5 minutes; remove from pan, and let cool completely on a wire rack. Yield: 1 loaf.   Julie Howalt

Not So Secret Recipes
4450th Tactical Group, Nellis Air Force Base
Las Vegas, Nevada

Apple-Pear Coffee Cake

½ cup butter or margarine, softened
1 cup sugar
2 eggs
2 cups all-purpose flour
1 teaspoon baking powder
1 teaspoon baking soda
½ teaspoon salt
1 (8-ounce) carton sour cream
1¼ cups peeled, finely chopped cooking apples (about 2 apples)

¾ cup peeled, finely chopped pear (about 1 pear)
1 teaspoon vanilla extract
1 cup firmly packed brown sugar
½ cup chopped pecans
2 tablespoons butter or margarine, softened
1 teaspoon ground cinnamon

Cream butter; gradually add sugar, beating well at medium speed of an electric mixer. Add eggs, one at a time, beating well after each addition. Combine flour and next 3 ingredients; add to creamed mixture alternately with sour cream, beginning and ending with flour mixture. Mix after each addition. Fold in apple and pear. Stir in vanilla.

Spread batter in a greased 13- x 9- x 2-inch baking pan. Combine 1 cup brown sugar, pecans, 2 tablespoons butter, and cinnamon; sprinkle evenly over batter. Bake at 350° for 45 to 50 minutes or until a wooden pick inserted in center comes out clean. Yield: 15 servings.   Vada Frank

You Make the Best Better
The Macoupin County 4-H Foundation
Carlinville, Illinois

Fresh Blueberry Coffee Cake

1¼ cups fresh blueberries
1⅓ cups sugar, divided
2 cups plus 2 tablespoons all-
  purpose flour, divided
½ cup butter, softened
2 eggs
1 teaspoon baking powder

½ teaspoon salt
1 (8-ounce) carton sour cream
1 teaspoon vanilla or almond
  extract
½ cup chopped pecans
Glaze (recipe follows)

Combine blueberries, ⅓ cup sugar, and 2 tablespoons flour in a small saucepan; cook over medium heat 5 minutes or until thickened, stirring constantly. Set aside.

Cream butter; gradually add remaining 1 cup sugar, beating well at medium speed of an electric mixer. Add eggs, one at a time, beating well after each addition.

Combine remaining 2 cups flour, baking powder, and salt; add to creamed mixture alternately with sour cream, beginning and ending with flour mixture. Stir in vanilla.

Spoon half of batter into a heavily greased 10-inch tube pan. Spoon half of reserved blueberry mixture over batter. Repeat procedure with remaining batter and blueberry mixture. Swirl through batter with a knife. Sprinkle with pecans. Bake at 350° for 50 minutes. Let cool in pan 5 minutes; transfer to a serving plate. Drizzle glaze over warm coffee cake. Yield: one 10-inch coffee cake.

Glaze

¾ cup sifted powdered sugar
1 tablespoon warm water

1 teaspoon vanilla or almond
  extract

Combine all ingredients in a small bowl; stir with a wire whisk until smooth. Yield: ¼ cup.   Betty Jo Van Sant

Cooks and Company
The Muscle Shoals District Service League
Sheffield, Alabama

Blueberry Streusel Muffins

1 cup all-purpose flour
½ cup whole wheat flour
2 teaspoons baking powder
½ teaspoon baking soda
¼ teaspoon salt
¾ cup sugar
¾ cup buttermilk
½ cup butter or margarine,
  melted and cooled
2 eggs, lightly beaten

1 teaspoon vanilla extract
2 cups fresh or frozen
  blueberries, thawed
¼ cup sugar
3 tablespoons all-purpose flour
½ teaspoon ground cinnamon
¼ teaspoon salt
1 tablespoon butter or
  margarine

Combine first 6 ingredients in a large bowl; stir well. Make a well in center of flour mixture.

Combine buttermilk, ½ cup melted butter, eggs, and vanilla, beating well with a wire whisk. Add to flour mixture, stirring just until dry ingredients are moistened. Gently fold in blueberries. Spoon batter into paper-lined muffin pans, filling two-thirds full.

Combine ¼ cup sugar, 3 tablespoons flour, cinnamon, and ¼ teaspoon salt. Cut in 1 tablespoon butter with a pastry blender until mixture resembles coarse meal. Sprinkle mixture evenly over batter. Bake at 375° for 20 to 25 minutes or until golden. Remove from pans immediately. Yield: 1½ dozen.   Richard Buro

Our Favorite Recipes
Hope Lutheran Church
Moose Lake, Minnesota

The Muscle Shoals District Service League's cookbook, Cooks and Company, *is an ongoing fund-raising project which enables the organization to provide services for the area's handicapped and underprivileged citizens. Muscle Shoals is located on the scenic Tennessee River in Alabama.*

Sweet Potato Muffins

1¼ cups regular oats,
　uncooked
1 cup all-purpose flour
1 teaspoon baking powder
½ teaspoon baking soda
½ teaspoon salt
1 teaspoon ground cinnamon
½ teaspoon ground nutmeg
1 cup cooked, mashed sweet
　potato

1 cup milk
¾ cup firmly packed brown
　sugar
½ cup vegetable oil
1 egg, beaten
1 teaspoon vanilla extract
⅓ cup chopped pecans
Topping (recipe follows)

Combine oats, flour, baking powder, soda, salt, cinnamon, and nutmeg; stir well.

Combine sweet potato and next 5 ingredients; stir well. Add sweet potato mixture to oat mixture, stirring just until dry ingredients are moistened. Stir in pecans.

Spoon batter into greased and floured muffin pans, filling three-fourths full. Sprinkle topping evenly over batter. Bake at 400° for 15 minutes or until a wooden pick inserted in center comes out clean. Remove from pans immediately. Yield: 1½ dozen.

Topping

¼ cup regular oats, uncooked
¼ cup all-purpose flour
¼ cup firmly packed brown
　sugar

¼ cup chopped pecans
1 teaspoon ground cinnamon
¼ cup butter or margarine

Combine first 5 ingredients in a small bowl; stir well. Cut in butter with a pastry blender until mixture resembles coarse meal. Yield: about 1 cup.

Good Cookin' from Giffin
The Giffin Elementary School PTA
Knoxville, Tennessee

Pumpkin Pancakes

2 cups all-purpose flour
2 teaspoons baking powder
1 teaspoon baking soda
½ teaspoon salt
1 teaspoon ground cinnamon
¼ teaspoon ground ginger
¼ teaspoon ground nutmeg

2 eggs, lightly beaten
1½ cups buttermilk
1 cup cooked, mashed
   pumpkin
¼ cup water
¼ cup vegetable oil

Sift together first 7 ingredients into a large bowl. Add eggs, buttermilk, pumpkin, water, and oil, stirring until blended.

For each pancake, pour about ¼ cup batter onto a hot, lightly greased griddle. Turn pancakes when tops are covered with bubbles and edges look cooked. Serve pancakes immediately. Yield: 20 (4-inch) pancakes.   Elsie Ford

Cookbook to benefit the Homeless
Lutheran Social Services of Southern California
Riverside, California

Wheat Germ Waffles

2 cups all-purpose flour
1 tablespoon baking powder
1 teaspoon salt
½ cup wheat germ
¼ cup sugar

½ teaspoon ground nutmeg
1¾ cups milk
⅓ cup vegetable oil
2 eggs, separated

Combine first 6 ingredients in a large bowl; stir well. Combine milk, oil, and egg yolks; add to dry ingredients, stirring until blended.

Beat egg whites at high speed of an electric mixer until stiff peaks form; gently fold into batter. Bake in preheated, oiled waffle iron. Yield: 14 (4-inch) waffles.   Linda Lehtola

Note-Worthy Recipes
Iowa Falls High School
Iowa Falls, Iowa

Swedish Apple Coffee Crown

4 to 5 cups all-purpose flour,
    divided
⅓ cup sugar
1 teaspoon salt
1 package dry yeast
1 cup milk
½ cup water
¼ cup butter or margarine
1 egg
1 (3-ounce) package cream
    cheese, softened
¼ cup butter or margarine,
    softened

¾ cup sugar
1 teaspoon ground cinnamon
2 cups peeled, chopped
    cooking apples
⅓ cup firmly packed brown
    sugar
½ teaspoon ground cinnamon
Glaze (recipe follows)
Garnish: marachino cherry
    halves

Combine 3 cups flour, ⅓ cup sugar, salt, and yeast in a large mixing bowl; stir well.

Combine milk, water, and ¼ cup butter in a saucepan; cook over low heat until butter melts, stirring occasionally. Let cool to 120° to 130°. Gradually add milk mixture and egg to flour mixture, beating well at low speed of an electric mixer. Beat an additional 2 minutes at medium speed. Gradually stir in enough remaining 2 cups flour to make a soft dough.

Turn dough out onto a floured surface, and knead until smooth and elastic (about 5 to 8 minutes). Place in a well-greased bowl, turning to grease top. Cover and let rise in a warm place (85°), free from drafts, 1 hour or until doubled in bulk.

Combine cream cheese and ¼ cup butter in a small mixing bowl; beat at medium speed until blended. Gradually add ¾ cup sugar and 1 teaspoon cinnamon, beating well. Set aside.

Combine apple, ⅓ cup brown sugar, and ½ teaspoon cinnamon in a small bowl; stir well, and set aside.

Punch dough down; turn out onto a lightly floured surface, and knead lightly 4 or 5 times. Divide dough in half. Roll one portion of dough to an 18- x 8-inch rectangle. Spread with half of reserved cream cheese mixture, leaving ½-inch margin on all sides; sprinkle half of reserved apple mixture over cream cheese layer. Roll up dough, jellyroll fashion, starting at long side, pressing firmly to eliminate air pockets; pinch seam and ends to seal. Place dough, seam side up, in a heavily greased 12-cup Bundt pan. Repeat procedure with remaining portion of dough, cream cheese mixture, and apple mixture, placing seam side down on top of dough in pan.

Cover and let rise in a warm place, free from drafts, 1 hour or until doubled in bulk. Bake at 350° for 40 minutes; cover loosely with aluminum foil to prevent excessive browning. Bake an additional 5 to 10 minutes or until bread sounds hollow when tapped. Remove from pan immediately. Drizzle glaze over warm coffee cake. Garnish, if desired. Yield: one 10-inch coffee cake.

Glaze

1 cup sifted powdered sugar   **1 tablespoon milk**
1 tablespoon butter or   **1 teaspoon lemon juice**
** margarine, melted**

Combine all ingredients in a small bowl, stirring until smooth. Yield: about ⅓ cup.   James Getzlaff, Bill Holloway

The Oregon County Cookbook
Milwaukie Elementary School
Milwaukie, Oregon

Milwaukie Elementary School created The Oregon County Cookbook *to help students learn about the agricultural and cultural influences of the state's seven geographic regions. Funds generated from the sale of the cookbook support the school's computer lab which is used in the student writing program. The children see firsthand the power of writing by observing their cookbook sales, newspaper coverage, and by making guest appearances as "chefs" on a local television show.*

Cinnamon Swirl Loaves

2 cups milk	2 eggs
½ cup shortening	½ cup sugar
7½ to 8 cups all-purpose flour	1 tablespoon ground cinnamon
½ cup sugar	1 cup sifted powdered sugar
2 teaspoons salt	1½ to 2 tablespoons milk
2 packages dry yeast	½ teaspoon vanilla extract

Combine 2 cups milk and shortening in a saucepan; heat until shortening melts, stirring occasionally. Let cool to 120° to 130°.

Combine 3½ cups flour, ½ cup sugar, salt, and yeast in a mixing bowl. Gradually add milk mixture to flour mixture, beating well at medium speed of an electric mixer. Add eggs, one at a time, beating well after each addition. Beat an additional 2 minutes at medium speed. Gradually add ¾ cup flour; beat 2 minutes. Stir in enough remaining 3¾ cups flour to make a soft dough.

Turn dough out onto a floured surface, and knead until smooth and elastic (about 10 minutes). Place in a well-greased bowl, turning to grease top. Cover and let rise in a warm place (85°), free from drafts, 1 hour or until doubled in bulk.

Punch dough down; let rest 10 minutes. Turn out onto a floured surface; knead lightly 4 or 5 times. Divide dough in half. Roll one portion to a 15- x 7-inch rectangle; brush with water. Combine ½ cup sugar and cinnamon. Sprinkle half of sugar mixture over dough. Roll up dough, jellyroll fashion, starting at narrow edge, pressing firmly to eliminate air pockets; pinch seam and ends to seal. Place dough, seam side down, in a greased 9- x 5- x 3-inch loafpan. Repeat procedure with remaining dough and sugar mixture. Cover and let rise in a warm place, free from drafts, 35 minutes or until doubled in bulk. Bake at 375° for 20 minutes. Cover with aluminum foil to prevent excessive browning. Bake an additional 15 to 20 minutes or until loaves sound hollow when tapped. Remove loaves from pans immediately; let cool on wire racks. Combine powdered sugar, 1½ to 2 tablespoons milk, and vanilla. Drizzle glaze over loaves. Yield: 2 loaves.   Jan Fraser

Montana 1889-1989 Centennial Cookbook
The Inter-Denominational Christian Fellowship
Noxon, Montana

Kasha Bread

2½ cups water
1 cup kasha (buckwheat groats)
¾ cup milk
3 tablespoons sugar
2 tablespoons butter or
  margarine
1 tablespoon salt
1 tablespoon molasses

2 packages dry yeast
¼ cup warm water (105° to
  115°)
4 cups all-purpose flour
2 cups whole wheat flour
1 cup diced onion
1 tablespoon butter or
  margarine, melted

Place 2½ cups water in a medium saucepan; bring to a boil. Add kasha, and cook 10 minutes or until liquid is absorbed. Stir in milk and next 4 ingredients; cook to 105° to 115°.

Dissolve yeast in ¼ cup warm water; let stand 5 minutes. Add yeast mixture to kasha mixture; stir well. Add flours to kasha mixture; stir well.

Turn dough out onto a floured surface, and knead until smooth and elastic (about 10 minutes). Shape dough into a ball. Place dough in a well-greased bowl, turning to grease top. Cover and let rise in a warm place (85°), free from drafts, 1 hour or until doubled in bulk.

Sauté onion in 1 tablespoon melted butter in a small skillet until tender; set aside.

Punch dough down. Turn out onto a lightly floured surface; add onion, and knead lightly 4 or 5 times. Divide dough in half. Roll one portion of dough to a 14- x 7-inch rectangle. Roll up dough, jellyroll fashion, starting at narrow edge, pressing firmly to eliminate air pockets; pinch ends to seal. Place dough, seam side down, in a heavily greased 9- x 5- x 3-inch loafpan. Repeat procedure with remaining portion of dough. Cover and let rise in a warm place, free from drafts, 35 to 40 minutes or until doubled in bulk.

Bake at 350° for 35 to 40 minutes or until loaves sound hollow when tapped. Remove bread from pans immediately, and let cool on wire racks. Yield: 2 loaves.   Evelyn Garb

Chef's EscORT
Women's American ORT, Southeast District
Hallandale, Florida

Onion Braid

1 cup milk
½ cup butter or margarine
¼ cup sugar
¼ cup water
1½ teaspoons salt
4 cups bread flour
1 package dry yeast
1 egg
1 cup finely chopped onion

¼ cup butter or margarine, melted
1 tablespoon grated Parmesan cheese
1 tablespoon poppy seeds
1 clove garlic, minced
1 egg yolk, beaten
1 teaspoon water
Additional poppy seeds

Combine first 5 ingredients in a saucepan; heat until sugar dissolves, stirring occasionally. Let cool to 120° to 130°.

Combine 2 cups flour and yeast in a large mixing bowl. Gradually add milk mixture to flour mixture, beating well at medium speed of an electric mixer. Add egg; beat 2 minutes at medium speed. Gradually stir in enough remaining 2 cups flour to make a soft dough. Turn dough out onto a floured surface; knead until smooth and elastic (about 10 minutes). Place in a well-greased bowl, turning to grease top. Cover and let rise in a warm place (85°), free from drafts, 1 hour or until doubled in bulk.

Combine onion, ¼ cup melted butter, Parmesan cheese, 1 tablespoon poppy seeds, and garlic. Punch dough down. Roll to an 18- x 12-inch rectangle. Cut lengthwise into three (4-inch) strips. Spread onion mixture lengthwise down center of each strip. Fold strips over lengthwise to form ropes, pinching seams to seal. Place ropes, side by side, on a greased baking sheet; braid ropes, and tuck ends under to seal. Cover and let rise in a warm place, free from drafts, 35 minutes or until doubled in bulk.

Combine egg yolk and 1 teaspoon water. Brush loaf with egg yolk mixture; sprinkle with poppy seeds. Bake at 350° for 35 to 40 minutes or until loaf sounds hollow when tapped. (Cover loosely with aluminum foil during the last 15 minutes of baking to prevent excessive browning, if necessary.) Remove from baking sheet; let cool on a wire rack. Yield: 1 loaf.   Louise Cole

The Fort Leavenworth Recollection
The Fort Leavenworth Officers' and Civilians' Wives' Club
Fort Leavenworth, Kansas

Cheese and Herb Ring

2½ cups all-purpose flour, divided
1 cup (4 ounces) shredded Cheddar cheese, divided
1 tablespoon dry yeast
1 teaspoon salt
¾ cup milk
2 tablespoons butter

1 egg
1 clove garlic, minced
¼ cup butter, melted
1 tablespoon minced fresh parsley
¼ teaspoon dried whole tarragon

Combine 1 cup flour, ½ cup cheese, yeast, and salt; set aside.

Combine milk and 2 tablespoons butter in a saucepan; heat until butter melts, stirring occasionally. Let cool to 120° to 130°. Gradually add milk mixture to flour mixture, beating well at high speed of an electric mixer. Add egg; beat 2 minutes at medium speed. Gradually add ¾ cup flour; beat 2 minutes. Stir in enough remaining ¾ cup flour to make a soft dough.

Turn dough out onto a floured surface, and knead until smooth and elastic (about 10 minutes). Place in a well-greased bowl, turning to grease top. Cover and let rise in a warm place (85°), free from drafts, 1 hour or until doubled in bulk.

Sauté garlic in ¼ cup melted butter in a skillet until tender; stir in parsley and tarragon. Set aside.

Punch dough down; let rest 10 minutes. Turn out onto a floured surface; knead lightly 4 or 5 times. Roll dough to a 20- x 9-inch rectangle. Brush with herb mixture; sprinkle with remaining ½ cup cheese. Roll up dough, jellyroll fashion, starting at long side, pressing firmly to eliminate air pockets; pinch ends to seal.

Cut roll of dough in half lengthwise. Place halves, side by side, cut side up. Twist halves together, and shape into a ring. Place loaf on a greased baking sheet. Cover and let rise in a warm place, free from drafts, 45 minutes or until doubled in bulk. Bake at 350° for 25 to 30 minutes or until loaf sounds hollow when tapped. Remove loaf from baking sheet immediately; let cool on a wire rack. Yield: 1 loaf.   Anna D'Agostino, Karen D'Agostino

Cookin' with the Crusaders
Most Holy Redeemer School
Tampa, Florida

Walnut Rolls

1 package dry yeast
2 tablespoons warm water
   (105° to 115°)
¼ cup sugar
¼ cup milk
3 tablespoons shortening
½ teaspoon salt
1 egg
2 cups all-purpose flour
1 teaspoon grated lemon rind
¼ teaspoon ground ginger

¼ cup butter or margarine
½ cup firmly packed brown
   sugar
2 tablespoons dark corn syrup
1 tablespoon water
½ cup walnut pieces
1 tablespoon butter or
   margarine, melted
½ cup chopped walnuts
¼ cup sugar
¼ teaspoon ground cinnamon

Dissolve yeast in 2 tablespoons warm water in a large bowl; let stand 5 minutes.

Combine ¼ cup sugar, milk, shortening, and salt in a small saucepan; heat until butter melts, stirring occasionally. Let cool to 105° to 115°.

Add milk mixture, egg, 1½ cups flour, lemon rind, and ginger to yeast mixture; beat at medium speed of an electric mixer until smooth. Gradually stir in enough remaining ½ cup flour to make a soft dough.

Turn dough out onto a floured surface, and knead until smooth and elastic (about 5 minutes). Place in a well-greased bowl, turning to grease top. Cover and let rise in a warm place (85°), free from drafts, 1 hour or until doubled in bulk.

Melt ¼ cup butter in a small saucepan over medium-low heat. Add brown sugar, corn syrup, and 1 tablespoon water; cook just until mixture comes to a boil, stirring constantly. Pour into a greased 9-inch round cakepan; sprinkle with ½ cup walnut pieces. Set aside.

Punch dough down; turn out onto a lightly floured surface. Roll to a 12- x 8-inch rectangle; brush with 1 tablespoon melted butter. Combine chopped walnuts, ¼ cup sugar, and cinnamon; sprinkle evenly over dough. Roll up dough, jellyroll fashion, starting at long side, pressing firmly to eliminate air pockets; pinch seam to seal (do not seal ends). Cut roll into 1-inch slices. Place slices, cut side down, in prepared pan. Cover and let rise in a warm place, free from drafts, 45 minutes or until doubled in bulk.

Bake at 375° for 20 to 25 minutes or until lightly browned. Immediately invert pan onto a serving plate. Let stand 1 minute to allow caramel mixture to drizzle over rolls. Remove rolls from pan. Yield: 1 dozen.   Jan McCabe

Return Engagement
The Junior Board of the Quad Symphony Orchestra Association
Davenport, Iowa

Coffee Dunkers

1 package dry yeast	1 tablespoon sugar
¼ cup warm water (105° to 115°)	¾ teaspoon salt
⅓ cup boiling water	1 egg yolk
⅔ cup shortening	¾ cup strawberry preserves
2 to 2¾ cups all-purpose flour, divided	1 cup sifted powdered sugar
	1 tablespoon milk
	1 teaspoon vanilla extract

Dissolve yeast in warm water in a large bowl; let stand 5 minutes.

Pour boiling water over shortening in a medium mixing bowl; beat at medium speed of an electric mixer until shortening melts. Add 2 cups flour, 1 tablespoon sugar, and salt; beat until well blended. Stir in yeast mixture and egg yolk. Gradually stir in enough remaining ¾ cup flour to make a soft dough.

Turn dough out onto a well-floured surface. Roll dough into 1-inch balls; place 2 inches apart on ungreased baking sheets. Press thumb into each ball, leaving an indentation. Spoon 1 teaspoon preserves into center of each ball. Cover and let rise in a warm place (85°), free from drafts, 1 hour or until doubled in bulk. Bake at 375° for 12 to 15 minutes or until lightly browned. Let cool slightly on baking sheets; transfer to wire racks.

Combine 1 cup powdered sugar, milk, and vanilla in a small bowl; stir with a wire whisk until smooth. Drizzle glaze over warm pastries. Yield: 3 dozen.   Rachael E. Downie

Treasured Recipes of the Past
The Pomeroy Sesquicentennial Committee
Pomeroy, Ohio

Grissini (Breadsticks)

1 package dry yeast
¼ cup warm water (105° to 115°)
1 cup milk
¼ cup butter or margarine

1 tablespoon sugar
1 teaspoon salt
1 egg white
3 to 3½ cups all-purpose flour
Sesame seeds (optional)

Dissolve yeast in warm water in a large bowl; let stand 5 minutes.

Combine milk and next 3 ingredients in a small saucepan; heat until butter melts, stirring occasionally. Let cool to 105° to 115°.

Add milk mixture, egg white, and 1½ cups flour to yeast mixture, beating well at high speed of an electric mixer. Beat an additional 2 minutes at medium speed. Gradually stir in enough remaining 2 cups flour to make a soft dough.

Turn dough out onto a lightly floured surface, and knead until smooth and elastic (about 10 minutes). Roll dough out to a 12- x 8-inch rectangle. Cut in half lengthwise; cut crosswise to make 16 pieces. Shape each piece into an 8- to 10-inch rope. Roll in sesame seeds, if desired.

Place ropes 1 inch apart on ungreased baking sheets. Cover and let rise in a warm place (85°), free from drafts, 1 hour or until doubled in bulk. Bake at 425° for 5 minutes; reduce heat to 350°, and bake an additional 10 minutes or until breadsticks are lightly browned. Serve warm. Yield: 1¼ dozen.   Marilyn McCann

The Walla Walla Italian Heritage Association Cookbook
Walla Walla Italian Heritage Association
Walla Walla, Washington

Cakes

Scout Rest Ranch, near North Platte, Nebraska, was once the home of William F. Cody, popularly known to fans as Buffalo Bill. This famous frontiersman and showman rehearsed his "Wild West" show at the ranch. The house now serves as the focal point of the Buffalo Bill State Historical Park.

Fresh Apple Cake with Rum Sauce

½ cup butter or margarine,
   softened
2 cups sugar
2 eggs
2 cups all-purpose flour
1 teaspoon baking powder
¾ teaspoon baking soda
½ teaspoon salt

½ teaspoon ground nutmeg
½ teaspoon ground cinnamon
3 cups peeled, chopped
   cooking apples
1½ cups chopped pecans or
   walnuts
Hot Buttered Rum Sauce

Cream butter; gradually add sugar, beating well at medium speed of an electric mixer. Add eggs, one at a time, beating well after each addition.

Combine flour and next 5 ingredients; add to creamed mixture, beating until blended. Stir in apple and pecans.

Pour batter into a greased and floured 13- x 9- x 2-inch baking pan. Bake at 325° for 50 to 55 minutes or until a wooden pick inserted in center comes out clean. Let cool completely in pan on a wire rack. Serve with Hot Buttered Rum Sauce. Yield: 15 servings.

Hot Buttered Rum Sauce

1 cup sugar
½ cup butter or margarine

½ cup half-and-half
1 teaspoon rum extract

Combine first 3 ingredients in a saucepan; cook over low heat, stirring occasionally, until sugar dissolves. Remove from heat, and stir in rum extract. Yield: 1½ cups.   Virginia Bowen

Grrr-eat Grub
Faith Bible Fellowship
Huston, Alaska

Julie's Favorite Applesauce Cake

1 cup butter or margarine,
  softened
2 cups sugar
2 eggs
4 cups all-purpose flour
1 teaspoon baking powder
1 teaspoon baking soda
1 teaspoon salt

1 teaspoon ground nutmeg
1 teaspoon ground cinnamon
1 teaspoon ground cloves
2 cups applesauce
1 (15-ounce) package raisins
1 cup chopped pecans or
  walnuts (optional)
Easy Caramel Frosting

Cream butter; gradually add sugar, beating well at medium speed of an electric mixer. Add eggs, one at a time, beating well after each addition.

Combine flour and next 6 ingredients; add to creamed mixture alternately with applesauce, beginning and ending with flour mixture. Mix after each addition. Stir in raisins and, if desired, pecans.

Pour batter into a greased and floured 13- x 9- x 2-inch baking pan. Bake at 325° for 65 to 70 minutes or until a wooden pick inserted in center comes out clean. Let cool completely in pan on a wire rack. Spread Easy Caramel Frosting on top of cake. Yield: 15 servings.

Easy Caramel Frosting

1 cup firmly packed brown
  sugar
¼ cup plus 1 tablespoon butter
  or margarine

¼ teaspoon salt
¼ cup milk
1½ cups sifted powdered sugar

Combine brown sugar, butter, and salt in a saucepan; bring to a boil over medium heat, stirring constantly. Add milk; cook over low heat 3 minutes, stirring occasionally. Remove from heat, and let cool. Add powdered sugar, and beat with a wooden spoon to almost spreading consistency. Yield: 1⅓ cups.   Joyce E. Huyett

eating
First Lutheran Church
Mission Hills, Kansas

Ring Around the Rum Cake

⅓ cup butter, softened
⅓ cup shortening
1½ cups sugar
3 eggs
3 cups all-purpose flour
1½ tablespoons baking powder

1½ teaspoons salt
1⅓ cups milk
½ cup ground pecans or
   walnuts
2 teaspoons vanilla extract
Rum Sauce

Cream butter and shortening; gradually add sugar, beating well at medium speed of an electric mixer. Add eggs, one at a time, beating after each addition.

Combine flour, baking powder, and salt; add to creamed mixture alternately with milk, beginning and ending with flour mixture. Mix just until blended after each addition. Stir in pecans and vanilla.

Pour batter into a greased and floured 12-cup Bundt pan. Bake at 350° for 55 to 60 minutes or until a wooden pick inserted in center comes out clean. Let cool in pan 10 minutes; remove from pan, and let cool completely on a wire rack. Pour 1 cup Rum Sauce over cake; serve with remaining sauce. Yield: one 10-inch cake.

Rum Sauce

1 (12-ounce) can apricot nectar
1 cup sugar
3 tablespoons cornstarch
3 tablespoons cold water

2 (11-ounce) cans mandarin
   oranges, drained
½ cup light rum

Combine nectar and sugar in a small saucepan. Bring to a boil over medium heat, stirring frequently; reduce heat, and simmer 8 minutes.

Combine cornstarch and water, stirring until smooth. Stir cornstarch mixture into nectar mixture; cook 1 minute, stirring constantly, or until sauce is thickened and bubbly. Let cool slightly. Stir in orange sections and rum. Yield: 4 cups.   Kathy Terry

Trinity Episcopal School, Classroom Classics
The Parents and Students of Trinity Episcopal School
Pine Bluff, Arkansas

Banana Cake

½ cup margarine, softened
1 cup sugar
2 eggs
1½ cups all-purpose flour
1 teaspoon baking soda

¼ cup sour cream
1 cup mashed bananas
1 teaspoon vanilla extract
1 (6-ounce) package semisweet
   chocolate morsels

Cream margarine; gradually add sugar, beating well. Add eggs, one at a time, beating well after each addition.

Combine flour and baking soda; add to creamed mixture alternately with sour cream, beginning and ending with flour mixture. Mix after each addition. Stir in banana and vanilla.

Pour batter into a greased 9-inch square baking pan. Sprinkle with morsels. Bake at 350° for 35 to 40 minutes or until a wooden pick inserted in center comes out clean. Let cool completely in pan on a wire rack. Yield: 9 servings.   Mary T. Reene

What's Cooking in Cazenovia
St. James Women's Council
Cazenovia, New York

Anna's Shortcake

½ cup butter, softened
1⅓ cups sugar
2 eggs
1 teaspoon vanilla extract
2 cups self-rising flour
1⅓ cups buttermilk

3 cups sliced fresh strawberries
   or peaches
½ cup sugar
2 tablespoons dark rum
2 cups whipping cream,
   whipped

Cream butter; gradually add 1⅓ cups sugar, beating well at medium speed of an electric mixer. Add eggs, one at a time, beating well after each addition. Stir in vanilla. Add flour to creamed mixture alternately with buttermilk, beginning and ending with flour. Mix after each addition.

Pour batter into a greased and floured 10-inch cast-iron skillet. Bake at 400° for 30 minutes or until a wooden pick inserted in center comes out clean. Let cool in skillet 10 minutes. Remove from skillet, and let cool completely on a wire rack.

Combine strawberries, ½ cup sugar, and rum; let stand 30 minutes. Spoon mixture over slices of cake; top with cream. Yield: 12 servings.

From a Lighthouse Window
The Chesapeake Bay Maritime Museum
St. Michaels, Maryland

Fig Preserve Cake

1½ cups sugar	1 teaspoon ground nutmeg
1 cup vegetable oil	1 teaspoon ground cinnamon
3 eggs	½ teaspoon ground allspice
1 cup buttermilk	½ teaspoon ground cloves
1 tablespoon vanilla extract	1 cup fig preserves
2 cups all-purpose flour	½ cup chopped pecans
1 teaspoon baking soda	Buttermilk Glaze
1 teaspoon salt	

Combine sugar and oil; beat well at medium speed of an electric mixer. Add eggs, one at a time, beating after each addition. Stir in buttermilk and vanilla. Combine flour and next 6 ingredients. Add to creamed mixture; beat well. Stir in preserves and pecans. Pour into a greased and floured 10-inch tube pan. Bake at 350° for 1 hour or until a wooden pick inserted in center comes out clean. Let cool in pan 15 minutes. Remove from pan; place on a wire rack. Pour glaze over cake. Yield: one 10-inch cake.

Buttermilk Glaze

½ cup sugar	1½ teaspoons cornstarch
¼ cup butter or margarine	¼ teaspoon baking soda
¼ cup buttermilk	1½ teaspoons vanilla extract

Combine first 5 ingredients in a medium saucepan; stir well. Bring to a boil; boil 4 minutes, stirring frequently. Remove from heat; stir in vanilla. Yield: 1 cup.   Barbara Landry

"From the Heart of the Teche"
Jeanerette Chamber of Commerce
Jeanerette, Louisiana

Cousin Betty's Fruitcake

2 cups butter, softened
2¼ cups sugar
1 cup molasses
½ cup cider vinegar
4 cups all-purpose flour
1 teaspoon baking soda
2 teaspoons ground nutmeg
1 teaspoon ground mace
1 teaspoon ground cinnamon
12 eggs, separated
2 (15-ounce) packages raisins

3 (10-ounce) packages currants
1 pound candied citron
½ pound red and green
   candied cherries
3 cups chopped blanched
   almonds
1½ cups chopped pecans
1½ cups chopped walnuts
1 cup brandy
Additional brandy

Grease four 9- x 5- x 3-inch loafpans. Line loafpans with wax paper, and set aside.

Cream butter; gradually add sugar, beating well at medium speed of an electric mixer. Add molasses and vinegar, beating until blended.

Combine flour and next 4 ingredients; stir well. Reserve ½ cup flour mixture. Beat egg yolks. Add remaining 3½ cups flour mixture to creamed mixture alternately with beaten egg yolks, beginning and ending with flour mixture (batter will be very thick).

Combine raisins, currants, citron, cherries, and nuts in a large bowl; sprinkle with ½ cup reserved flour mixture, tossing gently to coat. Stir in 1 cup brandy. Add fruit and nut mixture to batter; stir well.

Beat egg whites at high speed of an electric mixer until stiff peaks form. Gently fold beaten egg whites into batter.

Spoon batter evenly into prepared pans. Bake at 275° for 2½ hours or until a wooden pick inserted in center comes out clean. Let cool in pans 10 minutes; remove from pans, and let cool completely on wire racks.

Wrap fruitcakes in brandy-soaked cheesecloth. Store in an airtight container in a cool place. To serve, slice with an electric knife. Yield: 4 fruitcakes.

Mary Winslow Chapman

Gracious Goodness: The Taste of Memphis
The Symphony League of Memphis, Tennessee

Chocolate-Sauerkraut Surprise Cake

½ cup butter or margarine,
  softened
1½ cups sugar
3 eggs
2 cups all-purpose flour
½ cup cocoa
1 teaspoon baking powder
1 teaspoon baking soda

¼ teaspoon salt
1 cup water
1 (8-ounce) can shredded
  sauerkraut, rinsed, drained,
  and finely chopped
1 teaspoon vanilla extract
Sour Cream Chocolate Frosting

Cream butter; gradually add sugar, beating well at medium speed of an electric mixer. Add eggs, one at a time, beating well after each addition.

Combine flour and next 4 ingredients; add to creamed mixture alternately with water, beginning and ending with flour mixture. Mix after each addition. Stir in sauerkraut and vanilla.

Pour batter into a greased and floured 13- x 9- x 2-inch baking pan. Bake at 350° for 30 to 35 minutes or until a wooden pick inserted in center comes out clean. Let cool completely in pan on a wire rack. Spread Sour Cream Chocolate Frosting on top of cake. Yield: 15 servings.

Sour Cream Chocolate Frosting

1 (6-ounce) package semisweet
  chocolate morsels
¼ cup butter or margarine
½ cup sour cream

1 teaspoon vanilla extract
¼ teaspoon salt
4½ to 5 cups sifted powdered
  sugar

Combine chocolate and butter in a medium saucepan; cook over low heat until chocolate and butter melt, stirring frequently. Remove from heat; stir in sour cream, vanilla, and salt. Gradually add powdered sugar, beating well at medium speed of an electric mixer until frosting is smooth and spreading consistency. Yield: about 3 cups.   Helen Rodgers

Favorite Recipes of the Episcopal Churches on the Kenai
The Episcopal Churches on the Kenai
Nikiski, Alaska

Lil's Crater Cocoa Cake

1¾ cups all-purpose flour
1½ teaspoons baking soda
1 teaspoon salt
1½ cups sugar
⅔ cup cocoa
1 (16-ounce) carton sour cream
½ cup butter or margarine,
   softened

2 eggs, lightly beaten
1 tablespoon vanilla extract
Crater Filling
½ cup chopped pecans or
   walnuts (optional)
Powdered sugar (optional)

Combine first 5 ingredients in a large mixing bowl; stir well.
Combine sour cream, butter, eggs, and vanilla; add to flour
mixture, beating well at medium speed of an electric mixer 3
minutes or until well blended.

Pour batter into a greased and floured 13- x 9- x 2-inch baking
pan. Spoon Crater Filling, ½ teaspoon at a time, 1 inch apart on
top of batter. Gently streak filling through batter with a fork.
Sprinkle with pecans, if desired. Bake at 350° for 35 to 40 minutes
or until a wooden pick inserted in center comes out clean. Let
cool completely in pan on a wire rack. Sprinkle with powdered
sugar just before serving, if desired. Yield: 15 servings.

Crater Filling

3 tablespoons butter or
   margarine
3 tablespoons cocoa

⅔ cup sifted powdered sugar
1 tablespoon milk
¼ teaspoon vanilla extract

Melt butter in a small saucepan over low heat; add cocoa,
stirring until blended.

Combine powdered sugar, milk, and vanilla in a small mixing
bowl; add cocoa mixture, beating at high speed of an electric
mixer 2 minutes. Yield: ½ cup.   Edna Bess Greenblatt

The Center of Attention Cookbook
The Medical Center Foundation
Beaver, Pennsylvania

Chocolate-Orange Marble Cake

3 (1-ounce) squares
  unsweetened chocolate,
  chopped
1 cup plus 2 tablespoons
  unsalted butter, softened and
  divided
2 cups sugar
4 eggs
2½ cups all-purpose flour

1 teaspoon baking powder
¾ teaspoon baking soda,
  divided
½ teaspoon salt
1 cup buttermilk
2 teaspoons vanilla extract
1 tablespoon grated orange
  rind
¼ cup water

Combine chocolate and 2 tablespoons butter in top of a double boiler. Bring water to a boil; reduce heat to low, and cook until chocolate and butter melt, stirring occasionally. Let cool.

Cream remaining 1 cup butter; gradually add sugar, beating well at medium speed of an electric mixer. Add eggs, one at a time, beating well after each addition. Sift together flour, baking powder, ½ teaspoon baking soda, and salt; add to creamed mixture alternately with buttermilk, beginning and ending with flour mixture. Mix after each addition. Stir in vanilla.

Pour half of batter into a separate bowl. Stir in grated orange rind. Set aside.

Add melted chocolate to remaining half of batter; stir well. Add remaining ¼ teaspoon baking soda and water to chocolate batter; stir well.

Pour half of orange batter into a well-greased and floured 12-cup Bundt pan. Top with half of chocolate batter. Repeat layers with remaining batters. Gently swirl batters with a knife to create a marbled effect. Bake at 350° for 1 hour and 10 minutes or until a wooden pick inserted in center comes out clean. Let cool in pan 10 minutes; remove from pan, and let cool completely on a wire rack. Yield: one 10-inch cake.

Kathy Riechel

Out of This World
Wood Acres Elementary School
Bethesda, Maryland

Chocolate Chip Chiffon Cake

2¼ cups all-purpose flour
1 tablespoon baking powder
1 teaspoon salt
1¾ cups sugar
½ cup vegetable oil
¾ cup water
5 egg yolks

2 teaspoons vanilla extract
7 egg whites
½ teaspoon cream of tartar
3 (1-ounce) squares
   unsweetened chocolate,
   grated
Frosting (recipe follows)

Sift together flour, baking powder, salt, and sugar; make a well in center of dry ingredients. Add oil, water, yolks, and vanilla; beat at medium speed of an electric mixer 2 minutes.

Beat egg whites and cream of tartar at high speed until stiff peaks form. Pour egg yolk mixture in a thin, steady stream over entire surface of egg whites; gently fold whites into yolk mixture. Fold in grated chocolate.

Pour batter into an ungreased 10-inch tube pan, spreading evenly with a spatula. Bake at 325° for 55 minutes; increase temperature to 350°, and bake an additional 10 minutes or until cake springs back when lightly touched. Remove from oven; invert pan, and let cool 40 minutes. Loosen cake from sides of pan using a narrow metal spatula; remove from pan. Spread frosting on top and sides of cake. Yield: one 10-inch cake.

Frosting

3 (1-ounce) squares
   unsweetened chocolate
3 tablespoons shortening
2 cups sifted powdered sugar

¼ cup plus 1 tablespoon milk
¼ teaspoon salt
1 teaspoon vanilla extract

Combine chocolate and shortening in top of a double boiler. Bring water to a boil; reduce heat to low, and cook until chocolate melts, stirring occasionally. Add sugar, and stir until smooth. Add milk and remaining ingredients; stir until frosting is spreading consistency. Yield: 1½ cups.   Donna Kempkes

Bergan Family Favorites
Archbishop Bergan Mercy Hospital
Omaha, Nebraska

Cocoa-Walnut Brownie Loaf

¾ cup butter or margarine,
  softened
¾ cup sugar
¾ cup firmly packed brown
  sugar
2 eggs
1¾ cups all-purpose flour
½ cup cocoa
1 teaspoon baking powder

½ teaspoon baking soda
1 (8-ounce) carton plain low-fat
  yogurt
1 cup coarsely chopped
  walnuts
1 teaspoon vanilla extract
Cocoa Fudge Frosting
Additional coarsely chopped
  walnuts

Cream butter; gradually add sugars, beating well at medium speed of an electric mixer. Add eggs, one at a time, beating after each addition.

Combine flour and next 3 ingredients; add to creamed mixture alternately with yogurt, beginning and ending with flour mixture. Mix just until blended after each addition. Stir in 1 cup chopped walnuts and vanilla.

Pour batter into a greased and floured 9- x 5- x 3-inch loafpan. Bake at 350° for 55 to 60 minutes or until a wooden pick inserted in center comes out clean. Let cool in pan 10 minutes. Remove from pan, and let cool completely on a wire rack. Spread Cocoa Fudge Frosting on top and sides of cake. Sprinkle with chopped walnuts. Yield: 8 servings.

Cocoa Fudge Frosting

2½ cups sifted powdered sugar
¼ cup butter or margarine,
  melted

¼ cup cocoa
3 tablespoons milk
½ teaspoon vanilla extract

Combine all ingredients in a small mixing bowl; beat at medium speed of an electric mixer until frosting is smooth and spreading consistency. Yield: 1½ cups.   Dorothy Catena

Birthright Sampler
Birthright of Johnstown, Pennsylvania

Chocolate-Nut Torte

4 (1-ounce) squares
  unsweetened chocolate
¾ cup butter or margarine
4 eggs, separated
1 cup sugar
1 cup plus 1 tablespoon all-
  purpose flour

3 tablespoons toasted, skinned,
  and ground hazelnuts
¼ teaspoon salt
Hazelnut Buttercream
Chocolate Glaze

Combine chocolate and butter in top of a double boiler. Bring water to a boil; reduce heat to low, and cook until chocolate and butter melt, stirring occasionally. Remove from heat, and let cool slightly.

Beat egg yolks in a medium mixing bowl at high speed of an electric mixer until thick and lemon colored. Gradually add sugar, beating well. Add chocolate mixture, beating until blended. Combine flour, hazelnuts, and salt; gently fold into chocolate mixture (batter will be very thick).

Beat egg whites at high speed until stiff peaks form. Gently fold ½ cup beaten egg whites into chocolate mixture; fold in remaining egg whites.

Pour batter into a greased and floured 9-inch round cakepan. Bake at 350° for 20 to 25 minutes. (Cake will not test done.) Let cool in pan 1 hour; remove from pan, and let cool completely on a wire rack.

Place wax paper under cake on wire rack. Spread Hazelnut Buttercream on top and sides of cake, letting excess drip onto wax paper. Chill 30 minutes. Spread Chocolate Glaze on top and sides of cake. Yield: one 9-inch torte.

Hazelnut Buttercream

¾ cup hazelnuts, toasted and
  skinned
⅔ cup sifted powdered sugar
3 tablespoons butter, softened

3 tablespoons light corn
  syrup
1 tablespoon water

Position knife blade in food processor bowl; add hazelnuts, and process 2 to 3 minutes or until a paste forms. Add sugar, butter, corn syrup, and water, and process until smooth. Yield: 1 cup.

Chocolate Glaze

**4 (1-ounce) squares semisweet
  chocolate
1 tablespoon plus 1 teaspoon
  butter**

**⅔ cup sifted powdered sugar
3 tablespoons whipping cream
1 teaspoon vanilla extract**

Combine chocolate and butter in top of a double boiler. Bring water to a boil; reduce heat to low, and cook until chocolate and butter melt, stirring occasionally. Remove from heat. Add sugar, cream, and vanilla; beat at medium speed of an electric mixer until smooth. Yield: ¾ cup.   Chris McGrayel

Home Cookin' is a Family Affair
New Life Ladies Fellowship
Nashville, Indiana

Brown Sugar Angel Food

**10 egg whites
2 teaspoons vanilla extract
1½ teaspoons cream of tartar
1 teaspoon salt**

**2 cups firmly packed brown
  sugar, divided
1¼ cups sifted cake flour**

Beat egg whites and vanilla in a large mixing bowl at high speed of an electric mixer just until foamy. Add cream of tartar and salt; beat until soft peaks form. Press 1 cup brown sugar through a sieve; gradually sprinkle over egg white mixture, beating until stiff peaks form.

Sift together remaining 1 cup brown sugar and cake flour. Sprinkle flour mixture, ¼ cup at a time, over egg white mixture, and fold in gently. Pour batter into an ungreased 10-inch tube pan. Bake at 350° for 45 to 50 minutes or until cake springs back when lightly touched. Invert pan; let cake cool completely. Loosen cake from sides of pan using a narrow metal spatula; remove from pan. Yield: one 10-inch cake.   Ruth Beebe

Recipes to Come Home to
Oologah Area Chamber of Commerce
Oologah, Oklahoma

Toasted Butter Pecan Cake

2 cups chopped pecans
¼ cup butter, melted
1 cup butter, softened
2 cups sugar
4 eggs
3 cups all-purpose flour

2 teaspoons baking powder
½ teaspoon salt
1 cup milk
2 teaspoons vanilla extract
Frosting (recipe follows)

Combine pecans and ¼ cup butter in a 15- x 10- x 1-inch jellyroll pan. Bake at 350° for 20 to 25 minutes or until pecans are lightly toasted, stirring occasionally. Set aside.

Cream 1 cup butter; gradually add sugar, beating well at medium speed of an electric mixer. Add eggs, one at a time, beating well after each addition.

Combine flour, baking powder, and salt; add to creamed mixture alternately with milk, beginning and ending with flour mixture. Mix after each addition. Stir in 1⅓ cups toasted pecans and vanilla. (Reserve remaining ⅔ cup toasted pecans for frosting.)

Pour batter into 3 greased and floured 8-inch round cakepans. Bake at 350° for 20 to 25 minutes or until a wooden pick inserted in center comes out clean. Let cool in pans 10 minutes; remove from pans, and let cool completely on wire racks. Spread frosting between layers and on top and sides of cake. Yield: one 3-layer cake.

Frosting

½ cup butter, softened
2 (16-ounce) packages
  powdered sugar, sifted

½ cup whipping cream
2 teaspoons vanilla extract

Cream butter; gradually add powdered sugar, beating at medium speed of an electric mixer until light and fluffy. Add cream, beating until spreading consistency. Stir in reserved ⅔ cup toasted pecans and vanilla. Yield: 4 cups.   Billie Buchanan

The Cookbook
East Lake United Methodist Church
Birmingham, Alabama

Pecan Roll with Caramel-Nut Sauce

3 eggs
1 cup sugar
⅓ cup water
1 teaspoon vanilla extract
¾ cup all-purpose flour
1 teaspoon baking powder

¼ teaspoon salt
½ cup ground pecans
2 tablespoons powdered sugar
1 quart butter pecan ice cream,
   softened
Caramel-Nut Sauce

Grease bottom and sides of a 15- x 10- x 1-inch jellyroll pan with vegetable oil; line with wax paper, and grease wax paper with oil. Set pan aside.

Beat eggs in a large bowl at high speed of an electric mixer until thick and lemon colored. Gradually add 1 cup sugar, beating well. Gradually add water and vanilla, beating until well blended.

Combine flour and next 3 ingredients; stir well. Gradually fold flour mixture into egg mixture. Pour batter into prepared pan, spreading evenly. Bake at 375° for 15 minutes.

Sift powdered sugar in a 15- x 10-inch rectangle on a towel. When cake is done, immediately loosen from sides of pan, and turn out onto sugared towel. Carefully peel off wax paper. Starting at wide end, roll up cake and towel together; let cool completely on a wire rack, seam side down. Unroll cake. Spread softened ice cream over cake, and carefully reroll cake without towel. Cover and freeze 8 hours or until firm. To serve, cut diagonally into slices, and top with Caramel-Nut Sauce. Yield: 12 servings.

Caramel-Nut Sauce

½ cup firmly packed brown
   sugar
½ cup light corn syrup
2 tablespoons butter

⅛ teaspoon salt
¾ cup chopped pecans, toasted
¼ cup whipping cream
1 teaspoon vanilla extract

Combine brown sugar, corn syrup, butter, and salt in a small saucepan. Bring to a boil; reduce heat, and simmer 2 to 3 minutes or until sugar dissolves, stirring frequently. Remove from heat; let cool slightly. Stir in pecans, cream, and vanilla. Yield: 1⅓ cups.

Stirring Performances
The Junior League of Winston-Salem, North Carolina

Almond Cold-Oven Cake

1 cup butter, softened
½ cup margarine, softened
3 cups sugar
5 eggs
3 cups all-purpose flour

½ teaspoon baking powder
1 cup milk
1½ teaspoons almond extract
½ teaspoon vanilla extract
½ cup sliced almonds

Cream butter and margarine; gradually add sugar, beating well at medium speed of an electric mixer. Add eggs, one at a time, beating after each addition. Combine flour and baking powder; add to creamed mixture alternately with milk, beginning and ending with flour mixture. Mix after each addition. Stir in flavorings.

Sprinkle almonds in bottom of a greased and floured 10-inch tube pan; pour batter over almonds. Place pan in a cold oven. Turn oven to 350°; bake 1 hour and 10 minutes or until a wooden pick inserted in center comes out clean. Let cool in pan 10 minutes; remove from pan, and let cool completely on a wire rack. Yield: one 10-inch cake.

Cardinal Cuisine
The Mount Vernon Hospital Auxiliary
Alexandria, Virginia

Cream Cheese-Apple Cake

1 cup butter, softened
¾ cup sugar
2 eggs
2 cups all-purpose flour
½ teaspoon baking soda
¼ teaspoon salt
1 teaspoon cream of tartar
1 tablespoon vanilla extract, divided

2 (8-ounce) packages cream cheese, softened
⅓ cup sugar
2 teaspoons whipping cream
9 cooking apples, peeled and thinly sliced (about 3 pounds)
Custard Topping
⅓ cup chopped pecans

Cream butter; gradually add ¾ cup sugar, beating at medium speed of an electric mixer until light and fluffy. Add eggs, one at a time, beating after each addition. Combine flour and next 3 ingredients; add to creamed mixture, beating well. Stir in 1 teaspoon vanilla. Spoon batter into a greased 10-inch springform pan. Spread batter evenly on bottom and up sides of pan. Cover and chill.

Beat cream cheese at high speed until light and fluffy; gradually add ⅓ cup sugar, beating well. Stir in whipping cream and 2 teaspoons vanilla.

Spoon cream cheese mixture over bottom of chilled batter. Arrange apple slices over filling. Pour Custard Topping over apple slices. Sprinkle with pecans. Bake at 350° for 50 minutes; shield with aluminum foil to prevent excessive browning. Bake an additional 1 hour and 10 minutes or until a wooden pick inserted in center comes out clean. Remove foil, and let cool to room temperature in pan on a wire rack. Carefully remove sides of springform pan. Yield: one 10-inch cake.

Custard Topping

¾ cup plus 3 tablespoons
  whipping cream
2 eggs, beaten
½ cup sugar

1 tablespoon lemon juice
½ teaspoon ground cinnamon
⅛ teaspoon ground nutmeg

Beat cream in a mixing bowl until soft peaks form. Add eggs and remaining ingredients; mix well. Yield: 1 cup.   Marie B. Patin

The Cajun Connection Cookbook
Trinity Catholic School Booster Club
St. Martinville, Louisiana

Trinity Catholic School is located in St. Martinville, Louisiana—an area known as "Cajun country." Proceeds from the sale of its cookbook, The Cajun Connection Cookbook, are used to purchase necessities as well as luxuries for the school.

Hazelnut-Chocolate Chip Cheesecake

1½ cups vanilla wafer crumbs
¾ cup toasted, skinned, and finely chopped hazelnuts
⅓ cup semisweet chocolate morsels, finely chopped
¼ cup butter, melted
2 tablespoons sugar
3 (8-ounce) packages cream cheese, softened
1 cup sugar
3 eggs

3 tablespoons Frangelico or other hazelnut-flavored liqueur
1 cup semisweet chocolate morsels, coarsely chopped
10 to 15 whole hazelnuts, toasted and skinned
¼ cup semisweet chocolate morsels, melted
Glaze (recipe follows)

Combine first 5 ingredients in a medium bowl; stir well. Firmly press crumb mixture on bottom and up sides of a buttered 9-inch springform pan. Bake at 300° for 15 minutes; set aside.

Beat cream cheese at high speed of an electric mixer until light and fluffy; gradually add 1 cup sugar, beating well. Add eggs, one at a time, beating well after each addition. Stir in liqueur and 1 cup coarsely chopped morsels. Pour batter into prepared pan. Bake at 350° for 1 hour. Let cool to room temperature in pan on a wire rack; chill at least 8 hours.

Dip half of each whole hazelnut in melted chocolate. Place on wax paper; let stand until chocolate is set. Spread glaze over top of cheesecake. Arrange hazelnuts around edge of cheesecake. Carefully remove sides of springform pan. Yield: 12 servings.

Glaze

⅔ cup semisweet chocolate morsels
¼ cup sour cream

1 tablespoon Frangelico or other hazelnut-flavored liqueur

Place chocolate morsels in top of a double boiler. Bring water to a boil; reduce heat to low, and cook until chocolate melts, stirring occasionally. Remove from heat; stir in sour cream and liqueur. Yield: about 1 cup.

Savor the Flavor of Oregon
The Junior League of Eugene, Oregon

Praline Cheesecake

1 cup graham cracker crumbs
¼ cup finely chopped pecans
¼ cup butter, melted
3 (8-ounce) packages cream
  cheese, softened
1½ cups firmly packed brown
  sugar, divided

3 eggs
2 teaspoons vanilla extract
1 cup whipping cream
¼ cup butter
Candied Pecans

Combine first 3 ingredients; stir well. Firmly press crumb mixture in bottom of a 9-inch springform pan; set aside.

Beat cream cheese at high speed of an electric mixer until light and fluffy; gradually add 1 cup sugar, beating well. Add eggs and vanilla, beating just until blended. Stir in whipping cream.

Pour batter into prepared pan. Bake at 450° for 10 minutes; reduce temperature to 275°, and bake for 1 hour or until center is almost set. Let cool in pan on a wire rack. Chill at least 8 hours.

Combine remaining ½ cup sugar and ¼ cup butter in a saucepan. Cook over medium heat until butter melts and sugar dissolves, stirring constantly. Spread topping over cheesecake. Arrange Candied Pecans on top of cheesecake. Carefully remove sides of springform pan. Yield: 12 servings.

Candied Pecans

½ cup firmly packed brown
  sugar

2 tablespoons orange juice
1 cup pecan halves

Combine sugar and orange juice in a medium bowl; stir well. Add pecans; toss gently to coat. Spread pecans in a buttered 15- x 10- x 1-inch jellyroll pan; bake at 350° for 10 to 12 minutes or until lightly browned, stirring occasionally. Remove pecans from pan, and place on buttered aluminum foil. Let cool completely; break pecans apart, if necessary. Yield: 1 cup.   Sonny Gilmore

Plug in to Good Cooking
The National Management Association Corporate Headquarters
Chapter of Alabama Power Company
Birmingham, Alabama

Brownstone's Louisiana Coffee Cheesecake with Pecan Sauce

1 cup graham cracker crumbs
½ cup ground pecans
¼ cup butter, melted
3 (8-ounce) packages cream
   cheese, softened
1¼ cups firmly packed dark
   brown sugar

4 eggs
2 tablespoons strong brewed
   coffee
Garnishes: sweetened whipped
   cream and pecan halves
Pecan Sauce

Combine cracker crumbs, ground pecans, and melted butter; stir well. Firmly press crumb mixture on bottom and 2 inches up sides of a buttered 9-inch springform pan. Freeze 15 minutes.

Beat cream cheese at high speed of an electric mixer until light and fluffy; gradually add sugar, beating well. Add eggs, one at a time, beating after each addition. Stir in coffee.

Pour batter into prepared pan. Bake at 350° for 50 to 55 minutes or until cheesecake is almost set. Turn oven off. Partially open oven door, and let cheesecake cool in oven 1 hour. Let cool to room temperature in pan on a wire rack; chill at least 8 hours.

Carefully remove sides of springform pan. Garnish, if desired. Serve with warm Pecan Sauce. Yield: 12 servings.

Pecan Sauce

½ cup unsalted butter
1 cup firmly packed dark
   brown sugar
1 cup whipping cream

¼ cup strong brewed coffee
2 tablespoons bourbon
1 cup pecan halves

Melt butter in a heavy saucepan over low heat. Add sugar and next 3 ingredients, stirring well. Bring to a boil; reduce heat, and simmer, uncovered, 5 minutes. Remove from heat, and stir in pecan halves. Yield: about 3 cups.   Pat Allen

Cooking with Love
For Love of Children Foster Home Management Board
Washington, DC

Pineapple Mac Nut Cheesecake

1 (20-ounce) can crushed
   unsweetened pineapple,
   undrained
1½ cups vanilla wafer crumbs
¼ cup plus 2 tablespoons
   unsalted butter, melted
¼ cup firmly packed brown
   sugar
1 teaspoon vanilla extract
1 egg white, lightly beaten
2 (8-ounce) packages cream
   cheese, softened

⅔ cup sugar
4 eggs
¼ cup light rum
1 teaspoon vanilla extract
1 (12-ounce) package grated
   coconut
½ cup chopped macadamia
   nuts
1 (16-ounce) carton sour cream
¼ cup plus 2 tablespoons sugar
1 tablespoon light rum

Drain crushed pineapple, reserving ¼ cup juice. Set pineapple and juice aside.

Combine vanilla wafer crumbs and next 3 ingredients; stir well. Firmly press crumb mixture on bottom of a 10-inch springform pan. Brush with egg white; bake at 350° for 10 minutes. Set aside.

Beat cream cheese at medium speed of an electric mixer until light and fluffy; gradually add ⅔ cup sugar, beating well. Add eggs, one at a time, beating well after each addition. Stir in ¼ cup rum and 1 teaspoon vanilla. Fold in reserved pineapple, coconut, and macadamia nuts.

Pour batter into prepared pan. Bake at 350° for 1 hour. Remove cheesecake from oven; increase oven temperature to 450°.

Beat sour cream at medium speed 2 minutes. Add reserved pineapple juice, ¼ cup plus 2 tablespoons sugar, and 1 tablespoon rum; beat 1 minute. Spread mixture on top of cheesecake. Bake at 450° for 5 minutes. Turn oven off. Partially open oven door, and let cheesecake cool in oven 1 hour. Let cool to room temperature in pan on a wire rack; chill at least 2 hours. Carefully remove sides of springform pan. Yield: 12 servings.   Bill G. Weaver

Kona Kitchens
Kona Outdoor Circle
Kailua-Kona, Hawaii

Peppermint Cheesecake

1 cup chocolate wafer crumbs
3 tablespoons butter or
  margarine, melted
1 envelope unflavored gelatin
¼ cup cold water
2 (8-ounce) containers process
  cream cheese product,
  softened
½ cup sugar

½ cup milk
¼ cup crushed peppermint
  candy
1 cup whipping cream,
  whipped
2 (1.55-ounce) milk chocolate
  candy bars, finely chopped
Garnishes: whipped cream and
  crushed peppermint candy

Combine chocolate wafer crumbs and butter; stir well. Firmly press crumb mixture on bottom of a 9-inch springform pan. Bake at 350° for 10 minutes; set aside.

Sprinkle gelatin over cold water in a small saucepan; let stand 1 minute. Cook over low heat, stirring until gelatin dissolves. Beat cream cheese at high speed of an electric mixer until light and fluffy; gradually add sugar, beating well. Gradually add gelatin mixture, milk, and peppermint candy, beating until blended. Chill until slightly thickened. Gently fold in whipped cream and candy bars. Pour mixture into prepared pan. Chill until firm. Carefully remove sides of springform pan. Garnish, if desired. Yield: 8 servings.

Anne Ellett

View Beyond the Park
The Junior Women's Club of Fairview Park, Ohio

Cookies &
Candies

*Once the mainstay of public transportation, the St. Charles Line
now leisurely rumbles through New Orleans transporting eager
tourists to the French Quarter where they can sample New Orleans'
famous confection—pralines.*

Waffle Iron Cookies

**2 (1-ounce) squares
  unsweetened chocolate**
½ cup butter or margarine
2 eggs

¾ cup sugar
1 teaspoon vanilla extract
1 cup all-purpose flour
Frosting (recipe follows)

Combine chocolate and butter in top of a double boiler. Bring water to a boil; reduce heat to low, and cook until chocolate and butter melt, stirring occasionally. Set aside.

Combine eggs, sugar, and vanilla in a medium mixing bowl; beat at medium speed of an electric mixer until blended. Add flour and reserved chocolate mixture; mix well.

Preheat waffle iron. Drop dough by 2 teaspoonfuls onto iron. Close iron, and bake for 1 to 1½ minutes or until done. Let cool on wire racks. Top with frosting. Yield: 2½ dozen.

Frosting

**¼ cup butter or margarine,
  softened**
1½ tablespoons cocoa

1½ cups sifted powdered sugar
2 to 3 tablespoons milk
½ teaspoon vanilla extract

Cream butter; add cocoa, beating well at medium speed of an electric mixer. Gradually add powdered sugar, milk, and vanilla, beating until smooth. Yield: 1¼ cups.   Kathy Gemberling

Seasoned with Love
Metro Women's Auxiliary, Marcy-Newberry Association
Chicago, Illinois

Amish Oatmeal Cookies

1½ cups raisins
1 cup salted peanuts
6 cups all-purpose flour
1 tablespoon baking powder
1 teaspoon salt
1 teaspoon ground nutmeg
1 teaspoon ground cinnamon
1½ cups shortening

3 cups sugar
2 cups quick-cooking oats, uncooked
1 tablespoon baking soda
1 cup buttermilk
½ cup molasses
3 eggs, lightly beaten
1 egg

Position knife blade in food processor bowl; add raisins and peanuts, and process until ground. Set aside.

Sift together flour and next 4 ingredients into a large bowl. Cut in shortening with a pastry blender until mixture resembles coarse meal. Add ground raisin mixture, sugar, and oats; mix well. Set mixture aside.

Dissolve baking soda in buttermilk in a small bowl. Add molasses and 3 beaten eggs; beat with a wire whisk until blended. Add buttermilk mixture to flour mixture; mix well.

Drop dough by level tablespoonfuls 2 inches apart onto greased cookie sheets; slightly flatten each cookie with fingertips. Beat remaining egg; brush tops of cookies with beaten egg. Bake at 375° for 8 to 10 minutes or until lightly browned. Let cool on wire racks. Yield: 11 dozen.   Phyllis Backhaus

Grrr-eat Grub
Faith Bible Fellowship
Huston, Alaska

White Chocolate Chip Pecan Cookies

2 cups butter, softened
2 cups firmly packed dark brown sugar
1½ cups sugar
3 eggs
2 tablespoons vanilla extract
6 cups all-purpose flour

1½ teaspoons baking soda
¾ teaspoon salt
4 cups vanilla milk chips or 4 cups chopped white chocolate (about 1½ pounds)
2 cups chopped pecans

Cream butter; gradually add sugars, beating well at medium speed of an electric mixer. Add eggs and vanilla, beating well.

Combine flour, soda, and salt; add to creamed mixture, mixing well. Stir in chips and pecans.

Drop dough by rounded tablespoonfuls 2 inches apart onto lightly greased cookie sheets. Slightly flatten each cookie with fingertips. Bake at 350° for 12 to 14 minutes. Let cool slightly on cookie sheets; transfer to wire racks, and let cool completely. Yield: about 7½ dozen.   Dianne Hawkins

Home Cookin' "AT&T's Right Choices"
Western Electric Council Telephone Pioneers of America
Ballwin, Missouri

Chocolate Chip Angel Cookies

½ cup butter or margarine, softened	2 cups all-purpose flour
½ cup shortening	1 teaspoon baking soda
½ cup sugar	1 teaspoon cream of tartar
½ cup firmly packed brown sugar	¼ teaspoon salt
1 egg	1 (12-ounce) package semisweet chocolate morsels
1 teaspoon vanilla extract	1 cup chopped pecans
	Additional sugar

Cream butter and shortening in a large mixing bowl; gradually add sugars, beating well at medium speed of an electric mixer. Add egg and vanilla; beat well.

Combine flour, soda, cream of tartar, and salt; add to creamed mixture, mixing well. Stir in chocolate morsels and pecans.

Shape dough into 1-inch balls; roll in sugar. Place 2 inches apart on greased cookie sheets. Bake at 350° for 14 to 15 minutes. Let cool on wire racks. Yield: 5 dozen.   Monty Bordelon

The Cajun Connection Cookbook
Trinity Catholic Church Booster Club
St. Martinville, Louisiana

Chocolate-Peanut Butter Cookies

1 cup creamy or chunky peanut butter
¾ cup butter or margarine, softened
1½ cups firmly packed brown sugar
⅓ cup water
1 egg
1 teaspoon vanilla extract

3 cups regular oats, uncooked
1½ cups all-purpose flour
½ teaspoon baking soda
1½ cups semisweet chocolate morsels
1 tablespoon plus 1 teaspoon shortening
½ cup chopped peanuts

Cream peanut butter and butter; gradually add sugar, beating at medium speed of an electric mixer until light and fluffy. Add water, egg, and vanilla; beat well.

Combine oats, flour, and baking soda; add to peanut butter mixture, mixing well.

Shape dough into 1-inch balls; place on ungreased cookie sheets. Flatten with a fork dipped in sugar. Bake at 350° for 8 to 10 minutes or until edges are golden. Let cookies cool completely on wire racks.

Combine chocolate morsels and shortening in top of a double boiler. Bring water to a boil; reduce heat to low, and cook until chocolate and shortening melt, stirring occasionally. Spread about ½ teaspoon chocolate mixture on top of each cookie. Sprinkle each cookie with chopped peanuts. Chill cookies 20 minutes or until chocolate is set. Store cookies in an airtight container. Yield: about 6 dozen.   Kay D. Fortier

"From the Heart of the Teche"
Jeanerette Chamber of Commerce
Jeanerette, Louisiana

Macadamia Nut Blossoms

1 cup butter, softened
1 cup almond butter or
   macadamia nut butter
1 cup sugar
1 cup firmly packed brown
   sugar
2 eggs
¼ cup milk
4¼ cups all-purpose flour

2 teaspoons baking soda
1 teaspoon salt
⅛ teaspoon ground nutmeg
1 cup chopped macadamia
   nuts
2 teaspoons vanilla extract
Additional sugar
60 milk chocolate kisses,
   unwrapped

Cream butter and almond butter; gradually add 1 cup sugar and 1 cup brown sugar, beating at medium speed of an electric mixer until light and fluffy. Add eggs and milk, beating well.

Combine flour, baking soda, salt, and nutmeg; add to creamed mixture, mixing well. Stir in macadamia nuts and vanilla.

Shape dough into 1-inch balls; roll in sugar. Place 2 inches apart on ungreased cookie sheets. Bake at 375° for 10 to 12 minutes. Press a chocolate kiss into top of each cookie. Let cool on wire racks. Yield: 5 dozen.

Only in California
The Children's Home Society of California
Los Angeles, California

The Jeanerette Chamber of Commerce is an organization dedicated to projects that provide a more abundant life for the people of the Jeanerette, Louisiana, area. Monies earned from the sale of its cookbook, "From the Heart of the Teche," will benefit the organization's downtown beautification project. Members will purchase curbside trash receptacles to discourage littering, and trees, planters, and plants to beautify Main Street.

Clinton Pecan Classics

1 cup shortening
¾ cup sugar
¾ cup firmly packed brown
  sugar
2 eggs
1 teaspoon vanilla extract

1½ cups all-purpose flour
1 teaspoon baking soda
1 teaspoon salt
2 cups regular oats, uncooked
1 cup chopped pecans
Topping (recipe follows)

Cream shortening; gradually add sugars, beating well at medium speed of an electric mixer. Add eggs and vanilla, beating well.

Combine flour, soda, and salt; add to creamed mixture, mixing well. Stir in oats and pecans. Shape dough into 1-inch balls; place on ungreased cookie sheets. Press thumb into each ball of dough, leaving an indentation. Fill each indentation with about ½ teaspoon topping. Bake at 350° for 8 to 10 minutes. Let cool on wire racks. Yield: 5½ dozen.

Topping

1 cup chopped pecans
½ cup firmly packed brown
  sugar

¼ cup sour cream

Combine all ingredients in a small bowl; stir well. Yield: 1 cup.

Celebrate
Missouri Bankers Association
Jefferson City, Missouri

Walnut Cheesecake Cookies

½ cup butter or margarine,
  softened
1 (3-ounce) package cream
  cheese, softened
1 egg, separated
1 teaspoon grated lemon rind
1 teaspoon vanilla extract

1 cup all-purpose flour
1 cup sifted powdered sugar
¼ teaspoon salt
1½ cups finely chopped pecans
  or walnuts
Apricot or cherry jam

Cream butter and cream cheese. Add egg yolk, lemon rind, and vanilla, beating well at medium speed of an electric mixer.

Combine flour, sugar, and salt; add to creamed mixture, beating well. Cover and chill thoroughly.

Shape dough into 1-inch balls. Beat egg white until foamy. Dip each ball of dough into egg white; roll in chopped pecans. Place 2 inches apart on ungreased cookie sheets. Press thumb into each ball of dough, leaving an indentation. Bake at 325° for 12 to 15 minutes or until lightly browned. Transfer cookies to wire racks; fill each cookie with jam. Let cool completely. Yield: 2½ dozen.

Ocean County Fare and Bounty, Cookbook of the Jersey Shore
Ocean County Girl Scout Council
Toms River, New Jersey

Cinnamon Shortbread Cookies

2 cups butter, softened	½ cup sugar
1 cup sugar	2 teaspoons ground cinnamon
4 cups all-purpose flour	½ cup finely chopped walnuts
1 tablespoon vanilla extract	or almonds

Cream butter; gradually add 1 cup sugar, beating well at medium speed of an electric mixer. Add flour and vanilla; beat well. Press mixture into an ungreased 13- x 9- x 2-inch baking pan.

Combine ½ cup sugar, cinnamon, and chopped walnuts in a small bowl; stir well. Sprinkle walnut mixture over dough; press mixture lightly into dough with fingertips. Bake at 350° for 30 minutes. Let cool completely in pan on a wire rack. Cut into squares. Yield: 3 dozen.   Lydia Frankel

Culinary Briefs
The San Francisco Lawyers' Wives
San Francisco, California

Apple Harvest Squares

1½ cups all-purpose flour
⅔ cup sugar, divided
¾ teaspoon salt
½ cup butter or margarine
4 cups peeled and sliced
  Granny Smith apples
2 tablespoons lemon juice
1 teaspoon ground cinnamon

1⅓ cups flaked coconut
¾ cup chopped pecans or
  walnuts
½ cup sugar
⅓ cup evaporated milk
1 egg, beaten
1 teaspoon vanilla extract

Combine flour, ⅓ cup sugar, and salt in a medium bowl; stir well. Cut in butter with a pastry blender until mixture resembles coarse meal. Press mixture into an ungreased 13- x 9- x 2-inch baking pan. Set aside.

Combine apple slices, ⅓ cup sugar, lemon juice, and cinnamon; toss mixture gently. Spoon apple mixture over prepared crust. Bake at 375° for 20 minutes or until apple is tender. Remove from oven.

Combine coconut and remaining ingredients; stir well. Sprinkle coconut mixture evenly over apple slices, and bake an additional 25 minutes. Let cool in pan on a wire rack. Cut into squares. Yield: 2 dozen. Beverly Stoops

Cookbook to benefit the Homeless
Lutheran Social Services of Southern California
Riverside, California

Coconut Bars Lani

1½ cups all-purpose flour
½ cup firmly packed brown
  sugar
½ cup butter or margarine
1 cup firmly packed brown
  sugar
2 eggs, beaten

2 tablespoons all-purpose flour
½ teaspoon baking powder
¼ teaspoon salt
½ teaspoon vanilla extract
1¼ cups flaked coconut
½ cup chopped macadamia
  nuts

Combine 1½ cups flour and ½ cup brown sugar in a medium bowl, stirring well. Cut in butter with a pastry blender until mixture resembles coarse meal. Press mixture into a lightly greased 9-inch square baking pan. Bake at 350° for 15 minutes. Remove from oven, and set aside.

Combine 1 cup brown sugar and next 5 ingredients; stir well. Add coconut and macadamia nuts, stirring well. Spread brown sugar mixture over prepared crust; bake at 350° for 20 minutes. Let cool completely in pan on a wire rack. Cut into bars. Yield: about 1½ dozen.   Yvonne Khouri-Morgan

Kona Kitchens
Kona Outdoor Circle
Kailua-Kona, Hawaii

Date Loaf Bars

1 (8-ounce) package pitted
  dates, chopped
1 cup sugar
1½ cups water
2 cups all-purpose flour
2 cups quick-cooking oats,
  uncooked
1 cup firmly packed dark
  brown sugar

1 teaspoon baking soda
⅛ teaspoon salt
1 cup butter or margarine,
  melted
1 teaspoon vanilla extract
Powdered sugar

Combine dates, 1 cup sugar, and water in a medium saucepan. Bring to a boil; reduce heat, and simmer, uncovered, 10 minutes or until thickened, stirring frequently. Remove from heat; let cool.

Combine flour and next 4 ingredients in a large bowl, stirring well. Add butter and vanilla, stirring well. Press half of oat mixture into a greased and floured 13- x 9- x 2-inch baking pan. Pour cooled date mixture over crust. Crumble remaining half of oat mixture over date mixture. Bake at 350° for 30 minutes or until set and lightly browned. Let cool in pan on a wire rack. Cover and chill until firm. Cut into bars; gently roll bars in powdered sugar. Yield: 6 dozen.   Amelia Tucker

Sharing Recipes
St. John's Lutheran Church
Springfield, Illinois

Raspberry-Brandy Delights

1¼ cups all-purpose flour
1 teaspoon baking powder
½ teaspoon salt
1 teaspoon sugar
½ cup butter or margarine
2 tablespoons brandy or milk
1 egg yolk

¾ cup raspberry jam
2 eggs, beaten
1½ cups sugar
¼ cup plus 2 tablespoons
    butter or margarine, melted
2 teaspoons vanilla extract
2½ cups flaked coconut

Combine first 4 ingredients in a medium bowl; cut in ½ cup butter with a pastry blender until mixture resembles coarse meal. Sprinkle brandy over surface of flour mixture. Add egg yolk, and stir with a fork until dry ingredients are moistened. Press mixture into a lightly greased 11- x 7- x 1½-inch baking dish. Spread jam over crumb mixture.

Combine eggs, 1½ cups sugar, ¼ cup plus 2 tablespoons butter, and vanilla in a mixing bowl; beat at medium speed of an electric mixer until well blended. Stir in flaked coconut, and pour mixture over jam. Bake at 350° for 35 minutes. Let cool completely in baking dish on a wire rack. Cover and chill. Cut into squares. Yield: 2 dozen.   Janet Gould

People Food
Animal Rescue League of Southern Rhode Island
Wakefield, Rhode Island

White Chocolate Brownies

½ cup unsalted butter
4 ounces white chocolate,
    grated
2 eggs
½ cup sugar
⅛ teaspoon salt

1 cup all-purpose flour
4 ounces semisweet chocolate,
    coarsely chopped
4 ounces white chocolate,
    coarsely chopped
1½ teaspoons vanilla extract

Melt butter in a small saucepan over low heat. Remove from heat; add 4 ounces grated white chocolate, stirring until chocolate melts. Set aside, and let cool to room temperature.

Combine eggs, sugar, and salt in a large bowl; beat at medium speed of an electric mixer until thick and lemon colored. Gradually add cooled white chocolate mixture, mixing well. Add flour, beating until smooth. Stir in chopped chocolates and vanilla. Spread batter in a greased 8-inch square baking pan. Bake at 325° for 30 to 35 minutes. Let cool in pan on a wire rack. Cut into squares. Yield: 16 brownies.   John D. Case, Jr.

Friends Come in All Flavors
Buckingham Friends School
Lahaska, Pennsylvania

Buttery Cashew Brittle

2 cups sugar
1 cup light corn syrup
½ cup water
1 cup butter or margarine

3 cups roasted unsalted
  cashews
1 teaspoon baking soda

Combine sugar, corn syrup, and water in a large heavy saucepan; cook over medium-low heat until sugar dissolves, stirring occasionally. Add butter, stirring gently until butter melts. Cover and cook over medium heat 2 to 3 minutes to wash down sugar crystals from sides of pan. Uncover and cook to soft crack stage (280°), stirring occasionally. Add cashews; cook, stirring constantly, until mixture reaches hard crack stage (300°). Remove from heat. Stir in baking soda.

Working rapidly, pour mixture evenly into two buttered 15- x 10- x 1-inch jellyroll pans, and spread in a thin layer. Let cool completely; break into pieces. Store candy in an airtight container. Yield: 2½ pounds.   Ken Beardslee

The Secret Ingredient
The Cheer Guild of Indiana University Hospitals
Indianapolis, Indiana

Margaret's Elegant Toffee

1 cup whole natural almonds	¼ teaspoon salt
1 cup butter	1 (11½-ounce) package milk
1 cup sugar	chocolate morsels
½ teaspoon vanilla extract	2 cups finely ground walnuts

Line a 15- x 10- x 1-inch jellyroll pan with aluminum foil. Arrange almonds in a single layer in pan, spreading to within 1½ inches of edges. Set aside.

Combine butter, sugar, vanilla, and salt in a large heavy saucepan. Cook over medium-high heat to hard crack stage (300°), stirring constantly. Pour mixture immediately over almonds, spreading to cover nuts. Let cool completely. Break into large pieces.

Place chocolate morsels in top of a double boiler. Bring water to a boil; reduce heat to low, and cook until chocolate melts, stirring occasionally. Dip each piece of candy into melted chocolate. Holding candy with two forks, coat each piece in ground walnuts. Place on wax paper; let stand until chocolate is set. Store in an airtight container in the refrigerator. Yield: 2 pounds.   Pat Tate

Trinity Episcopal School, Classroom Classics
The Parents and Students of Trinity Episcopal School
Pine Bluff, Arkansas

Carrie's Fudge

4½ cups sugar	1 (12-ounce) package
1 (12-ounce) can evaporated milk	semisweet chocolate morsels
½ cup butter or margarine	3 (4-ounce) packages sweet baking chocolate
1½ cups marshmallows (8 ounces)	2 cups chopped pecans or walnuts
2 (1-ounce) squares unsweetened chocolate	1 tablespoon vanilla extract
	Pecan or walnut halves

Combine first 3 ingredients in a large heavy saucepan. Bring mixture to a boil over medium heat, stirring constantly. Cover and boil 5 minutes. Remove from heat; add marshmallows, stirring until marshmallows melt. Add chocolates, one at a time, stirring until chocolates melt. Stir in chopped pecans and vanilla.

Pour fudge mixture into a buttered 15- x 10- x 1-inch jellyroll pan. Cover and chill until firm. Cut fudge into squares. Gently press a pecan or walnut half on top of each square of fudge. Yield: about 5 pounds.   Dee Oberman

The Best Specialties of the House . . . and More
North Suburban Guild of Children's Memorial Medical Center
Chicago, Illinois

Rocky Road Candy

1 (14-ounce) can sweetened
  condensed milk
1 (12-ounce) package
  semisweet chocolate morsels
2 tablespoons butter or
  margarine

2 cups unsalted dry roasted
  peanuts
1 (10-ounce) package
  miniature marshmallows

Butter a 13- x 9- x 2-inch baking pan; line pan with wax paper, and set aside.

Combine first 3 ingredients in a large heavy saucepan. Cook over low heat, stirring occasionally, until chocolates and butter melt. Remove from heat; stir in peanuts and marshmallows. Spread mixture into prepared pan. Cover and chill 2 hours or until firm. Remove candy from pan; remove wax paper. Cut into squares. Yield: about 3 pounds.   Susan Morrow

The Broker's Cookbook, Second Edition
The Robinson-Humphrey Company, Inc.
Atlanta, Georgia

Bourbon-Soaked Chocolate Truffles

6½ (1-ounce) squares
   semisweet chocolate
1½ (1-ounce) squares
   unsweetened chocolate
¼ cup bourbon or dark rum
2 tablespoons brewed coffee
½ cup unsalted butter,
   softened and cut into
   1-inch pieces

1 cup ground gingersnaps
Ground pecans, almonds,
   pistachios, hazelnuts,
   gingersnaps, or powdered
   sugar

Combine first 4 ingredients in top of a double boiler. Bring water to a boil; reduce heat to low, and cook until chocolates melt, stirring occasionally. Add butter, one piece at a time, stirring with a wire whisk until butter melts and mixture is smooth. Remove from heat, and stir in gingersnap crumbs. Cover and chill 8 hours.

Shape mixture into 1-inch balls. Roll balls in ground nuts, gingersnaps, or powdered sugar. Place truffles in paper candy cups. Store truffles in an airtight container in refrigerator. Yield: 2½ dozen.

Second Round, Tea-Time at the Masters®
The Junior League of Augusta, Georgia

Desserts

After many of Savannah, Georgia's, 18th-century homes were destroyed by the fires of 1796 and 1820, builders and architects from the northern states and England joined forces to work on their reconstruction. The Owen-Thomas house is a lovely example of the collaboration of architectural styles.

Baked Apples with Figs

6 fig-filled bar cookies,
  crumbled
⅓ cup orange juice
1 tablespoon light corn syrup
6 large Rome apples, peeled
  and cored

1 cup sugar
½ cup boiling water
1 tablespoon butter or
  margarine
1 teaspoon grated orange rind

Combine first 3 ingredients in a small bowl; stir well, and let stand 10 minutes.

Place apples upright in an 11- x 7- x 1½-inch baking dish. Spoon cookie mixture evenly into center of apples. Combine sugar, boiling water, and butter, stirring until sugar dissolves. Stir in orange rind. Pour sugar mixture over apples. Bake, uncovered, at 350° for 45 to 50 minutes or until apples are tender, basting frequently. Serve warm. Yield: 6 servings.

Celebrate
Missouri Bankers Association
Jefferson City, Missouri

Bananas in Grand Marnier

1 tablespoon margarine
⅓ cup orange juice
2 tablespoons Grand Marnier
  or other orange-flavored
  liqueur

1½ teaspoons honey
¼ teaspoon vanilla extract
3 large bananas, sliced
Ground cinnamon

Melt margarine in a saucepan over medium heat. Add orange juice, Grand Marnier, honey, and vanilla; stir well. Add banana, and cook 3 minutes or until thoroughly heated, stirring frequently. Sprinkle with cinnamon, and serve immediately. Yield: 4 servings.

Simply Colorado
Colorado Dietetic Association
Littleton, Colorado

Poached Pears with White Chocolate and Raspberries

8 firm ripe pears with stems
1½ quarts strained fresh
   orange juice
1½ cups Chablis or other dry
   white wine
1 cup sugar
2 (4-inch) sticks cinnamon

½ teaspoon fennel seeds
8 ounces white chocolate,
   finely chopped
½ cup milk
Fresh raspberries
Garnish: fresh mint sprigs

Peel pears, leaving stems intact. Trim bottom of pears so pears will stand upright.

Combine orange juice and next 4 ingredients in a large saucepan; bring to a boil. Add pears, standing them upright; cover, reduce heat, and simmer 12 to 15 minutes or until pears are tender, basting often with orange juice mixture. Remove from heat; drain pears on paper towels.

Combine chocolate and milk in top of a double boiler; bring water to a boil. Reduce heat to low; cook until chocolate melts, stirring occasionally. Spoon white chocolate sauce evenly onto 8 dessert plates. Place pears upright on sauce; sprinkle raspberries over sauce. Garnish, if desired. Yield: 8 servings.

A Taste of San Francisco
The Symphony of San Francisco, California

Frantic Elegance *is a collection of recipes from parents, alumni, and friends of Arendell Parrott Academy. Proceeds from the sale of the cookbook will be used to further the academic excellence of the students through the purchase of items such as a facsimile machine, audio and video materials, and a new bus.*

Fresh Fruit Grand Marnier

4 medium oranges
2 medium bananas, sliced
2 medium apples, peeled and
   diced
2 cups fresh strawberries,
   hulled and halved
2 cups fresh blueberries
1½ cups seedless green grapes
1 cup milk

4 egg yolks
½ cup sugar
1 teaspoon cornstarch
¼ cup Grand Marnier or other
   orange-flavored liqueur
1 teaspoon vanilla extract
1 teaspoon grated orange rind
½ cup whipping cream

Peel and section oranges, catching juice in a small bowl. Place orange sections in a large bowl; set aside. Dip banana slices in orange juice to prevent browning; add to orange sections. Add apple, strawberries, blueberries, and grapes, tossing gently to combine. Cover and chill.

Cook milk in a small saucepan over medium heat until thoroughly heated. Position knife blade in food processor bowl; add egg yolks, sugar, and cornstarch, and process 1 to 2 minutes or until thick and lemon colored. Slowly pour warm milk through food chute with processor running, processing just until mixture is smooth. Transfer to a medium saucepan; cook over medium-low heat, stirring constantly, until mixture is slightly thickened and coats a metal spoon. Remove from heat; stir in Grand Marnier, vanilla, and orange rind. Cover and chill thoroughly.

Beat whipping cream at high speed of an electric mixer until stiff peaks form; gently fold whipped cream into Grand Marnier mixture. To serve, spoon fruit mixture evenly into individual dessert dishes; top each serving with whipped cream mixture. Yield: 8 to 10 servings.   Kay Gross

Frantic Elegance
Arendell Parrott Academy
Kinston, North Carolina

Olde English Trifle

⅓ cup sugar
2 teaspoons cornstarch
3 cups milk
6 eggs, beaten
1½ teaspoons vanilla extract
½ to 1 cup seedless raspberry
   jam
24 ladyfingers

¼ cup cream sherry
1 (16-ounce) can sliced peaches
   in heavy syrup, drained
3 bananas, sliced
1 cup whipping cream,
   whipped
Maraschino cherries, quartered
Sliced almonds

Combine sugar and cornstarch in a medium saucepan; stir well. Gradually add milk; cook over medium heat, stirring constantly, until mixture thickens and comes to a boil. Boil 1 minute, stirring constantly. Remove from heat.

Gradually stir about one-fourth of hot milk mixture into beaten eggs; add to remaining hot milk mixture, stirring constantly. Cook over medium heat, stirring constantly, until mixture thickens (do not boil). Remove from heat, and stir in vanilla. Let custard cool.

Spread jam between halves of ladyfingers; reassemble. Brush both sides of ladyfingers with sherry. Arrange ladyfingers in bottom of a 12-cup trifle bowl. Cover with sliced peaches and bananas. Pour cooled custard over fruit. Cover and chill at least 2 hours. Top trifle with whipped cream, cherries, and almonds. Yield: 12 servings.

10,000 Tastes of Minnesota
The Woman's Club of Minneapolis, Minnesota

Summer Cantaloupe Cooler

3 cups cantaloupe balls, chilled
   and divided
2 envelopes unflavored gelatin
1 cup boiling lemonade

¼ cup lemonade, chilled
1 cup vanilla ice cream
1 cup ice cubes

Place ½ cup cantaloupe balls in container of an electric blender, and process until smooth. Sprinkle gelatin over cantaloupe puree in blender; let stand 1 minute. Add 1 cup boiling lemonade, and process at low speed 2 minutes. Add ¼ cup chilled lemonade, ½ cup cantaloupe balls, and ice cream; process until smooth. Add ice cubes, one at a time, processing until smooth. Let stand 3 minutes or until mixture is slightly thickened.

Spoon about ½ cup ice cream mixture into each of four 12-ounce parfait glasses; top each with about ¼ cup cantaloupe balls. Repeat layers once. Cover and chill 30 minutes or until set. Yield: 4 servings.

Favorite Recipes from Union Baptist Church Cooks
Union Baptist Church
Tylertown, Mississippi

Lime Mousse

5 eggs	**1 cup fresh lime juice**
1 cup sugar	**2 cups whipping cream**
½ cup butter, melted and	**1 tablespoon grated lime rind**
cooled	**Garnish: fresh raspberries**

Beat eggs at medium speed of an electric mixer; gradually add sugar, beating until thick and lemon colored. Slowly add melted butter in a thin stream, mixing well. Stir in lime juice.

Pour egg mixture into top of a double boiler. Bring water to a boil. Reduce heat to medium; cook 12 to 15 minutes or until mixture thickens and coats a metal spoon, stirring constantly with a wire whisk. Pour mixture into a large bowl. Cover and chill at least 1 hour, stirring twice.

Beat whipping cream at high speed of an electric mixer until soft peaks form. Gently fold whipped cream and lime rind into chilled mixture. To serve, spoon mousse into individual dessert dishes. Garnish, if desired. Yield: 12 servings.

It's Our Serve!
The Junior League of Long Island
Roslyn, New York

Baked Fruit Custard

3 cups fresh raspberries, sliced
   cooking apples, or sliced
   peaches
2 tablespoons sugar
¼ to ½ teaspoon ground
   cinnamon
2 cups evaporated milk

3 eggs
¼ cup all-purpose flour
3 tablespoons sugar
1 teaspoon vanilla extract
¼ teaspoon salt
Powdered sugar or vanilla
   ice cream

Arrange fruit in a buttered 11- x 7- x 1½-inch baking dish. Combine 2 tablespoons sugar and cinnamon; sprinkle over fruit.

Combine milk and next 5 ingredients in container of an electric blender, and process 1 minute or until smooth. Pour milk mixture over fruit; bake, uncovered, at 350° for 35 to 40 minutes or until set and lightly browned. To serve, cut into squares. Sprinkle with powdered sugar or top with ice cream. Serve immediately. Yield: 6 servings.   Susan Spiggle

Command Performances
The Southwest Virginia Opera Society
Roanoke, Virginia

Baked Apple Pudding

½ cup shortening
2 cups sugar
2 eggs
2¼ cups all-purpose flour
2 teaspoons baking soda
½ teaspoon salt
2 teaspoons ground cinnamon
1½ teaspoons ground nutmeg
4 cups applesauce

1 cup firmly packed brown
   sugar
1 cup chopped pecans or
   walnuts
2 tablespoons butter or
   margarine
Whipped cream or vanilla
   ice cream

Cream shortening; gradually add 2 cups sugar, beating well at medium speed of an electric mixer. Add eggs, one at a time, beating well after each addition.

Combine flour and next 4 ingredients in a medium bowl; stir well. Add flour mixture to creamed mixture alternately with applesauce, beginning and ending with flour mixture. Mix well after each addition. (Mixture will be very wet.)

Pour batter into a greased and floured 13- x 9- x 2-inch baking pan. Combine 1 cup brown sugar, pecans, and butter in a small bowl; mix well with a fork. Sprinkle brown sugar mixture over batter, lightly pressing into batter. Bake at 350° for 45 to 55 minutes or until a wooden pick inserted in center comes out clean.

To serve, cut into squares; invert each square onto a dessert plate. Serve warm topped with whipped cream or ice cream. Yield: 10 to 12 servings. Janet Trowbridge

Holladay 7th Ward Cookbook
The Holladay 7th Ward Relief Society
Salt Lake City, Utah

Cranberry Bread Pudding

½ (16-ounce) loaf day-old French bread, torn into pieces
1 cup cranberries, coarsely chopped
1 cup chopped pecans or walnuts
2 cups milk
2 cups half-and-half
3 eggs, beaten
1 cup firmly packed brown sugar
½ cup sugar
¼ cup dark rum
1 tablespoon vanilla extract
Maple syrup or hard sauce

Combine bread, cranberries, and pecans in a large bowl; toss gently. Combine milk and half-and-half; pour over bread mixture. Cover and chill 1 hour.

Combine eggs, sugars, rum, and vanilla; stir well. Add egg mixture to chilled bread mixture, stirring gently to combine. Pour into a greased 13- x 9- x 2-inch baking pan. Bake, uncovered, at 325° for 1 hour or until set and lightly browned. Let cool in pan 5 minutes. Cut into squares; serve warm with maple syrup or hard sauce. Yield: 10 to 12 servings.

More Than a Tea Party
The Junior League of Boston, Massachusetts

Triple Chocolate Bread Pudding

2 cups day-old French bread, torn into pieces
8 (1-ounce) squares semisweet chocolate, cut into ½-inch pieces
¼ cup butter, melted
4 eggs
2 cups chocolate milk

1 cup sugar
½ cup cocoa
⅛ teaspoon salt
½ teaspoon vanilla extract
Powdered sugar
Garnishes: whipped cream, chocolate shavings, and fresh strawberries

Combine bread, chocolate, and butter in a large bowl; toss gently. Divide mixture evenly among eight 8-ounce ramekins.

Beat eggs; gradually add milk and next 4 ingredients, mixing well. Pour egg mixture evenly over bread mixture in ramekins. Let stand 30 minutes, stirring occasionally.

Place ramekins in a large shallow baking pan. Pour hot water into pan to a depth of 1 inch. Bake, uncovered, at 350° for 40 to 45 minutes or until set. Sprinkle with powdered sugar. Garnish, if desired. Yield: 8 servings. Trisha Pape

Our Favorite Recipes
St. Anne's Roman Catholic Church
Rock Hill, South Carolina

Ed Macauley's Bread Pudding

2 cups milk
3 eggs, beaten
¼ cup plus 2 tablespoons sugar
½ teaspoon salt
½ teaspoon vanilla extract

4 slices white bread, crusts removed
1 teaspoon ground cinnamon
Dash of ground nutmeg
Vanilla Sauce

Heat milk in a small saucepan over low heat until hot (do not boil). Combine eggs, sugar, and salt in a medium bowl; stir well. Gradually stir about one-fourth of hot milk into egg mixture; add to remaining milk, stirring constantly. Add vanilla, stirring well.

Place bread slices in a buttered shallow 2-quart baking dish. Pour milk mixture over bread. Combine cinnamon and nutmeg; sprinkle over pudding mixture. Bake, uncovered, at 300° for 50 minutes or until a knife inserted in center comes out clean. Serve warm with Vanilla Sauce. Yield: 6 servings.

Vanilla Sauce

1 cup water
½ cup sugar
1 tablespoon cornstarch

2 tablespoons butter
2 teaspoons vanilla extract
Pinch of salt

Bring water to a boil in a small saucepan. Combine sugar and cornstarch; stir well. Add sugar mixture to boiling water. Reduce heat to medium, stirring constantly, or until mixture thickens. Remove from heat; add butter, vanilla, and salt, stirring until butter melts. Yield: ¾ cup.   Ed Macauley

What the Winners Eat
Sugar Creek Swim Club
St. Louis, Missouri

Pumpkin Rice Pudding

1 (16-ounce) can cooked, mashed pumpkin
1 (12-ounce) can evaporated milk
¾ cup sugar
2 eggs, lightly beaten

1 teaspoon ground cinnamon
½ teaspoon salt
½ teaspoon ground ginger
¼ teaspoon ground cloves
⅔ cup instant rice, uncooked
½ cup raisins

Combine first 8 ingredients in a medium bowl; stir well. Add rice and raisins, stirring well.

Pour pumpkin mixture into a lightly greased 1½-quart baking dish. Place dish in a 13- x 9- x 2-inch baking pan; pour hot water into pan to a depth of 1 inch. Bake, uncovered, at 350° for 15 minutes. Stir pumpkin mixture, and bake an additional 50 to 60 minutes or until a knife inserted in center comes out clean. Serve immediately. Yield: 8 servings.   Kathy Owen

Favorite Recipes of the Episcopal Churches on the Kenai
The Episcopal Churches on the Kenai
Nikiski, Alaska

Chocolate Meringue Gâteau

3 eggs, separated
½ cup sugar
⅓ cup sugar
1 teaspoon cornstarch
½ cup milk
2 ounces milk chocolate,
  broken into pieces

¾ cup unsalted butter,
  softened
½ cup whipping cream,
  whipped
Milk chocolate stars

Line a baking sheet with parchment paper; draw two 7-inch circles on paper. Turn paper over, and set aside.

Beat egg whites in a large bowl at high speed of an electric mixer just until foamy; gradually add ½ cup sugar, 1 tablespoon at a time, beating until stiff peaks form and sugar dissolves (about 2 to 4 minutes). Spoon half of meringue mixture into center of each circle on prepared baking sheet. Using the back of a spoon, shape meringue mixture into smooth circles. Bake at 300° for 1 hour. Turn oven off, and let meringue cool in oven. Peel off paper. Let meringues dry completely on wire racks, away from drafts.

Combine ⅓ cup sugar and cornstarch in a medium saucepan; stir well. Gradually add milk, stirring well. Add chocolate; cook over medium heat, stirring constantly, until chocolate melts. Beat egg yolks until thick and lemon colored. Gradually stir about one-fourth of hot milk mixture into beaten egg yolks. Add to remaining hot mixture, stirring constantly. Cook over medium heat until mixture thickens and coats a metal spoon. Remove from heat; let cool completely.

Cream butter; gradually add cooled chocolate mixture, beating at medium speed of an electric mixer until well blended.

To assemble, spread filling between layers and on top of meringue. Pipe whipped cream over top of dessert; arrange milk chocolate stars on whipped cream. Place in an airtight container; chill at least 2 hours. Yield: 6 servings.   Tamara Montgomery

Cooks and Company
The Muscle Shoals District Service League
Sheffield, Alabama

Frozen Apricot Bombe with Mocha Sauce

25 large marshmallows
¾ cup apricot brandy
½ cup chopped canned apricot
  halves
2 teaspoons grated lemon rind

2 cups whipping cream,
  whipped
Mocha Sauce
Garnish: fresh strawberries

Line a 6-cup mold or medium bowl with plastic wrap. Set aside.

Combine marshmallows and apricot brandy in top of a double boiler; bring water to a boil. Reduce heat to low; cook 3 to 4 minutes or until marshmallows melt, stirring occasionally. Remove from heat; let cool.

Add apricots and lemon rind to cooled marshmallow mixture; stir well. Gently fold whipped cream into apricot mixture. Spoon into prepared mold. Cover and freeze 8 hours or until firm.

To unmold, place a damp, warm towel around mold; run a sharp knife or a small metal spatula around edges. Invert mold onto a chilled serving platter. Peel off plastic wrap. Spoon ½ cup Mocha Sauce over bombe. Serve bombe with remaining sauce. Garnish, if desired. Yield: 10 to 12 servings.

Mocha Sauce

1 (12-ounce) package
  semisweet chocolate morsels
2 (1-ounce) squares
  unsweetened chocolate
1 tablespoon instant coffee
  granules

1 (12-ounce) can evaporated
  milk
1 teaspoon vanilla extract

Place chocolates in top of a double boiler. Bring water to a boil; reduce heat to low, and cook until chocolates melt, stirring occasionally. Dissolve coffee granules in milk; gradually add to chocolate mixture, stirring with a wire whisk until smooth. Stir in vanilla. Yield: 2¾ cups.

RiverFeast: Still Celebrating Cincinnati
The Junior League of Cincinnati, Ohio

Ice Cream Crunch

1 cup all-purpose flour
¼ cup quick-cooking oats,
   uncooked
¼ cup firmly packed brown
   sugar
½ cup butter or margarine

½ cup chopped pecans
½ cup chocolate syrup, divided
½ cup caramel topping,
   divided
1 quart vanilla ice cream,
   softened

Combine flour, oats, and brown sugar; stir well. Cut in butter with a pastry blender until mixture resembles coarse meal. Stir in pecans. Press crumb mixture in bottom of a 13- x 9- x 2-inch baking pan. Bake at 400° for 10 minutes. Stir crumb mixture, and let cool in pan.

Sprinkle half of crumb mixture in a 9-inch square baking pan. Drizzle ¼ cup chocolate syrup and ¼ cup caramel topping over crumb mixture in pan. Spoon ice cream into pan, spreading evenly. Top with remaining half of crumb mixture, chocolate syrup, and caramel topping. Cover and freeze until firm. Cut into squares. Yield: 9 servings.   Joanne Johnson

Harvest of Home Cookin'
Trailways Girl Scout Council
Joliet, Illinois

Heavenly Chocolate Ice Cream

12 (1¾-ounce) chocolate-
   coated caramel and smooth
   nougat bars, cut into 1-inch
   pieces
1 (14-ounce) can sweetened
   condensed milk

2 quarts plus 1½ cups milk,
   divided
1 (5½-ounce) can chocolate
   syrup

Combine candy and condensed milk in a large saucepan; cook over medium-low heat until candy melts, stirring constantly.

Gradually add 1 quart milk and chocolate syrup, stirring with a wire whisk until well blended. Add remaining 1 quart plus 1½ cups milk, stirring well. Pour mixture into freezer can of a 5-quart

hand-turned or electric freezer. Freeze according to manufacturer's instructions. Let ice cream ripen 1 hour before serving.
Yield: about 5 quarts.   Elizabeth Walker

Evening Shade
Future Homemakers of America, Evening Shade High School
Evening Shade, Arkansas

Freezer Vanilla Ice Cream

2 cups whipping cream
3 cups sugar
1 (12-ounce) can evaporated
   milk

1 tablespoon vanilla extract
4 cups milk

Combine cream and sugar; stir well. Add evaporated milk and
vanilla; beat at medium speed of an electric mixer until foamy. Stir
in 4 cups milk. Pour into freezer can of a 1-gallon hand-turned or
electric freezer. Freeze according to manufacturer's instructions.
Let ripen 1 hour before serving. Yield: 1 gallon.

Second Round, Tea-Time at the Masters®
The Junior League of Augusta, Georgia

Beautiful Grape Ice Cream

4 cups whipping cream
2½ cups sugar
1 (20-ounce) can unsweetened
   crushed pineapple, drained

1 (12-ounce) can frozen grape
   juice concentrate, thawed
1 teaspoon grated lemon rind
1 cup fresh lemon juice

Combine all ingredients in a large bowl; stir well. Pour into
freezer can of a 1-gallon hand-turned or electric freezer. Freeze
according to manufacturer's instructions. Let ripen 1 hour before
serving. Yield: 2½ quarts.   Joanne C. Moore

Gracious Goodness: The Taste of Memphis
The Symphony League of Memphis, Tennessee

Three-Fruit Ice Cream

1 cup fresh orange juice	**3 cups sugar**
¾ cup fresh lemon juice	**3 cups milk**
3 ripe bananas, mashed	**3 cups half-and-half**

Combine orange juice, lemon juice, and bananas in a small bowl; stir well. Set aside.

Combine sugar, milk, and half-and-half, stirring until sugar dissolves. Pour milk mixture into freezer can of a 5-quart hand-turned or electric freezer. Turn about 20 minutes or until mixture is partially frozen. Remove dasher, and add reserved banana mixture. Return dasher to freezer, and freeze mixture according to manufacturer's instructions.

Spoon ice cream mixture into a 13- x 9- x 2-inch dish. Cover and freeze at least 4 hours before serving. Yield: 3 quarts.

A Touch of Atlanta
Marist School
Atlanta, Georgia

Pineapple Sherbet

3 cups milk	**½ (12-ounce) can frozen**
1 (15¼-ounce) can	**pineapple juice concentrate,**
unsweetened crushed	**thawed and undiluted**
pineapple, undrained	**⅓ cup sugar**
¾ cup evaporated milk	**½ teaspoon vanilla extract**

Combine all ingredients in a large bowl; stir until sugar dissolves. Pour mixture into freezer can of a 1-gallon hand-turned or electric freezer. Freeze according to manufacturer's instructions. Yield: about 9 cups.   Kimberly Klaver

Note-Worthy Recipes
Iowa Falls High School
Iowa Falls, Iowa

Frozen Fruit Yogurt

1 teaspoon unflavored gelatin
2 tablespoons cold water
2 cups fresh strawberries,
  hulled
1 banana, sliced

1 (16-ounce) carton plain
  low-fat yogurt
1 tablespoon plus 1 teaspoon
  sugar
½ teaspoon vanilla extract

Sprinkle gelatin over cold water in a saucepan; let stand 1 minute. Cook over low heat, stirring until gelatin dissolves.

Position knife blade in food processor bowl; add reserved gelatin mixture, strawberries, and remaining ingredients, and process until smooth. Pour strawberry mixture into a 9-inch square pan; freeze 3 to 4 hours, stirring every 30 minutes or until mixture is thickened. Yield: 1 quart.

Just Like Mom Used to Make
The Northfield Community Nursery School
Northfield, Illinois

Strawberry-Orange Ice

6 cups fresh strawberries,
  hulled
1¾ cups sugar

1¾ cups orange juice
½ cup lemon juice
⅛ teaspoon salt

Combine all ingredients in a large bowl; stir well. Pour half of strawberry mixture into container of an electric blender or food processor, and process until smooth. Pour mixture into a 13- x 9- x 2-inch pan. Repeat procedure. Freeze until almost firm (about 4 hours), stirring occasionally.

Spoon strawberry mixture into a large chilled mixing bowl; beat at medium speed of an electric mixer just until smooth. Return mixture to pan; freeze until firm. Let stand at room temperature 10 minutes before serving. Yield: 2 quarts.   Audrey Wenner

100th Anniversary Cookbook
Auxiliary of Harrisburg Hospital
Harrisburg, Pennsylvania

Kiwi Sorbet

1½ cups fresh orange juice
3 ripe kiwifruit, peeled and
   chopped

1 banana, chopped
Garnish: fresh strawberries

Position knife blade in food processor bowl; add first 3 ingredients, and process 45 to 60 seconds or until smooth. Pour mixture into freezer can of a 2-quart hand-turned or electric freezer. Freeze according to manufacturer's instructions. Let ripen 1 hour. To serve, scoop sorbet into stemmed glasses. Garnish, if desired. Yield: 3 cups.

The Fine Art of Cooking
The Women's Committee of the Philadelphia Museum of Art
Philadelphia, Pennsylvania

Strawberry Margarita Sorbet

1 cup sugar
1 cup water
1 quart fresh strawberries,
   hulled
¼ cup plus 2 tablespoons fresh
   lime juice

¼ cup plus 1½ teaspoons
   tequila
3 tablespoons Triple Sec or
   other orange-flavored liqueur
Garnish: fresh mint leaves

Combine sugar and water in a small saucepan. Bring to a boil, stirring until sugar dissolves. Remove from heat, and let cool.

Position knife blade in food processor bowl. Add strawberries; process until smooth. Add lime juice, tequila, and Triple Sec; process until blended. Combine sugar syrup and strawberry mixture. Pour into an 8-inch square pan; freeze until firm.

Position knife blade in processor bowl. Add half of frozen strawberry mixture; process until fluffy, but not thawed. Set aside. Repeat procedure with remaining mixture. Return mixture to pan. Freeze until firm. To serve, scoop sorbet into individual dessert dishes. Garnish, if desired. Yield: 4¾ cups.

Stirring Performances
The Junior League of Winston-Salem, North Carolina

Eggs & Cheese

The one-room Adams Chapel School, built in 1898, once seated children from grades one through twelve. Located in the old North Hull Historic District, the school is one of a group of restored 19th-century buildings in downtown Montgomery, Alabama.

Hoppelpoppel

1 large onion, chopped
¼ cup plus 1 tablespoon butter
  or margarine, melted
3½ cups cooked, peeled,
  and diced red
  potatoes

1 cup diced cooked pork or
  roast beef
4 eggs, beaten
1 tablespoon chopped fresh
  parsley
Salt and pepper to taste

Sauté onion in butter in a large skillet 1 minute. Add potato, and cook 3 minutes. Add meat, and cook 2 minutes. Combine eggs, parsley, and salt and pepper to taste, beating with a wire whisk until blended. Pour egg mixture over potato mixture; cook over low heat until eggs are set, stirring occasionally. Yield: 6 servings.

Connecticut Cooks III
The American Cancer Society, Connecticut Division, Inc.
Wallingford, Connecticut

Baked Sicilian Frittata

5 medium-size red potatoes,
  peeled and sliced
¼ cup olive oil
1 cup chopped onion
¼ cup chopped green pepper
3 cloves garlic, minced
4 cups frozen chopped
  broccoli

12 eggs, beaten
¾ cup grated Parmesan cheese
½ cup water
1 teaspoon dried whole basil
½ teaspoon salt
½ teaspoon pepper
1½ cups (6 ounces) shredded
  Monterey Jack cheese

Sauté potato in oil in a large skillet 10 minutes. Add onion, green pepper, and garlic; sauté until tender. Add broccoli; cover and cook 5 minutes. Arrange mixture in an 11- x 7- x 1½-inch baking dish. Combine eggs and next 5 ingredients; beat until blended. Pour over potato mixture. Sprinkle with Monterey Jack cheese. Bake, uncovered, at 350° for 25 to 30 minutes or until set. Yield: 8 servings.

Savor the Flavor of Oregon
The Junior League of Eugene, Oregon

Eggs Florentine

1 (10-ounce) package frozen
  chopped spinach
1 cup (4 ounces) shredded
  Cheddar cheese
1 pound bulk pork sausage
2 cups sliced fresh mushrooms
½ cup chopped green onions
2 tablespoons butter or
  margarine, melted
12 eggs, lightly beaten
2 cups whipping cream
1 cup (4 ounces) shredded
  Swiss cheese
Paprika

Cook spinach according to package directions; drain well. Sprinkle Cheddar cheese in bottom of a buttered 13- x 9- x 2-inch baking dish; spread spinach evenly over cheese.

Cook sausage in a skillet over medium heat until browned, stirring to crumble meat; drain and sprinkle over spinach.

Sauté mushrooms and green onions in butter in a large skillet until tender. Sprinkle sautéed vegetables over sausage. Combine eggs and cream, beating with a wire whisk until blended. Pour egg mixture over vegetable mixture. Top evenly with Swiss cheese; sprinkle with paprika. Bake, uncovered, at 350° for 40 to 45 minutes or until set. Yield: 12 servings.   Nancy Schorr

Delectable Edibles from the Livable Forest
The Women's Club of Kingwood, Texas

Swiss Pie Florentine with Cheese Crust

1¼ cups (5 ounces) shredded
  sharp Cheddar cheese
¾ cup all-purpose flour
1 teaspoon salt
¼ teaspoon dry mustard
¼ cup butter or margarine,
  melted
½ cup finely chopped onion
1½ cups sliced fresh
  mushrooms
¼ cup butter or margarine,
  melted
¼ cup all-purpose flour
½ cup milk
½ cup whipping cream
1 (10-ounce) package frozen
  chopped spinach, cooked
  and drained
3 eggs, beaten
1 teaspoon salt
¼ teaspoon ground nutmeg
Dash of pepper

Combine first 5 ingredients in a bowl; stir well. Firmly press mixture on bottom and up sides of a 9-inch pieplate; set aside.

Sauté onion and mushrooms in ¼ cup melted butter in a large skillet until tender. Add ¼ cup flour, stirring until blended. Cook 1 minute, stirring constantly. Gradually add milk and whipping cream; cook over medium heat, stirring constantly, until mixture is slightly thickened. Remove from heat. Add spinach, eggs, 1 teaspoon salt, nutmeg, and pepper, stirring well to combine.

Pour mixture into prepared crust. Bake, uncovered, at 400° for 15 minutes. Reduce heat to 325°, and bake an additional 25 minutes or until set and lightly browned. Let stand 10 minutes before serving. Yield: 6 servings.

It's Our Serve!
The Junior League of Long Island
Roslyn, New York

Crustless Quiche

½ **pound sliced fresh mushrooms**
2 **tablespoons butter or margarine, melted**
4 **eggs**
1 **(8-ounce) carton sour cream**
½ **cup small-curd cottage cheese**
½ **cup grated Parmesan cheese**
¼ **cup all-purpose flour**
1 **teaspoon onion powder or 1 small onion, chopped**
4 **drops of hot sauce**
2 **cups (8 ounces) shredded Monterey Jack cheese**

Sauté mushrooms in butter in a skillet until tender. Set aside.

Combine eggs and next 6 ingredients in container of an electric blender or food processor, and process until smooth. Stir in reserved mushrooms and Monterey Jack cheese. Pour into a greased 10-inch quiche dish. Bake, uncovered, at 350° for 45 minutes or until set and lightly browned. Let stand 5 minutes before serving. Yield: one 10-inch quiche.   Peggy Gaier

The Family Affair
Lincolnshire Community Nursery School
Lincolnshire, Illinois

Garden Vegetable Quiche

1 cup all-purpose flour
½ cup butter or margarine,
  softened
1 (3-ounce) package cream
  cheese, softened
½ cup diced fresh mushrooms
½ cup diced green pepper
½ cup diced zucchini
1 small onion, diced
1 small carrot, scraped and
  diced
1 teaspoon minced garlic
2 tablespoons butter or
  margarine, melted

1 teaspoon paprika
½ teaspoon salt
¼ teaspoon pepper
1 cup (4 ounces) shredded
  mozzarella or Muenster
  cheese
3 eggs
1 cup milk
3 tablespoons chopped onion
1 tablespoon butter or
  margarine, melted

Combine flour, ½ cup butter, and softened cream cheese in a medium bowl, stirring until blended. Shape into a ball. Cover and chill 30 minutes.

Sauté mushrooms and next 5 ingredients in 2 tablespoons melted butter in a large skillet until vegetables are crisp-tender. Remove from heat; stir in paprika, salt, and pepper. Set aside.

Press chilled pastry evenly on bottom and up sides of a 10-inch pieplate. Sprinkle mozzarella cheese over bottom of pastry shell. Spoon reserved sautéed vegetables evenly over cheese. Combine eggs and milk in a medium bowl; beat with a wire whisk until blended. Pour egg mixture over vegetables.

Sauté chopped onion in 1 tablespoon butter in a small skillet until tender; drain and sprinkle over quiche. Bake, uncovered, at 350° for 40 to 45 minutes or until set and lightly browned. Let stand 5 minutes before serving. Yield: one 10-inch quiche.

Spice and Spirit: The Complete Kosher Jewish Cookbook
Lubavitch Women's Organization
Brooklyn, New York

Feta Compli

1¼ cups matzo meal
1 tablespoon sugar
½ cup margarine
1 egg, lightly beaten
¾ cup finely chopped
  blanched almonds or walnuts
1¼ pounds fresh spinach,
  washed and trimmed
1¼ cups chopped onion
3 tablespoons vegetable oil
1 cup (4 ounces) shredded
  Swiss cheese

1¼ cups half-and-half
2 eggs
½ (8-ounce) package cream
  cheese, softened
½ teaspoon salt
¼ teaspoon pepper
⅛ teaspoon ground nutmeg
6 ounces feta cheese,
  crumbled

Combine matzo meal and sugar; cut in margarine with a pastry blender until mixture resembles coarse meal. Add 1 lightly beaten egg; stir well to combine. Stir in almonds. Firmly press mixture on bottom and up sides of a 10-inch deep-dish pieplate. Prick bottom and sides of pastry with a fork. Bake at 400° for 7 minutes. Set aside, and let cool completely.

Cook spinach in a small amount of boiling water 3 to 4 minutes; drain. Press spinach between paper towels to remove excess moisture. Set aside.

Sauté onion in oil in a medium skillet until tender. Combine onion, reserved spinach, and Swiss cheese. Set aside.

Combine half-and-half and next 5 ingredients in container of an electric blender, and process until smooth. Set aside.

Spread spinach mixture over prepared crust; top with feta cheese. Pour half-and-half mixture over cheese. Bake, uncovered, at 350° for 50 minutes or until set. (Shield with aluminum foil to prevent excessive browning, if necessary.) Let stand 5 minutes before serving. Yield: one 10-inch quiche.   Kirk Cashmere

The When You Live in Hawaii You Get Very Creative During Passover
Cookbook
Congregation Sof Ma'arav
Honolulu, Hawaii

Zucchini Torte

1¼ cups all-purpose flour
½ teaspoon salt
½ teaspoon anise seeds,
  crushed
1½ cups (6 ounces) shredded
  Cheddar cheese, divided
½ cup butter or margarine,
  softened
¾ cup long-grain rice,
  uncooked
1 cup water
1 cup Chablis or other dry
  white wine

8 slices bacon
2 cups thinly sliced zucchini
¾ cup chopped onion
3 cloves garlic, minced
6 eggs, beaten
1 (8-ounce) carton sour cream
Salt and pepper to taste
Garnishes: paprika, poached
  zucchini slices, grated
  Parmesan cheese

Position knife blade in food processor bowl; add flour, salt, anise seeds, ½ cup shredded Cheddar cheese, and butter. Process until dough begins to form a ball and leaves sides of bowl. Press dough evenly on bottom and 1 inch up sides of a 9-inch springform pan. Set aside.

Cook rice in water and wine according to package directions. Set rice aside.

Cook bacon in a large skillet until crisp; remove bacon, reserving 2 tablespoons drippings in skillet. Crumble bacon, and set aside.

Sauté 2 cups zucchini, onion, and garlic in bacon drippings in skillet until vegetables are tender.

Combine zucchini mixture, remaining 1 cup Cheddar cheese, reserved rice, reserved bacon, eggs, sour cream, and salt and pepper to taste. Pour into prepared pan.

Bake, uncovered, at 350° for 55 minutes or until set and lightly browned. Let stand 5 minutes before serving. Carefully remove sides of pan. Garnish, if desired. Yield: one 9-inch torte.

A Touch of Atlanta
Marist School
Atlanta, Georgia

Deluxe Cheese Grits Soufflé

2 tablespoons grated Parmesan
  cheese
4 cups water
½ teaspoon salt
1 cup regular grits, uncooked
3 tablespoons butter or
  margarine
3 tablespoons all-purpose flour

1 cup milk
1 cup whipping cream
1 cup (4 ounces) shredded
  Cheddar cheese
½ cup grated Parmesan cheese
6 eggs, separated
Pinch of cream of tartar

Lightly butter a 3-quart soufflé dish. Cut a piece of aluminum foil long enough to fit around the dish, allowing a 1-inch overlap. Fold foil lengthwise into thirds, and lightly butter one side. Wrap foil around outside of soufflé dish, buttered side against dish, allowing it to extend 3 inches above rim to form a collar; secure with string. Sprinkle bottom and sides of dish with 2 tablespoons Parmesan cheese.

Combine water and salt in a large saucepan; bring to a boil. Stir in grits; cover, reduce heat, and simmer 10 minutes, stirring occasionally. Remove from heat, and set aside.

Melt butter in a large saucepan over low heat. Add flour, stirring until smooth. Cook 1 minute, stirring constantly. Gradually add milk and cream; cook over medium heat, stirring constantly, until mixture is thickened and bubbly. Add reserved grits, Cheddar cheese, and ½ cup Parmesan cheese, stirring until cheeses melt. Set aside.

Beat egg yolks at high speed of an electric mixer until thick and lemon colored; add to reserved grits mixture, stirring well. Set aside.

Beat egg whites in a large mixing bowl at high speed just until foamy. Add cream of tartar; beat at high speed until stiff peaks form. Gently fold beaten egg whites into grits mixture. Spoon into prepared soufflé dish. Place in 400° oven; reduce temperature to 375°, and bake for 1 hour and 5 minutes or until soufflé is puffed and golden. Serve immediately. Yield: 10 servings.   Shirley Smith

Kentucky Kitchens, Volume II
Telephone Pioneers of America, Kentucky Chapter No. 32
Louisville, Kentucky

Miniature Cheese and Herb Soufflés

1 tablespoon unsalted butter,
  softened
8 slices white bread, crusts
  removed
1 cup whipping cream
1 cup milk
5 eggs
½ teaspoon salt

½ teaspoon freshly ground
  pepper
Dash of hot sauce
1 pound Camembert cheese
½ pound sliced bacon, cooked
  and crumbled
1 tablespoon dried whole
  rosemary, crushed

Lightly butter eight 6-ounce soufflé dishes with 1 tablespoon unsalted butter. Cut each slice of bread in half lengthwise; place ½ slice bread in bottom of each soufflé dish. Set soufflé dishes and remaining bread aside.

Combine whipping cream and next 5 ingredients; beat with a wire whisk until blended. Set aside.

Remove rind from cheese; cut cheese into ½-inch cubes. Layer half each of cheese, bacon, and rosemary in order in soufflé dishes; repeat layers with remaining half of bread slices, cheese, bacon, and rosemary. Divide whipping cream mixture evenly among soufflé dishes. Gently press mixture down with the back of a spoon. Cover and chill 30 minutes. Line a 15- x 10- x 1-inch jellyroll pan with aluminum foil; place soufflé dishes in pan. Bake, uncovered, at 350° for 30 minutes or until soufflés are puffed and lightly browned. Serve immediately. Yield: 8 servings.

The Fine Art of Cooking
The Women's Committee of the Philadelphia Museum of Art
Philadelphia, Pennsylvania

Proceeds generated from the sale of View Beyond the Park, *a cookbook compiled by the Fairview Park Junior Women's Club, enable the members to participate in programs that assist the disabled and provide college scholarships.*

Tomato-Cheese Casserole

2 large purple onions, sliced
¼ cup plus 2 tablespoons
   butter or margarine, melted
1 (6-ounce) package plain
   croutons
6 large tomatoes, sliced

1 teaspoon salt
½ teaspoon pepper
½ teaspoon dried whole basil
3 cups (12 ounces) shredded
   Monterey Jack cheese

Sauté onion in butter in a large skillet 5 minutes. Add croutons, and sauté 3 minutes. Set aside.

Place tomato slices in a bowl. Sprinkle with salt, pepper, and basil; toss gently. Spoon half of reserved onion mixture into a greased 13- x 9- x 2-inch baking dish. Arrange half of tomato slices over onion mixture; sprinkle with half of cheese. Repeat layers. Bake, uncovered, at 350° for 35 to 40 minutes or until hot and bubbly. Yield: 8 servings.   Elaine Voinovich

View Beyond the Park
The Junior Women's Club of Fairview Park, Ohio

Andrea's Deluxe Grilled Cheese

1 cup (4 ounces) shredded
   Swiss cheese
1 cup (4 ounces) shredded
   Cheddar cheese
⅓ cup mayonnaise
1 tablespoon prepared mustard

1 tablespoon finely chopped
   green onion
8 slices bread
¼ cup butter or margarine,
   softened

Combine first 5 ingredients. Spread mixture evenly on one side of 4 slices of bread to within ¼ inch of edges. Top with remaining bread slices. Spread outside of sandwiches with butter. Place sandwiches on a hot griddle; cook over medium heat until bread is golden, turning once. Yield: 4 servings.   Andrea Spadoni

Trinity Episcopal School, Classroom Classics
The Parents and Students of Trinity Episcopal School
Pine Bluff, Arkansas

Never-To-Be-Forgotten Garlic Loaf

1 (16-ounce) loaf French bread
¼ cup plus 2 tablespoons
  butter or margarine
2 to 8 cloves garlic, crushed
2 tablespoons plus 1 teaspoon
  sesame seeds
2 cups (8 ounces) diced
  Monterey Jack or mozzarella
  cheese
1½ cups sour cream

¼ cup grated Parmesan cheese
2 tablespoons minced fresh
  parsley
2 teaspoons lemon-pepper
  seasoning
1 (14-ounce) can artichoke
  hearts, drained and coarsely
  chopped
1 cup (4 ounces) shredded
  Cheddar cheese

Slice bread in half horizontally. Hollow out each half of loaf, leaving a ¼-inch-thick shell. Place bread shells on a baking sheet. Set aside. Cut soft bread into 1-inch cubes, and set aside.

Melt butter in a large skillet; add garlic and sesame seeds, stirring well. Add reserved bread cubes; cook over medium heat, stirring constantly, until bread begins to brown and butter has been absorbed. Remove from heat, and set aside.

Combine Monterey Jack cheese, sour cream, Parmesan cheese, parsley, and lemon-pepper seasoning; stir well. Add reserved bread mixture and artichoke hearts, stirring well. Spoon evenly into bread shells; sprinkle with Cheddar cheese. Bake, uncovered, at 350° for 30 minutes or until thoroughly heated. Yield: 10 to 12 servings.

Only in California
The Children's Home Society of California
Los Angeles, California

Fish & Shellfish

The "Blue Moon" floats peacefully with other boats on waters that are surrounded by snow-covered mountains. After a successful day of fishing in this typical small Alaskan port, fishermen might have salmon, King crab, halibut, shrimp, and scallops among their catch.

Sesame Cod

¼ cup fresh orange juice
1 tablespoon brown sugar
2 tablespoons catsup
2 tablespoons soy sauce
1 tablespoon lemon juice
1 teaspoon vegetable oil

¼ teaspoon freshly ground
  pepper
4 (4-ounce) cod or other fish
  fillets
1 tablespoon sesame seeds,
  toasted

Place first 7 ingredients in a small bowl; stir well to combine.

Arrange fillets in a single layer in an 11- x 7- x 1½-inch baking dish. Pour orange juice mixture over fillets; cover and marinate fillets in refrigerator 2 hours, turning once.

Remove fillets from marinade, reserving marinade. Pour marinade into a small saucepan. Bring to a boil; reduce heat, and simmer 5 minutes. Set half of marinade aside.

Place fillets on a lightly greased rack in a shallow roasting pan. Broil fillets 6 inches from heat 10 to 12 minutes or until fish flakes easily when tested with a fork, basting occasionally with marinade.

Transfer fillets to a serving platter. Sprinkle toasted sesame seeds evenly over fillets. Serve fillets with reserved marinade. Yield: 4 servings.   Ellie Abramowitz

Literally Delicious
Abington Friends School Parents' Association
Jenkintown, Pennsylvania

Mahimahi with Shrimp and Scallops

½ cup butter
1½ cups sliced fresh
  mushrooms
2 green onions, sliced
1½ pounds mahimahi or other
  fish fillets, cut into 1-inch
  cubes
½ pound unpeeled medium-
  size fresh shrimp, peeled and
  deveined
½ pound bay scallops
1 cup Chablis or other dry
  white wine

½ cup canned diluted chicken
  broth
⅓ cup half-and-half
1 teaspoon salt
½ teaspoon pepper
3 tablespoons cornstarch
¼ cup cold water
¼ cup plus 2 tablespoons fine,
  dry breadcrumbs
Paprika
2 tablespoons butter, melted

Clarify ½ cup butter by melting it over low heat. Skim off the white froth that appears on top. Strain off the clear, yellow butter, keeping back the sediment of milk solids.

Sauté mushrooms and green onions in 2 tablespoons clarified butter in a large skillet until tender. Set aside, and keep warm.

Heat remaining clarified butter in skillet; add mahimahi, shrimp, and scallops, and sauté 3 to 5 minutes, stirring frequently. Add wine, broth, half-and-half, salt, and pepper; cook over medium heat 10 minutes, stirring frequently. Add reserved mushroom mixture, and bring just to a boil. Combine cornstarch and water; stir well. Gradually add cornstarch mixture to seafood mixture, and cook until thickened, stirring frequently.

Pour mixture into a buttered 2-quart gratin dish. Sprinkle with breadcrumbs and paprika. Drizzle with 2 tablespoons melted butter; broil 6 inches from heat 1½ to 2 minutes or until golden. Yield: 4 to 6 servings.   Helen Larson

Kona Kitchens
Kona Outdoor Circle
Kailua-Kona, Hawaii

Orange Roughy with Orange-Basil Butter

6 (4-ounce) orange roughy or
   other fish fillets
½ teaspoon salt
¼ teaspoon pepper
¾ cup Chablis or other dry
   white wine

Orange-Basil Butter
Garnishes: orange twists and
   fresh basil leaves

Sprinkle both sides of fillets with salt and pepper, and place in an ungreased 13- x 9- x 2-inch baking dish. Pour wine over fillets. Bake, uncovered, at 375° for 12 to 15 minutes or until fish flakes easily when tested with a fork. Transfer to a serving platter. Top with Orange-Basil Butter. Garnish, if desired. Yield: 6 servings.

Orange-Basil Butter

1 small onion, chopped
1 tablespoon butter, melted
¾ cup Chablis or other dry
   white wine

½ cup orange juice
½ cup loosely packed chopped
   fresh basil

Sauté onion in butter in a large skillet until tender. Add wine and remaining ingredients, and cook until thoroughly heated. Yield: 1½ cups.   Colleen Runkel

Heavenly Delights
St. Mary's Catholic Church Christian Women
Waukesha, Wisconsin

Proceeds from the sale of Kona Kitchens *will be returned to the Honolulu community through beautification projects. The Kona Outdoor Circle, publisher of the cookbook, finances community-wide landscaping and spearheaded an effort that banned roadside billboards in Hawaii.*

Fish Fillets with Mushroom-Lemon Sauce

½ pound sliced fresh
   mushrooms
4 to 6 green onions, chopped
¼ cup butter or margarine,
   melted
2 tablespoons all-purpose flour
1 cup milk

1 tablespoon chopped fresh
   parsley
1 teaspoon salt
1 teaspoon grated lemon rind
⅛ teaspoon pepper
6 (4-ounce) orange roughy or
   other fish fillets

Sauté mushrooms and green onions in butter in a large skillet until vegetables are tender. Add flour, stirring well. Cook 1 minute, stirring constantly. Gradually stir in milk. Add parsley and next 3 ingredients; bring to a boil. Arrange fillets in a single layer over sauce in skillet; carefully spoon sauce over fillets. Cover, reduce heat, and simmer 12 to 15 minutes or until fish flakes easily when tested with a fork. Transfer fillets to a serving platter, and top with sauce. Yield: 6 servings.   Debra McKinney

Best Friends
Terranova West Women's Club
Spring, Texas

Savory Cheese-Topped Fish Fillets

2 pounds orange roughy or
   other fish fillets
1 tablespoon vegetable oil
1¼ cups sliced fresh
   mushrooms
2 tablespoons minced green
   onions
3 tablespoons butter or
   margarine, melted

1 medium tomato, peeled,
   seeded, and chopped
1 cup (4 ounces) shredded
   Cheddar cheese
1 egg, beaten
¾ teaspoon salt
½ teaspoon dried whole basil
¼ teaspoon lemon-pepper
   seasoning

Place fillets in a lightly greased 13- x 9- x 2-inch baking pan; drizzle with vegetable oil. Bake at 500° for 8 to 10 minutes or until fish flakes easily when tested with a fork. Set aside.

Sauté mushrooms and onions in butter in a skillet until tender. Stir in tomato and remaining ingredients; cook 1 minute. Spoon mixture over fillets; broil 6 inches from heat 3 minutes or until cheese melts. Yield: 6 servings.   Caryol Adrian

Harrington Cooks
Harrington Homemakers
Harrington, Washington

Puget Sound Baked Salmon

1 (6- to 8-pound) salmon, cleaned and dressed
2 tablespoons fresh lemon juice
1 tablespoon salt, divided
1 medium onion, chopped
2 tablespoons butter or margarine, melted
1 (14.5-ounce) can whole tomatoes, undrained and chopped
½ teaspoon dried whole basil
¼ teaspoon freshly ground pepper
Pinch of sugar
3 large tomatoes, sliced
1 medium onion, sliced
1 medium-size green pepper, cut into strips
Additional freshly ground pepper to taste
4 slices bacon
2 tablespoons chopped fresh parsley

Rub fish cavity with lemon juice and 1 teaspoon salt; set aside. Sauté chopped onion in butter in a large skillet until tender. Stir in chopped tomatoes, 1 teaspoon salt, basil, ¼ teaspoon pepper, and sugar. Reduce heat; simmer, uncovered, until mixture is slightly thickened. Set aside.

Combine sliced tomato, sliced onion, green pepper, remaining 1 teaspoon salt, and freshly ground pepper to taste, stirring gently; spoon mixture into fish cavity. Close cavity with skewers. Make 4 slashes crosswise on one side of salmon; insert bacon in slashes.

Place salmon in a 15- x 10- x 1-inch jellyroll pan lined with aluminum foil. Spoon reserved tomato sauce over salmon. Bake, uncovered, at 425° for 45 to 50 minutes or until fish flakes easily when tested with a fork. Sprinkle with parsley; serve immediately. Yield: 12 servings.   Louise Brown

Favorite Recipes of Edmonds
Edmonds United Methodist Women
Edmonds, Washington

Country Salmon Pie

1½ cups whole wheat flour
½ cup grated Parmesan cheese
¾ cup shortening
2 to 3 tablespoons cold water
1 large onion, finely chopped
1 clove garlic, crushed
2 tablespoons butter or
  margarine, melted
1 (16-ounce) carton sour
  cream

4 eggs, lightly beaten
1 (14¾-ounce) can pink
  salmon, drained and flaked
1½ cups (6 ounces) shredded
  Gruyère cheese, divided
1 teaspoon dried whole
  dillweed, crushed
¼ teaspoon salt

Combine flour and Parmesan cheese in a medium bowl; cut in shortening with a pastry blender until mixture resembles coarse meal. Sprinkle cold water (1 tablespoon at a time) evenly over surface; stir with a fork until dry ingredients are moistened.

Press pastry on bottom and up sides of an 8-inch springform pan. Bake at 375° for 10 to 15 minutes. Set pastry shell aside.

Sauté onion and garlic in melted butter in a skillet over medium-high heat until onion is tender; set aside.

Combine sour cream and eggs in a large bowl, beating with a wire whisk until blended. Add salmon, reserved onion mixture, 1 cup Gruyère cheese, dillweed, and salt; stir well.

Pour salmon mixture into prepared pastry shell; sprinkle with remaining ½ cup Gruyère cheese. Bake, uncovered, at 375° for 1 hour and 10 minutes or until set and lightly browned. Let cool in pan 15 minutes. Carefully remove sides of pan. Serve immediately. Yield: 8 servings. June S. Hollingsworth

The Cookbook
East Lake United Methodist Church
Birmingham, Alabama

Salmon Brunch Squares

3 eggs
2 cups milk
1 cup (4 ounces) shredded
  Cheddar cheese
1 (2¼-ounce) can sliced ripe
  olives, drained
¼ cup sliced green onions
2 tablespoons chopped fresh
  parsley

2 teaspoons Worcestershire
  sauce
3 cups cooked long-grain rice
1 (15½-ounce) can red salmon,
  drained and flaked
Paprika
Fresh Zucchini Sauce

Combine eggs and milk in a large bowl; beat with a wire whisk until blended. Add cheese and next 4 ingredients; stir well. Fold in rice and salmon. Spoon mixture into a lightly greased 11- x 7- x 1½-inch baking dish. Sprinkle with paprika. Bake, uncovered, at 325° for 1 hour or until a knife inserted in center comes out clean. Let stand 10 minutes before serving. Serve with Fresh Zucchini Sauce. Yield: 8 servings.

Fresh Zucchini Sauce

¼ cup butter or margarine
1 cup shredded zucchini
¼ cup sliced green onions
¼ cup diced pimiento, drained
¼ cup all-purpose flour

½ teaspoon salt
½ teaspoon seasoned salt
¼ teaspoon pepper
1¾ cups milk

Melt butter in a saucepan over medium heat. Add zucchini, green onions, and pimiento, and sauté 5 minutes or until vegetables are crisp-tender. Sprinkle flour and next 3 ingredients over vegetables; stir well. Gradually add milk; cook, stirring constantly, until mixture is thickened and bubbly. Serve warm. Yield: 2 ½ cups.   Doris Dobyns

Historic Lexington Cooks: Rockbridge Regional Recipes
Historic Lexington Foundation
Lexington, Virginia

Red Snapper with Matchstick Vegetables

2 tablespoons butter or
    margarine
6 (4-ounce) red snapper fillets
¼ teaspoon salt
Freshly ground white pepper to
    taste
2 shallots, minced
12 sprigs fresh lemon thyme or
    thyme
¾ cup diagonally sliced snow
    pea pods

½ cup scraped and julienned
    carrots
½ cup julienned zucchini
½ cup julienned sweet red
    pepper
½ cup julienned yellow squash
¼ cup plus 2 tablespoons
    Chablis or other dry white
    wine
6 thin slices lemon

Cut six 12- x 9-inch pieces of parchment paper or aluminum foil; fold in half lengthwise, creasing firmly. Trim each piece into a large heart shape. Place parchment hearts on baking sheets.

Place 1 teaspoon butter on each parchment heart. Place fillets, skin side down, on top of butter on each piece of parchment near the crease. Sprinkle with salt and pepper to taste. Top evenly with shallots; place 2 sprigs of lemon thyme over each fillet. Surround fillets evenly with snow peas and julienned vegetables. Drizzle 1 tablespoon wine over each fillet; top each with a lemon slice.

Fold over remaining halves of parchment hearts. Starting with rounded edge of each heart, pleat and crimp edges together to seal. Twist end tightly to seal. Bake at 400° for 15 to 20 minutes or until bags are puffed and lightly browned and fish flakes easily when tested with a fork. Immediately transfer bags to serving plates. To serve, cut a cross in top of each bag with scissors, and fold paper back. Yield: 6 servings.

Connecticut Cooks III
The American Cancer Society, Connecticut Division, Inc.
Wallingford, Connecticut

Grilled Marinated Swordfish with Avocado Butter

8 (8-ounce) swordfish steaks
½ cup vegetable oil
¼ cup soy sauce
1 teaspoon grated lemon rind
¼ cup fresh lemon juice

2 cloves garlic, crushed
Avocado Butter
Garnishes: lime wedges and
   fresh parsley sprigs

Place steaks in two 13- x 9- x 2-inch baking dishes. Combine vegetable oil and next 4 ingredients in a small bowl; stir well. Pour marinade mixture over steaks; cover and marinate in refrigerator 2 hours, turning occasionally.

Remove steaks from marinade, reserving marinade. Place marinade in a small saucepan. Bring to a boil; reduce heat, and simmer 5 minutes. Set aside.

Grill steaks over hot coals (400° to 500°) 9 minutes on each side or until fish flakes easily when tested with a fork, basting frequently with reserved marinade. Serve with Avocado Butter. Garnish, if desired. Yield: 8 servings.

Avocado Butter

½ cup butter, softened
½ cup mashed ripe avocado
¼ cup plus 1 tablespoon fresh
   lime juice

2 tablespoons minced fresh
   flat-leaf parsley
2 cloves garlic, minced
½ teaspoon salt

Combine butter and avocado in a small mixing bowl; beat at medium speed of an electric mixer until smooth. Add lime juice, parsley, garlic, and salt; stir well. Cover and chill until firm. If desired, shape butter mixture into small balls before serving. Yield: 1 cup.   Joanne Lennon

Cohasset Entertains, Encore
The Community Garden Club of Cohasset, Massachusetts

Marinated Broiled Speckled Trout Fillets

8 (3½- to 4-ounce) trout fillets
½ cup Chablis or other dry
   white wine
¼ cup fresh lemon juice
¼ cup soy sauce
¼ teaspoon ground white
   pepper
¼ cup butter or margarine,
   cubed
Paprika
Garnish: lemon wedges

Rinse and drain fillets; place in a shallow baking dish. Combine wine and next 3 ingredients in a small bowl; stir well. Pour marinade mixture over fillets. Cover and marinate in refrigerator 2 to 8 hours. Remove fillets from marinade, discarding marinade.

Place fillets on a rack in a broiler pan; dot with butter, and sprinkle with paprika. Broil 6 inches from heat 5 to 6 minutes or until fish flakes easily when tested with a fork. Serve immediately. Garnish, if desired. Yield: 8 servings.   Mrs. Frank L. Myrick

Camellia Delights
The Altrusa Club of Gulfport, Mississippi

Grandma's Crab Cakes

3 tablespoons butter or
   margarine
2 tablespoons all-purpose flour
1 cup milk
1 teaspoon salt
½ teaspoon dry mustard
2 cups fresh crabmeat, drained
   and flaked
1 cup soft breadcrumbs
¾ cup finely chopped celery
½ cup finely chopped onion
1 teaspoon finely chopped
   fresh parsley
½ teaspoon lemon juice
Dash of nutmeg
2 eggs, beaten
¼ cup water
2 cups fine, dry breadcrumbs
Vegetable oil

Melt butter in a heavy saucepan over low heat; add flour, stirring until smooth. Cook 1 minute, stirring constantly. Gradually add milk; cook over medium heat, stirring constantly, until mixture is thickened and bubbly. Stir in salt and mustard. Remove from heat, and let cool 5 minutes. Add crabmeat and next 6 ingredients; stir well to combine.

Shape crab mixture into 12 patties. Combine eggs and water, beating with a wire whisk until blended. Dredge each patty in fine, dry breadcrumbs; dip in egg mixture, and dredge again in breadcrumbs. Fry patties in oil in a large skillet over medium-high heat 3 to 4 minutes on each side or until lightly browned. Yield: 6 servings.

Gracious Goodness
Penn Laurel Girl Scout Council
York, Pennsylvania

Scallops with Angel Hair Pasta and Chives

1½ cups Chablis or other dry
  white wine
1 teaspoon grated lemon rind
1 pound bay scallops
1 tablespoon Dijon mustard
½ cup butter or margarine, cut
  into pieces

¼ teaspoon salt
⅛ teaspoon freshly ground
  pepper
1 (8-ounce) package angel hair
  pasta
2 tablespoons minced fresh
  chives

Combine wine and lemon rind in a large skillet. Bring to a boil over medium heat; add scallops, reduce heat, and simmer 1 minute. Transfer scallops to a bowl using a slotted spoon, reserving wine mixture in skillet. Set scallops aside.

Bring wine mixture to a boil over medium heat; boil 8 minutes or until reduced to ½ cup. Reduce heat, and add mustard, stirring until smooth. Add butter, one piece at a time, stirring until butter melts. Add reserved scallops, and cook until thoroughly heated. Stir in salt and pepper.

Cook pasta according to package directions; drain well. Combine pasta and scallop mixture, tossing gently. Sprinkle with chives. Serve immediately. Yield: 4 servings.

Gateways
Auxiliary-Twigs . . . Friends of St. Louis Children's Hospital
St. Louis, Missouri

Bay Scallops with Vegetables

½ cup water
½ cup Chablis or other dry
  white wine
½ teaspoon salt
1½ pounds bay scallops
½ pound fresh mushrooms,
  sliced
⅔ cup sliced green onions
⅔ cup sliced celery
3 tablespoons butter or
  margarine, melted

1 (6-ounce) package frozen
  snow pea pods, thawed
1 tablespoon soy sauce
2 teaspoons cornstarch
1 teaspoon cracked pepper
2 teaspoons lemon juice
¼ teaspoon hot sauce
1 tablespoon diced pimiento
Hot cooked rice

Combine water, wine, and salt in a saucepan; bring to a boil. Add scallops; cover, reduce heat, and simmer 3 to 4 minutes. Drain scallops, reserving ½ cup liquid. Set scallops and liquid aside.

Sauté mushrooms, green onions, and celery in butter in a large skillet until vegetables are tender. Add snow peas, and sauté 1 to 2 minutes. Combine reserved ½ cup liquid, soy sauce, and next 4 ingredients; stir well. Add cornstarch mixture to vegetable mixture, and cook until thickened and bubbly, stirring frequently. Stir in reserved scallops and pimiento; cook until thoroughly heated. Serve immediately over rice. Yield: 4 to 6 servings.   Pat Leary

Trinity Episcopal School, Classroom Classics
The Parents and Students of Trinity Episcopal School
Pine Bluff, Arkansas

Prawns in Pommerey Sauce

8 unpeeled prawns or jumbo
  fresh shrimp
1 tablespoon butter, melted
2 tablespoons Chablis or other
  dry white wine
1 tablespoon dry sherry
1 teaspoon minced shallot
⅛ teaspoon salt

⅛ teaspoon pepper
½ cup whipping cream
1 tablespoon coarse-grained
  Pommerey mustard
½ teaspoon fish-flavored
  bouillon granules
Garnish: lemon leaves

Peel, devein, and butterfly prawns, leaving tails intact. Sauté prawns in melted butter in a small skillet over medium heat 3 to 4 minutes or until prawns turn pink. Remove prawns with a slotted spoon; set aside and keep warm.

Add wine, sherry, shallot, salt, and pepper to skillet. Bring to a boil; reduce heat, and simmer 2 minutes. Stir in whipping cream, mustard, and bouillon; simmer 3 minutes, stirring constantly. Add reserved prawns, and cook 2 minutes or until thoroughly heated.

To serve, spoon sauce evenly onto 2 individual serving plates. Top evenly with prawns. Serve immediately. Garnish, if desired. Yield: 2 servings.   Scott Rinn

Livre de Cuisine
Pikes Peak Region, American Culinary Federation
Colorado Springs, Colorado

New Orleans-Style Scampi

2 pounds unpeeled jumbo fresh shrimp	**1½ teaspoons finely chopped fresh parsley**
¾ cup butter or margarine	**2 large cloves garlic, crushed**
½ cup fresh lemon juice	**1 teaspoon salt**
1 tablespoon finely chopped shallot or green onions	**Dash of hot sauce**
	½ teaspoon paprika

Peel and devein shrimp, leaving tails intact; set shrimp aside.

Melt butter in a small saucepan over low heat. Add lemon juice and next 5 ingredients; stir well to combine.

Arrange shrimp in a single layer in a large shallow baking pan. Brush shrimp with butter mixture; sprinkle with paprika. Broil 6 inches from heat 5 to 6 minutes or until shrimp turn pink, basting frequently with butter mixture. Serve immediately. Yield: 6 servings.

"From the Heart of the Teche"
Jeanerette Chamber of Commerce
Jeanerette, Louisiana

Battered-Fried Shrimp with Tangy Sauce

2 pounds unpeeled large fresh
  shrimp
½ teaspoon garlic powder
1 (12-ounce) jar orange
  marmalade
3 tablespoons lemon juice
2 tablespoons orange juice
1½ to 2 tablespoons prepared
  horseradish

1½ teaspoons Dijon mustard
1½ cups all-purpose flour
1 tablespoon baking powder
1 teaspoon salt
1 teaspoon paprika
½ cup vegetable oil
1 cup cold water
Additional vegetable oil

Peel, devein, and butterfly shrimp, leaving tails intact. Sprinkle butterflied shrimp lightly with garlic powder. Cover and chill thoroughly.

Combine orange marmalade, lemon juice, orange juice, horseradish, and mustard in container of an electric blender, and process until blended. Set sauce aside.

Combine flour, baking powder, salt, and paprika in a large bowl; stir well. Gradually add ½ cup oil, stirring until mixture leaves sides of bowl and forms a ball. Gradually add water, stirring until blended. (Batter will be very thick.)

Dip several shrimp into batter. Fry shrimp, a few at a time, in deep hot oil (360°) 2 to 3 minutes or until golden. Remove shrimp with a slotted spoon, and drain well on paper towels.

Place shrimp on a large baking sheet; keep warm in a 200° oven. Repeat procedure with remaining shrimp and batter. Serve shrimp with reserved sauce. Yield: 4 servings.

Stirring Performances
The Junior League of Winston-Salem, North Carolina

Seafood Imperial

3 cups water
¾ pound unpeeled medium-
   size fresh shrimp
1 cup fresh crabmeat, drained
   and flaked
1 cup chopped cooked lobster
1 cup diced celery
1 cup mayonnaise
¾ cup chopped onion
¾ cup chopped green pepper

½ cup sour cream
2 hard-cooked eggs, chopped
1 tablespoon Worcestershire
   sauce
1 teaspoon salt
½ teaspoon cracked pepper
1 cup soft breadcrumbs
2 tablespoons butter or
   margarine, melted
Chopped fresh parsley

Bring 3 cups water to a boil; add shrimp, and cook 3 to 5 minutes. Drain well; rinse with cold water. Peel and devein shrimp. Combine shrimp and next 11 ingredients in a large bowl; stir well. Spoon mixture into a buttered 2-quart casserole.

Combine breadcrumbs and butter in a small bowl; stir well. Sprinkle breadcrumb mixture evenly over seafood mixture. Bake, uncovered, at 350° for 30 minutes or until thoroughly heated. Sprinkle with parsley. Serve immediately. Yield: 6 to 8 servings.

From a Lighthouse Window
The Chesapeake Bay Maritime Museum
St. Michaels, Maryland

Funds generated from the sale of From a Lighthouse Window *will support the Chesapeake Bay Maritime Museum in efforts to preserve the heritage of the Chesapeake Bay. The museum is dedicated to furthering interest, understanding, and appreciation of the culture and maritime heritage of the Chesapeake Bay and its tributaries through educational activities that include collection, documentation, exhibition, research, and publication.*

Conchita's Paella

3 chicken breast halves,
   skinned, boned, and cut into
   1-inch pieces
½ cup olive oil
½ cup chopped onion
1 teaspoon minced garlic
12 to 14 clams, cleaned
3 lobster tails, cut into rings
3 pounds unpeeled medium-
   size fresh shrimp, peeled and
   deveined
1 pound fresh crabmeat,
   drained and flaked
½ pound cooked ham, cubed
1 (8-ounce) can tomato sauce
1 teaspoon salt
¼ teaspoon pepper
1 pound red snapper, cut into
   pieces
2 cups long-grain rice,
   uncooked
6 cups canned diluted chicken
   broth
1 (12-ounce) can beer
1 cup dry sherry
1 medium-size green pepper,
   chopped
1 cup frozen English peas
1 large bay leaf
Few threads of saffron
1 (7-ounce) jar sliced pimiento,
   drained

Brown chicken in oil in a large Dutch oven; remove chicken, reserving oil in Dutch oven. Set chicken aside. Add onion and garlic, and sauté 2 minutes. Stir in clams and next 7 ingredients; cook 5 minutes or until clam shells are barely open. Remove clams, and set aside.

Add reserved chicken to Dutch oven. Add red snapper, rice, broth, beer, sherry, green pepper, peas, bay leaf, and saffron. Bring to a boil; cover and simmer 25 minutes or until rice is tender. Remove and discard bay leaf. Spoon mixture into a paella dish or onto a serving platter. Top with reserved clams and pimiento strips. Yield: 12 to 14 servings.   Conchita Alonso

First Gentleman's Cookbook
Governor's Mansion Restoration Foundation
Lincoln, Nebraska

Meats

Devil's Tower, rising 1,280 feet above the Belle Fourche River in the Black Hills region of Wyoming, is the United States' first national monument. This soaring tower was formed over 20 million years ago by the cooling of molten volcanic rock.

Marinated Eye of Round
with Horseradish Sauce

1 (4-pound) eye of round roast
1 cup soy sauce
½ cup vegetable oil

¼ cup gin
3 cloves garlic, crushed
Horseradish Sauce

Place roast in an 11- x 7- x 1½-inch baking dish. Combine soy sauce and next 3 ingredients in a small bowl; stir well. Pour marinade mixture over roast. Cover and marinate in refrigerator 8 hours, turning occasionally.

Remove roast from marinade, discarding marinade. Place roast on a rack in a roasting pan; insert meat thermometer into thickest part of roast. Bake at 350° for 1 hour or until thermometer registers 150° (medium rare). Chill roast, and thinly slice. Serve with Horseradish Sauce. Yield: 8 to 10 servings.

Horseradish Sauce

1 cup whipping cream,
  whipped
1 cup mayonnaise

¼ cup prepared horseradish
⅛ teaspoon salt

Combine whipped cream and mayonnaise in a small bowl; stir well. Fold in horseradish and salt. Yield: 3¼ cups.

Marblehead Cooks
Tower School Associates
Marblehead, Massachusetts

Spiced Apple Butter Brisket

1 (4- to 4½-pound) beef brisket
1 small onion, quartered
10 whole cloves
1 clove garlic, halved
1 cup apple butter
½ cup Chablis or other dry
  white wine

3 tablespoons prepared
  mustard
2 tablespoons minced green
  onions
1½ teaspoons salt
¾ teaspoon curry powder
½ teaspoon pepper

Place brisket, onion, cloves, and garlic in a large Dutch oven; add water to cover. Bring to a boil; cover, reduce heat, and simmer 2½ hours. Remove brisket from Dutch oven; place brisket in a roasting pan.

Combine apple butter and remaining ingredients in a medium saucepan. Cook over medium heat 3 to 4 minutes, stirring occasionally. Brush ½ cup apple butter mixture over brisket. Bake, uncovered, at 325° for 30 minutes, basting occasionally with remaining apple butter mixture. Yield: 8 to 10 servings.

Spice and Spirit: The Complete Kosher Jewish Cookbook
Lubavitch Women's Organization
Brooklyn, New York

Glazed Corned Beef

1 (3-pound) corned beef
  brisket
4 cups water
½ cup coarse-grained mustard
2 cups red currant jelly
½ cup ruby port or other sweet
  red wine
½ cup chopped shallots
1½ tablespoons grated lemon
  rind

¼ cup fresh lemon juice
1 tablespoon grated orange
  rind
1 tablespoon dry mustard
1½ teaspoons ground ginger
1½ teaspoons pepper
½ teaspoon salt
½ cup firmly packed brown
  sugar

Place brisket in a large Dutch oven. Add water, and bring to a boil. Cover, reduce heat, and simmer 2½ hours. Drain; place brisket in an 8-inch square baking dish. Spread mustard over brisket, and set aside.

Combine jelly and next 9 ingredients in a medium saucepan; stir well. Cook over medium-low heat until jelly melts, stirring constantly. Pour jelly mixture over reserved brisket. Sprinkle with brown sugar. Bake, uncovered, at 350° for 45 minutes, basting occasionally with pan juices. Transfer brisket to a serving platter. Yield: 6 to 8 servings.

RiverFeast: Still Celebrating Cincinnati
The Junior League of Cincinnati, Ohio

Stuffed Flank Steak

1 (2-pound) flank steak
1 (4-ounce) can mushroom
  stems and pieces, undrained
½ cup chopped onion
¼ cup chopped fresh parsley
4 slices bacon, finely chopped
2 tablespoons vegetable oil

2 (8-ounce) cans tomato sauce
1 beef-flavored bouillon cube
1 teaspoon sugar
1 teaspoon prepared mustard
½ teaspoon Worcestershire
  sauce
¼ teaspoon pepper

Trim fat from steak; score in a diamond design ⅛-inch deep on one side.

Drain mushrooms, reserving liquid. Combine mushrooms, onion, parsley, and bacon in a large skillet. Cook over medium heat until onion is tender, stirring occasionally. Spread vegetable mixture evenly over unscored side of steak to within 1 inch of outside edges. Roll up jellyroll fashion, starting with short side. Tie with heavy string at 2-inch intervals.

Brown steak roll in vegetable oil in a large Dutch oven. Reduce heat to low; stir in reserved mushroom liquid, tomato sauce, and remaining ingredients. Bring mixture to a boil; cover, reduce heat, and simmer 2 to 2½ hours or until meat is tender. Yield: 4 to 6 servings.
Michelle Taylor

Best Friends
Terranova West Women's Club
Spring, Texas

Shaker Steak

1 (1½-pound) flank steak
2 tablespoons all-purpose flour
2 tablespoons butter or
  margarine, melted
1 large onion, finely chopped
1 medium-size green pepper,
  finely chopped
1 stalk celery, finely chopped

1 carrot, scraped and finely
  chopped
1 tablespoon lemon juice
½ teaspoon salt
¼ teaspoon pepper
2 tablespoons catsup
½ to 1 cup water
Hot cooked rice or egg noodles

Score steak in a diamond design ¼-inch deep on both sides; rub flour onto both sides of steak.

Cook steak in butter in a large skillet over medium heat until browned on both sides. Add onion and next 3 ingredients; sprinkle with lemon juice, salt, and pepper. Combine catsup and ½ cup water; pour over meat, and bring to a boil. Cover, reduce heat, and simmer 1½ hours or until meat is tender, adding an additional ½ cup water, if necessary. Serve over rice or noodles. Yield: 4 to 6 servings.   Marilyn Shelly

Treasured Recipes from Wellington Christian School
Parent Teacher Fellowship of Wellington Christian School
West Palm Beach, Florida

Flank Steak Oriental

½ cup dark soy sauce
½ cup rice wine vinegar
¼ cup chili oil
1 jalapeño pepper, seeded and
  minced
2 cloves garlic, minced
2 tablespoons chopped fresh
  basil

2 tablespoons chopped fresh
  cilantro
2 tablespoons chopped fresh
  mint leaves
1 tablespoon minced fresh
  gingerroot
1 (1½-pound) flank steak

Combine first 9 ingredients in a small bowl, stirring well. Place steak in an 11- x 7- x 1½-inch baking dish. Pour marinade mixture over steak; cover and marinate in refrigerator 3 hours.

Remove steak from marinade, reserving marinade. Place marinade in a small saucepan; bring to a boil. Reduce heat, and simmer 5 minutes. Set marinade aside.

Place steak on a rack in a broiler pan; broil 6 inches from heat 6 to 8 minutes on each side or to desired degree of doneness.

To serve, slice steak diagonally across grain into thin slices. Serve with reserved marinade. Yield: 4 to 6 servings.   Nick Mawford

The Western Gentlemen's Cookbook
The Men's Culinary Cup
Cheyenne, Wyoming

Ginger Beef Kabobs

1 pound sirloin steak, cut into
** 1-inch cubes**
½ cup vegetable oil
½ cup Burgundy or other dry
** red wine**
1 large clove garlic, minced
2 tablespoons finely chopped
** crystallized ginger**

2 tablespoons catsup
2 tablespoons molasses
½ teaspoon salt
½ teaspoon curry powder
½ teaspoon pepper
1 medium-size green pepper,
** cut into 1-inch pieces**

Place meat in a shallow dish. Combine oil and next 8 ingredients; stirring well. Pour marinade mixture over meat. Cover and marinate in refrigerator 8 hours.

Remove meat from marinade, reserving marinade. Place marinade in a small saucepan. Bring to a boil; reduce heat, and simmer 5 minutes. Set aside.

Alternate meat and pepper pieces on four 10-inch metal skewers. Grill over medium-hot coals (350° to 400°) 10 to 12 minutes or to desired degree of doneness, turning and basting frequently with reserved marinade. Yield: 4 servings.

Sound Seasonings
The Junior League of Westchester on the Sound
Larchmont, New York

Steak in a Garden

1 pound boneless sirloin steak
3 tablespoons peanut oil,
　divided
2 tablespoons soy sauce,
　divided
2 tablespoons cornstarch,
　divided
½ teaspoon garlic powder
½ teaspoon salt
¼ teaspoon pepper
¾ cup canned diluted beef
　broth

¼ teaspoon sugar
⅛ teaspoon ground ginger
2 carrots, scraped and thinly
　sliced
3 green peppers, cut into strips
¾ cup diagonally sliced celery
8 green onions, cut into ½-inch
　pieces
1 (6-ounce) package frozen
　snow pea pods, thawed and
　drained
Hot cooked rice

Partially freeze steak; slice diagonally across grain into 2- x ¼-inch strips. Combine 1 tablespoon peanut oil, 1 tablespoon soy sauce, 1 tablespoon cornstarch, and next 3 ingredients; stir well. Pour soy sauce mixture over steak; cover and let stand 20 minutes.

Combine remaining 1 tablespoon soy sauce, 1 tablespoon cornstarch, beef broth, sugar, and ginger; stir well, and set aside.

Pour remaining 2 tablespoons oil around top of a preheated wok, coating sides; heat at medium-high (325°) for 2 minutes. Add reserved steak mixture, and stir-fry 4 to 5 minutes. Add carrot, and stir-fry 3 minutes. Add green pepper strips, and stir-fry 3 minutes. Add celery, green onions, and snow peas; stir-fry 1 to 2 minutes. Add reserved broth mixture to steak mixture, and cook, stirring constantly, until mixture is thickened and bubbly. Serve over rice. Yield: 6 servings.   Lucille E. Treat

Birthright Sampler
Birthright of Johnstown, Pennsylvania

Ginger-Orange Beef

1 (1-pound) top round steak
¼ cup soy sauce
1 to 1½ tablespoons grated
   orange rind
1 tablespoon grated fresh
   gingerroot
1½ teaspoons cornstarch
1 teaspoon ground cinnamon
2 teaspoons vegetable oil,
   divided

¼ pound fresh snow pea pods
1 medium carrot, scraped and
   sliced
1 medium-size green pepper,
   cut into strips
1 medium-size sweet red
   pepper, cut into strips
¼ cup sliced water chestnuts
1 medium head iceberg lettuce,
   shredded

Trim fat from steak. Partially freeze steak; slice diagonally across grain into 2- x ¼-inch strips, and place in a medium bowl.

Combine soy sauce, orange rind, gingerroot, cornstarch, and cinnamon in a small bowl; stir well. Pour soy sauce mixture over steak, tossing gently to combine.

Brown steak in 1 teaspoon oil in a large skillet. Remove steak from skillet, reserving drippings in skillet. Set steak aside, and keep warm.

Heat remaining 1 teaspoon oil in skillet. Add snow peas, carrot, peppers, and water chestnuts; sauté 3 minutes or until vegetables are crisp-tender. Return steak to skillet, and cook until thoroughly heated.

Arrange lettuce on a serving platter; top with steak mixture, and serve immediately. Yield: 4 servings.   Steph Taylor

The Oregon County Cookbook
Milwaukie Elementary School
Milwaukie, Oregon

Sour Cream Enchilada Casserole

1 cup water
¼ cup plus 2 tablespoons
   picante sauce, divided
12 (6-inch) corn tortillas
2 pounds ground beef
1 medium onion, chopped
¾ cup sliced ripe olives
1 tablespoon chili powder
2 teaspoons ground cumin

1½ teaspoons salt
1 teaspoon garlic powder
⅛ teaspoon pepper
½ cup butter or margarine
2 tablespoons all-purpose flour
1½ cups milk
1 (16-ounce) carton sour cream
2 cups (8 ounces) shredded
   Cheddar cheese, divided

Combine water and 2 tablespoons picante sauce in a large shallow dish; top with tortillas. Let stand 5 minutes. Drain, and set tortillas aside.

Cook ground beef and onion in a large skillet until meat is browned, stirring to crumble meat. Drain, and return meat mixture to skillet. Add remaining ¼ cup picante sauce, olives, and next 5 ingredients; stir well. Set aside, and keep warm.

Melt butter in a heavy saucepan over low heat; add flour, stirring until smooth. Cook 1 minute, stirring constantly. Gradually add milk; cook over medium heat, stirring constantly, until mixture is thickened and bubbly. Remove from heat, and stir in sour cream.

Place half of corn tortillas in the bottom of a 13- x 9- x 2-inch baking dish. Pour half of sour cream mixture over tortillas. Top with half of ground beef mixture. Sprinkle with 1 cup Cheddar cheese. Repeat layers once. Bake, uncovered, at 375° for 25 minutes. Yield: 8 to 10 servings.   Edith McMullen

Methodist Blessings
The United Methodist Women, First United Methodist Church
New Iberia, Louisiana

Grilled Blue Cheese Burgers

3 pounds lean ground beef
1 teaspoon salt
½ teaspoon freshly ground
  pepper
2 (3-ounce) packages cream
  cheese, softened
2 tablespoons crumbled blue
  cheese

2 tablespoons minced onion
2 teaspoons cream-style
  horseradish
2 teaspoons prepared mustard
½ pound sliced fresh
  mushrooms
2 tablespoons butter or
  margarine, melted

Combine ground beef, salt, and pepper in a large bowl; mix well, and shape into 16 thin patties.

Combine cream cheese and next 4 ingredients in a small mixing bowl; beat at medium speed of an electric mixer until blended. Divide cheese mixture evenly among 8 patties; spread to within ½-inch of edges. Top with remaining patties, pressing edges to seal.

Grill hamburgers over medium-hot coals (350° to 400°) 10 minutes on each side or to desired degree of doneness. Set aside, and keep warm.

Sauté mushrooms in melted butter in a skillet until tender. Top hamburgers with sautéed mushrooms. Yield: 8 servings.

Stirring Performances
The Junior League of Winston-Salem, North Carolina

Founded in 1923, The Junior League of Winston-Salem has contributed over three-quarters of a million dollars to the community. The league has been instrumental in founding the Arts Council, Horizons, Nature Science Center, Juvenile Justice Council, Child's Guidance Clinic, and Cancer Patient Support Services. Funds from the sale of Stirring Performances *will ensure that the league can continue to make a difference in the North Carolina community.*

Meatball Sandwiches

1 cup soft French breadcrumbs
½ cup milk
1 pound mild bulk pork
   sausage
1 pound lean ground beef
2 eggs, beaten
¼ cup minced onion
2 cloves garlic, minced
¼ teaspoon salt
½ teaspoon dried whole basil
¼ teaspoon dried whole
   oregano
1 large green pepper, cut into
   strips
1 large onion, chopped

2 cloves garlic, minced
2 tablespoons vegetable oil
2 (14-ounce) cans Italian-style
   tomatoes, undrained and
   chopped
1 (6-ounce) can tomato paste
¾ cup Burgundy or other dry
   red wine
½ cup water
2 tablespoons sugar
1½ teaspoons dried whole basil
¼ teaspoon dried whole
   oregano
8 (6-inch) French bread rolls
Softened butter or margarine

Combine breadcrumbs and milk in a large bowl; let stand 5 minutes. Add sausage and next 7 ingredients; mix well. Shape meat mixture into 1½-inch balls. Place meatballs in a 13- x 9- x 2-inch baking dish. Bake at 450° for 15 to 20 minutes or until browned. Set aside.

Sauté green pepper, chopped onion, and 2 cloves minced garlic in oil in a large saucepan until vegetables are tender. Add tomatoes, tomato paste, wine, water, sugar, 1½ teaspoons basil, and ¼ teaspoon oregano; stir well. Bring to a boil; reduce heat, and simmer, uncovered, 45 minutes or until slightly thickened. Add reserved meatballs; cover and simmer 1 hour.

Slice rolls in half lengthwise; place rolls, cut side up, on a baking sheet. Brush cut side of each roll with softened butter. Broil 6 inches from heat until lightly toasted. Spoon meatball mixture over bottom halves of toasted rolls. Cover with tops of rolls. Yield: 8 servings.

Hearts & Flour
The Women's Club of Pittsford, New York

Liver with Mustard Cream and Broiled Onions

6 medium onions, sliced
¼ cup vegetable oil
1½ pounds thinly sliced calf liver
¼ teaspoon salt
¼ teaspoon freshly ground pepper
½ cup all-purpose flour

3 tablespoons olive oil
3 tablespoons butter
¼ cup Chablis or other dry white wine
½ cup whipping cream
2 tablespoons Pommerey mustard

Line a broiler pan with aluminum foil; place onion slices in pan, and brush with oil. Broil 6 inches from heat 6 to 8 minutes or until onion is tender and lightly browned, turning occasionally. Set onion aside, and keep warm.

Sprinkle both sides of liver slices with salt and pepper. Dredge liver slices in flour. Heat oil and butter in a large skillet over medium-high heat until hot; add half of liver slices, and cook 2 minutes on each side or until done. Transfer liver to a serving platter; set aside, and keep warm. Repeat cooking procedure with remaining half of liver slices.

Add wine to skillet; gradually stir in whipping cream and mustard. Bring to a boil; boil 1 to 2 minutes or until slightly thickened. Pour wine mixture over liver. Serve immediately with reserved onions. Yield: 6 servings.   Mary Carter Hudgins

Tastes in Plaid: Alamance County Entertains
Alamance County Historical Museum
Burlington, North Carolina

Veal Chops with Sorrel Sauce

1 bunch fresh sorrel (about 36
  large leaves)
6 boneless veal loin chops
  (about 2 pounds)
½ teaspoon salt
¼ teaspoon pepper
1 cup all-purpose flour

2 tablespoons virgin olive oil
2 tablespoons butter, melted
1 tablespoon minced shallot
⅓ cup Chablis or other dry
  white wine
1½ cups whipping cream

Remove stems and large veins from sorrel; wash leaves, and drain. Pat dry with paper towels. Cut into thin shreds; set aside.

Sprinkle veal with salt and pepper; dredge in flour. Cook veal in oil and butter in a large skillet 10 minutes on each side. Transfer veal to a serving platter, reserving drippings in skillet. Set aside, and keep warm.

Sauté shallot in drippings 3 minutes. Add wine; cook over high heat, deglazing pan by scraping particles that cling to bottom. Add reserved sorrel, and simmer 2 minutes. Stir in cream. Cook sauce over medium-high heat 3 minutes or until thickened. Spoon sauce over veal. Yield: 6 servings.

A Taste of San Francisco
The Symphony of San Francisco, California

Veal Piccata

1½ pounds veal cutlets
¼ teaspoon salt
¼ teaspoon pepper
½ cup all-purpose flour
3 tablespoons butter or
  margarine, melted
1 tablespoon olive oil
½ pound fresh mushrooms,
  sliced

2 cloves garlic, minced
½ cup Chablis or other dry
  white wine
2 tablespoons lemon juice
2 teaspoons capers with liquid,
  undrained
3 tablespoons minced fresh
  parsley
Garnish: thin lemon slices

Place veal between 2 sheets of wax paper; flatten veal to ¼-inch thickness, using a meat mallet or rolling pin. Sprinkle veal with salt and pepper, and dredge in flour.

Cook veal in melted butter and oil in a large skillet until browned on both sides. Remove veal, reserving drippings in skillet. Set aside, and keep warm.

Sauté mushrooms and garlic in drippings 1 to 2 minutes. Return veal to skillet; add wine and lemon juice. Bring to a boil; cover, reduce heat, and simmer 20 minutes. Add capers and liquid, and simmer an additional minute.

Transfer veal mixture to a serving platter. Sprinkle with parsley. Garnish, if desired. Yield: 4 to 6 servings.

Celebrate
Missouri Bankers Association
Jefferson City, Missouri

Veal Sabrosa

½ cup grated Parmesan cheese
¼ cup all-purpose flour
½ to 1 teaspoon salt
⅛ teaspoon pepper
1½ pounds (¼-inch-thick) veal cutlets, cut into 2-inch strips
1 clove garlic, halved
2 tablespoons olive oil

½ cup Chablis or other dry white wine
½ cup canned diluted beef consommé
1 tablespoon lemon juice
1 tablespoon chopped fresh parsley

Combine cheese, flour, salt, and pepper; stir well. Dredge veal in flour mixture. Set aside.

Sauté garlic in olive oil in a large skillet 1 minute. Add veal, and cook until browned. Remove and discard garlic. Add wine, consommé, and lemon juice; bring to a boil. Cover, reduce heat, and simmer 30 minutes. Transfer veal mixture to a serving platter; sprinkle with parsley. Yield: 6 servings.

Seasoned with Sun
The Junior League of El Paso, Texas

Veal St. André

¼ pound finely chopped fresh mushrooms
1 teaspoon chopped shallot
1 anchovy fillet, chopped
1 teaspoon butter or margarine, melted
¼ cup all-purpose flour
¼ teaspoon salt
¼ teaspoon pepper
4 (2-ounce) veal cutlets
2 teaspoons butter or margarine, melted

1 teaspoon olive oil
1 (3-ounce) package cream cheese, softened
½ teaspoon crumbled blue cheese
2 sheets frozen phyllo pastry, thawed
¼ cup butter or margarine, melted
¼ cup fine, dry breadcrumbs
1 egg, beaten

Sauté mushrooms, shallot, and anchovy in 1 teaspoon butter in a large skillet until liquid evaporates. Set aside, and let cool completely.

Combine flour, salt, and pepper; stir well. Dredge veal in flour mixture. Sauté veal in 2 teaspoons melted butter and olive oil in a large skillet 2 minutes on each side or until browned. Remove veal from skillet; set aside, and let cool completely.

To assemble, spread cream cheese evenly over 2 veal cutlets; top each with ¼ teaspoon blue cheese and half of reserved mushroom mixture. Top with remaining 2 veal cutlets. Set aside.

Place one sheet of phyllo on a damp towel. Lightly brush phyllo with melted butter; fold in half crosswise. Brush again with butter. Sprinkle 2 tablespoons breadcrumbs evenly over phyllo; place 1 piece prepared veal in center of phyllo sheet. Brush edges of phyllo with beaten egg. Fold phyllo over veal, pinching seams and ends to seal. Brush phyllo with beaten egg. Repeat procedure with remaining ingredients. Place seam side down in a greased 15- x 10- x 1-inch jellyroll pan. Brush phyllo with any remaining beaten egg. Bake at 375° for 15 to 18 minutes or until golden. Yield: 2 servings.

Patsy Clark's Mansion

Spokane Cooks! © Northwest
The Community Centers Foundation of Spokane, Washington

Ragoût de Veau

3 to 4 strips bacon
2 pounds veal, cubed
2 to 3 shallots, chopped
1 large green pepper, chopped
¼ cup brandy
1 tablespoon all-purpose flour
4 sprigs fresh parsley
1 sprig fresh thyme
1 bay leaf
1½ cups canned diluted beef broth

1 (14-ounce) can Italian-style tomatoes, undrained
½ cup Chablis or other dry white wine
2 stalks celery
1 clove garlic, crushed
Freshly ground pepper to taste
1 pound small fresh mushrooms
Chopped fresh parsley

Cook bacon in a Dutch oven until crisp; remove bacon, reserving drippings in Dutch oven.

Cook veal in drippings until browned on all sides. Remove veal from Dutch oven, reserving drippings in Dutch oven. Set aside, and keep warm.

Sauté shallots and green pepper in drippings in Dutch oven until tender. Add brandy, and heat until warm (do not boil). Ignite with long match; stir until flames die down.

Return veal to Dutch oven. Add flour, stirring well. Place parsley, thyme, and bay leaf on a piece of cheesecloth; tie ends of cheesecloth securely, and add to Dutch oven. Add broth and next 5 ingredients; stir well. Bring to a boil; reduce heat, and simmer, uncovered, 1 hour. Add mushrooms, and simmer an additional 30 minutes. Remove and discard cheesecloth bag and celery.

To serve, ladle into individual serving bowls. Sprinkle with parsley. Yield: 6 servings.

It's Our Serve!
The Junior League of Long Island
Roslyn, New York

Grilled Butterflied Leg of Lamb with Tarragon

1 (5- to 6-pound) leg of lamb,
  boned and butterflied
1 tablespoon minced garlic
½ teaspoon pepper
¼ cup tarragon vinegar

¼ cup olive oil
3 tablespoons mustard seeds
3 tablespoons minced fresh
  tarragon

Trim fat from lamb. Rub garlic and pepper over entire surface of lamb. Place lamb in a 13- x 9- x 2-inch baking dish. Combine vinegar and remaining ingredients; stir well. Pour marinade mixture over lamb. Cover and marinate in refrigerator 8 hours, turning occasionally.

Remove lamb from marinade; discard marinade. Grill over medium coals (300° to 350°) 20 minutes; turn and insert meat thermometer into thickest part of meat. Grill 20 minutes or until thermometer registers 160°. Let stand 10 minutes. Slice diagonally across grain into thin slices. Yield: 8 servings.

10,000 Tastes of Minnesota
The Woman's Club of Minneapolis, Minnesota

Tonya's Herbed Leg of Lamb

2 tablespoons olive oil
2 cloves garlic, crushed
1 (5-pound) leg of lamb
1 tablespoon cider vinegar
2 teaspoons Worcestershire
  sauce
1 teaspoon seasoned salt
1 teaspoon dried whole
  rosemary

½ teaspoon dried whole
  marjoram
½ teaspoon dried whole thyme
Pepper to taste
1 tablespoon water (optional)
1 tablespoon all-purpose flour
  (optional)

Combine olive oil and crushed garlic; rub over entire surface of lamb. Combine vinegar and Worcestershire sauce; brush over entire surface of lamb. Combine salt and next 4 ingredients; stir well. Sprinkle salt mixture evenly over lamb.

Place lamb, fat side up, on a rack in a shallow roasting pan. Insert meat thermometer, making sure it does not touch fat or bone. Bake at 350° for 2 hours or until thermometer registers 160°. Transfer lamb to a serving platter, reserving drippings in pan. Set aside, and keep warm.

If desired, combine water and flour, stirring until smooth. Stir flour mixture into reserved pan drippings. Cook over medium heat, stirring constantly, until thickened and bubbly. Serve lamb with gravy. Yield: 8 servings.   Tonya T. Marley

Family Secrets . . . the Best of the Delta
Lee Academy
Clarksdale, Mississippi

Lemon-Ginger Lamb Chops

½ cup pineapple juice
½ cup firmly packed brown
  sugar
2 teaspoons minced fresh
  gingerroot

2 teaspoons grated lemon rind
Salt and pepper to taste
8 (1-inch-thick) lamb chops

Combine pineapple juice and next 4 ingredients in a small saucepan. Cook over medium heat until sugar dissolves, stirring occasionally.

Place lamb chops on a rack in a roasting pan; brush with pineapple juice mixture. Broil 6 inches from heat 5 to 7 minutes on each side or to desired degree of doneness, basting frequently with remaining pineapple juice mixture. Yield: 4 servings.

Simply Colorado
Colorado Dietetic Association
Littleton, Colorado

Glazed Ginger Pork

¼ cup soy sauce
¼ cup Chablis or other dry
  white wine
2 tablespoons honey
1 tablespoon grated fresh
  gingerroot

1 clove garlic, minced
1 (3-pound) rolled boneless
  pork loin roast
¾ cup red currant jelly

Combine first 5 ingredients; stir well. Place roast in a shallow dish. Pour marinade mixture over roast; cover and marinate in refrigerator 6 hours, turning occasionally.

Remove roast from marinade, reserving marinade. Place marinade in a small saucepan. Bring to a boil; reduce heat, and simmer 5 minutes. Set aside.

Combine currant jelly and reserved 3 tablespoons marinade in a small saucepan. Cook over low heat 5 minutes or until jelly melts, stirring constantly. Set aside, and let cool completely.

Place roast on a rack in roasting pan. Insert meat thermometer into thickest part of roast, making sure it does not touch fat. Bake at 325° for 2 hours and 15 minutes or until thermometer registers 160°, basting frequently with any remaining reserved marinade.

Transfer roast to a serving platter; brush with glaze until thoroughly coated. Serve roast with any remaining glaze. Yield: 8 to 10 servings.   Stealth Donor

Not So Secret Recipes
4450th Tactical Group, Nellis Air Force Base
Las Vegas, Nevada

The mission of the Greater Pittsburgh Commission for Women is to improve the economic status and quality of life for women. Recipes in Cooking by Male *were contributed by men and represent a positive approach to changing the stereotypes of women and men.*

Roast Pork with Sinner Stuffing

1 cup bourbon
1 cup pitted prunes, halved
½ cup dried apricots, halved
¾ cup peeled, cubed cooking
　apples
1 tablespoon honey
1 teaspoon grated lemon rind
1 teaspoon grated orange rind
1 (5- to 6-pound) rolled
　boneless pork loin roast

Salt and pepper
1 clove garlic, sliced
¼ cup butter or margarine,
　softened
2 tablespoons all-purpose flour
1 tablespoon dried whole
　thyme
1 cup apple cider

Combine bourbon, prunes, and apricots in a small bowl; let stand 2 to 3 hours to soften. Stir in apple and next 3 ingredients; drain fruit, reserving bourbon mixture. Set fruit and bourbon mixture aside.

Remove strings from roast; slice roast in half lengthwise, if not purchased sliced. Slice pork pieces lengthwise in half again, cutting to but not through one side. Open cut pieces to enlarge roast. Lay pieces side by side, and sprinkle with salt and pepper. Spoon reserved fruit mixture evenly over pork pieces. Roll roast jellyroll fashion, beginning at long side; tie securely with heavy string at 2-inch intervals. Place roast in a lightly greased shallow roasting pan.

Make several small slits in roast, ¼-inch deep, and insert garlic slices. Rub butter over entire surface of roast. Sprinkle with flour and thyme. Pour reserved bourbon mixture and cider over roast. Insert meat thermometer into thickest part of roast, making sure it does not touch fat.

Place aluminum foil tent over roast. Bake at 325° for 1 hour. Remove foil, and bake an additional 2½ hours or until meat thermometer registers 160°, basting frequently with pan drippings. Let roast stand 10 minutes before serving. Yield: 12 to 14 servings.　　　　　　　　　　　　　　　　　　John Lovelace

Cooking by Male
The Greater Pittsburgh Commission for Women
Pittsburgh, Pennsylvania

Sautéed Pork Medaillons with Port

2 (¾-pound) pork tenderloins
2 teaspoons ground cumin
1 teaspoon paprika
½ teaspoon salt
¼ teaspoon pepper
2 tablespoons olive oil
½ cup finely chopped onion
1 teaspoon minced garlic

¼ cup port or other sweet red wine
¼ cup water
1 tablespoon red wine vinegar
2 tablespoons butter or margarine
2 tablespoons chopped fresh cilantro

Cut each tenderloin into 8 slices; sprinkle with cumin, paprika, salt, and pepper. Sauté pork slices in oil in a large skillet 6 to 8 minutes on each side or until browned. Transfer pork to a serving platter; set aside, and keep warm.

Drain fat from skillet; add onion and garlic, and sauté 3 to 4 minutes or until lightly browned. Add wine, water, and vinegar; stir well. Bring to a boil; reduce heat, and simmer, uncovered, until liquid is reduced to ⅓ cup. Add butter, stirring until butter melts. Spoon sauce over pork; sprinkle with cilantro. Yield: 4 servings.   Adonia Curry

The Galloping Chef
The Combined Training Equestrian Team Alliance
Woodside, California

Savory Pork Chops

2 tablespoons all-purpose flour
¼ teaspoon seasoned salt
¼ teaspoon dry mustard
Dash of pepper
4 (1-inch-thick) pork loin chops
Vegetable oil

¼ cup water
¼ cup soy sauce
2 tablespoons catsup
2 tablespoons orange marmalade
Chopped green onions

Combine flour, seasoned salt, mustard, and pepper in a small bowl, stirring well. Dredge chops in flour mixture; cook in oil in a large skillet until browned on both sides. Remove chops, and discard drippings. Return chops to skillet.

Combine water and next 3 ingredients; pour over chops. Bring to boil; cover, reduce heat, and simmer 20 minutes or until chops are tender, turning once. Sprinkle with green onions. Yield: 4 servings.   Dan Wendeborn

Treasured Recipes
Ketchikan Volunteer Fire Department
Ketchikan, Alaska

Apple Butter Country Ribs

4 pounds country-style pork ribs
Salt and pepper
1 (14-ounce) jar apple butter
½ cup water
¼ cup white vinegar
3 tablespoons lemon juice
2 teaspoons prepared horseradish

1 teaspoon prepared mustard
½ teaspoon sugar
½ teaspoon salt
½ teaspoon garlic powder
½ teaspoon celery seeds
⅛ teaspoon pepper
Dash of ground red pepper
Dash of ground cumin

Place ribs in a large Dutch oven; add water to cover. Bring to a boil; cover, reduce heat, and simmer 45 minutes or until tender. Drain well; sprinkle with salt and pepper. Set aside.

Combine apple butter and remaining ingredients in a saucepan; stir well. Bring to a boil; reduce heat, and simmer, uncovered, for 25 minutes, stirring occasionally.

Coat ribs generously with apple butter sauce. Grill ribs over low coals (275° to 300°) 45 minutes, turning every 5 to 10 minutes, and basting frequently with remaining apple butter sauce. Yield: 6 to 8 servings.   Alma McPherson

Home Cookin' "AT&T's Right Choices"
Western Electric Council Telephone Pioneers of America
Ballwin, Missouri

Stick-to-Your-Ribs Ribs

6½ pounds spareribs
1 onion, coarsely chopped
½ cup cider vinegar

12 black peppercorns
1 teaspoon salt
Jasmeen's Jazzi Barbecue Sauce

Cut ribs into serving-size pieces. Place ribs in a large Dutch oven; add water to cover. Add onion, vinegar, peppercorns, and salt. Bring to a boil; cover, reduce heat, and simmer 1 hour. Drain well.

Grill ribs over low coals (275° to 300°) 15 minutes, turning after 8 minutes. Baste ribs generously with Jasmeen's Jazzi Barbecue Sauce, and grill 8 minutes. Turn ribs; baste generously with sauce. Grill ribs an additional 7 minutes or to desired degree of doneness. Yield: 6 to 8 servings.

Jasmeen's Jazzi Barbecue Sauce

1 medium onion, finely
  chopped
½ cup chopped green pepper
1 tablespoon vegetable oil
1 (24-ounce) bottle catsup
½ cup firmly packed brown
  sugar

½ cup honey
3 tablespoons prepared
  mustard
½ cup water

Sauté onion and green pepper in oil in a large saucepan until vegetables are tender. Add catsup, brown sugar, honey, and mustard; bring mixture to a boil. Stir in water; reduce heat, and simmer, uncovered, 15 minutes. Yield: 4 cups.   Jasmeen L. Williams

Holiday Recipes
Gulf Pines Girl Scout Council
Hattiesburg, Mississippi

Sweet-and-Sour Pork

½ cup all-purpose flour
¼ cup cornstarch
½ cup cold water
2 teaspoons salt, divided
1 egg
2 pounds boneless pork, cut
  into ¾-inch pieces
Vegetable oil
1 (20-ounce) can unsweetened
  pineapple chunks, undrained
2 carrots, scraped and thinly
  sliced

½ cup firmly packed brown
  sugar
½ cup white vinegar
2 teaspoons soy sauce
1 clove garlic, minced
2 tablespoons cornstarch
2 tablespoons cold water
1 medium-size green pepper,
  cut into ¾-inch pieces
Hot cooked rice

Combine first 5 ingredients in a medium bowl; beat with a wire whisk until well blended. Add pork, stirring well. Carefully drop pork, one piece at a time, into deep hot oil (375°); fry until golden, turning once. Set aside.

Drain pineapple chunks, reserving juice. Set pineapple chunks aside. Add enough water to juice to make 1 cup. Combine pineapple juice, carrot, brown sugar, vinegar, soy sauce, and garlic in a Dutch oven. Bring to a boil over medium heat; cover, reduce heat, and simmer 6 minutes or until carrot is tender.

Combine 2 tablespoons cornstarch and 2 tablespoons water, stirring well. Add cornstarch mixture to carrot mixture, stirring well to combine. Stir in reserved cooked pork, reserved pineapple chunks, and green pepper. Bring mixture to a boil, stirring constantly; reduce heat, and simmer, uncovered, 1 minute. Serve with rice. Yield: 4 to 6 servings.   Katherine Sanford

Musical Tastes
Chancel and Bell Choir, First United Methodist Church
Charlottesville, Virginia

Stuffed Baked Ham

1 cup fine, dry breadcrumbs
¼ cup firmly packed brown
   sugar
2 tablespoons butter or
   margarine, melted
½ teaspoon ground allspice
½ teaspoon ground cloves
½ teaspoon ground mace

¼ teaspoon pepper
¼ cup water
1 (10-pound) smoked, fully
   cooked ham
1 egg, beaten
¼ cup fine, dry breadcrumbs
3 tablespoons sugar

Combine first 7 ingredients in a bowl; stir well. Gradually add water, stirring just until blended. Set aside.

Slice skin from ham. Score fat on ham in a diamond design, making 2-inch slits, 2 inches apart. Press reserved breadcrumb mixture into slits. Brush ham with egg; sprinkle with ¼ cup breadcrumbs and sugar.

Place ham, fat side up, on a rack in a shallow roasting pan. Insert meat thermometer, making sure it does not touch fat or bone. Bake, uncovered, at 325° for 2 to 2½ hours or until meat thermometer registers 140°. Yield: 15 to 20 servings.

Cardinal Cuisine
The Mount Vernon Hospital Auxiliary
Alexandria, Virginia

Pasta, Rice
& Grains

Shocks of grain are gathered in this finely combed Oklahoma field. An agriculturally rich state, Oklahoma is a leading producer of wheat, cotton, corn, oats, spinach, and watermelons, as well as broomcorn, from which stiff brooms and brushes are made.

Pasta with Asparagus

1 pound fresh asparagus spears
1 (12-ounce) package
   fettuccine
1 medium onion, minced
2 to 3 cloves garlic, minced
½ cup butter or margarine,
   melted
½ pound sliced fresh
   mushrooms
1 medium carrot, scraped and
   sliced
1 cup half-and-half

½ cup canned diluted chicken
   broth
2 teaspoons dried whole basil
½ cup chopped green pepper
½ cup chopped sweet red
   pepper
1 cup freshly grated Parmesan
   cheese
Salt and freshly ground pepper
   to taste
Additional freshly grated
   Parmesan cheese

Snap off tough ends of asparagus. Remove scales from stalks with a knife or vegetable peeler, if desired. Cut asparagus diagonally into 1-inch pieces; set aside.

Cook fettuccine according to package directions. Drain well, and set aside.

Sauté onion and garlic in melted butter in a large skillet over medium heat 3 minutes. Add reserved asparagus, mushrooms, and carrot, and sauté 7 minutes. Add half-and-half, chicken broth, and basil; cook over high heat 5 minutes or until liquid is reduced by about one-third. Stir in green pepper and sweet red pepper; cook 3 minutes.

Add reserved fettuccine, 1 cup Parmesan cheese, and salt and pepper to taste; cook over low heat, stirring constantly, until mixture is thoroughly heated. Sprinkle with additional Parmesan cheese. Serve immediately. Yield: 6 to 8 servings.

Honest to Goodness
The Junior League of Springfield, Illinois

Vegetable Fettuccine

2 small zucchini, cut into
   julienne strips
2 medium carrots, scraped and
   cut into julienne strips
1 cup sliced fresh mushrooms
4 green onions, cut into 1-inch
   pieces
1 clove garlic, minced
¼ cup butter or margarine,
   melted
1 (15-ounce) can garbanzo
   beans, drained

½ teaspoon dried whole basil
Salt and pepper to taste
1 (8-ounce) package fettuccine
½ (8-ounce) package spinach
   fettuccine
1 cup grated Parmesan cheese,
   divided
2 egg yolks
1 cup whipping cream

Sauté zucchini, carrot, mushrooms, green onions, and garlic in butter in a large skillet 5 minutes. Add beans, basil, and salt and pepper to taste, stirring gently to combine. Remove from heat, and set aside.

Cook fettuccine according to package directions; drain well. Place fettuccine and reserved vegetable mixture in a large Dutch oven; toss gently. Cook over medium heat until thoroughly heated. Stir in ¾ cup Parmesan cheese.

Combine egg yolks and whipping cream in a medium mixing bowl; beat at medium speed of an electric mixer until foamy. Add to fettuccine mixture, tossing gently to combine. Cook over medium heat until thickened, stirring gently. Sprinkle with remaining ¼ cup Parmesan cheese. Serve immediately. Yield: 8 servings.

Betty Russell

Recipes to Come Home to
Oologah Area Chamber of Commerce
Oologah, Oklahoma

Vegetable Stroganoff

1½ cups broccoli flowerets
1½ cups cauliflower flowerets
1½ cups scraped, thinly sliced
   carrots
3 cups sliced fresh mushrooms
1 small onion, chopped
1 clove garlic, minced
3 tablespoons butter or
   margarine, melted
2 tablespoons all-purpose flour

2 cups milk
½ teaspoon chicken-flavored
   bouillon granules
1 (2½-ounce) can sliced ripe
   olives, drained (optional)
1 cup ricotta cheese
¾ cup sour cream
½ cup grated Parmesan cheese,
   divided
1 (16-ounce) package linguine

Cook broccoli, cauliflower, and carrot in a small amount of boiling water 5 minutes or until vegetables are crisp-tender; drain well, and set aside.

Sauté mushrooms, onion, and garlic in melted butter in a large Dutch oven over medium heat until vegetables are tender. Add flour, stirring well. Cook 1 minute, stirring constantly. Gradually add milk and bouillon granules; cook over medium heat, stirring constantly, until mixture is thickened and bubbly. Add reserved vegetables and, if desired, olives; stir well, and set aside.

Combine ricotta cheese, sour cream, and ¼ cup Parmesan cheese; stir well. Add ricotta cheese mixture to reserved vegetable mixture; stir well. Cook over medium heat until thoroughly heated.

Cook linguine according to package directions; drain well. Combine linguine and vegetable mixture in a large serving bowl, tossing gently. Sprinkle with remaining ¼ cup Parmesan cheese. Serve immediately. Yield: 8 servings.

Thyme & Monet
The Krasl Art Center
St. Joseph, Michigan

Linguine with Ham and Cheese Sauce

1 (8-ounce) package linguine
½ cup chopped onion
¼ cup butter or margarine, melted
1 tablespoon all-purpose flour
2 cups milk
½ teaspoon salt
⅛ teaspoon pepper

1 (10-ounce) package frozen English peas, thawed
1 (4-ounce) package sliced cooked ham, cut into thin strips
½ cup (2 ounces) shredded Swiss cheese

Cook linguine according to package directions. Drain well, and set aside.

Sauté onion in butter in a large skillet until tender. Add flour, and stir until blended. Cook 1 minute, stirring constantly. Gradually add milk; cook over medium heat, stirring constantly, until mixture is slightly thickened and bubbly. Stir in salt and pepper. Add peas; cook over medium heat 2 to 3 minutes or until tender. Add ham; cook until thoroughly heated. Remove from heat; add cheese, stirring until cheese melts. Place linguine and sauce in a large serving bowl, and toss gently to combine. Serve immediately. Yield: 6 servings.   Cathy Danner

What the Winners Eat
Sugar Creek Swim Club
St. Louis, Missouri

The Sugar Creek Swim Club has compiled its members' favorite recipes to create a cookbook for parents of athletic children. With an emphasis on healthy food, this cookbook is designed to promote proper nutrition as an integral part of their youngsters' training regimen. Proceeds from the sale of What the Winners Eat *will benefit the young swimmers of the Sugar Creek Swim Club.*

Hot Chicken and Pasta

2 tablespoons peanut oil,
  divided
1 clove garlic, minced
1 teaspoon grated fresh
  gingerroot
2 pounds boneless chicken
  breasts, cut into 1-inch pieces
4 ounces linguine, uncooked
6 ounces fresh snow pea pods

1 medium-size sweet red
  pepper, cut into strips
2 green onions, chopped
3 tablespoons soy sauce
1 tablespoon rice wine vinegar
1 teaspoon chili oil
½ teaspoon crushed red
  pepper
¼ cup chopped peanuts

Pour 1 tablespoon peanut oil around top of preheated wok, coating sides; heat at medium-high (325°) for 2 minutes. Add garlic and gingerroot, and stir-fry 30 seconds. Add half of chicken pieces; increase temperature to high (375°), and stir-fry 5 minutes. Remove chicken, and set aside. Add remaining chicken pieces to wok, and stir-fry 5 minutes. Remove chicken from wok; set aside, and keep warm.

Cook linguine according to package directions. Drain well, and set aside.

Pour remaining 1 tablespoon peanut oil around top of wok, coating sides; heat at medium-high (325°) for 2 minutes. Add snow peas, sweet red pepper, and green onions; stir-fry 2 minutes. Return reserved chicken to wok. Add linguine, soy sauce, and next 3 ingredients; stir-fry until thoroughly heated. Sprinkle with peanuts. Serve immediately. Yield: 6 servings.

"One Lump or Two?"
All Children's Hospital Foundation
St. Petersburg, Florida

Linguine with Shrimp and Anchovy Tomato Sauce

3 cloves garlic, minced
¼ cup plus 1 tablespoon
  vegetable oil, divided
¼ cup unsalted butter, divided
6 anchovy fillets, chopped
⅔ cup Chablis or other dry
  white wine
2 tablespoons fresh lemon
  juice
4 medium tomatoes, peeled
  and chopped

½ cup chopped fresh basil
¼ cup whipping cream
1 clove garlic, minced
24 large unpeeled fresh
  shrimp, peeled and deveined
1 (12-ounce) package linguine
1 tablespoon grated Parmesan
  cheese
Additional grated Parmesan
  cheese

Sauté 3 cloves minced garlic in 2 tablespoons oil and 2 tablespoons butter in a large skillet until tender. Add anchovies, and sauté 1 to 2 minutes. Add wine and lemon juice; cook over medium-high heat 2 to 3 minutes. Stir in tomato; reduce heat, and simmer, uncovered, 5 minutes. Add basil, and simmer an additional minute. Slowly stir in whipping cream. Gradually add remaining 2 tablespoons butter, stirring until butter melts. Remove from heat, and set aside.

Sauté 1 clove minced garlic in 2 tablespoons oil in a large skillet 1 minute. Add shrimp, and sauté over medium-high heat until shrimp turn pink; drain. Combine shrimp and reserved tomato mixture; stir well, and set aside.

Cook linguine according to package directions; drain well. Add remaining 1 tablespoon oil and 1 tablespoon Parmesan cheese to linguine; toss gently to combine. Place linguine mixture on a large serving platter; top with shrimp mixture. Serve with additional Parmesan cheese. Serve immediately. Yield: 6 servings.

The Fine Art of Cooking
The Women's Committee of the Philadelphia Museum of Art
Philadelphia, Pennsylvania

Hot Shrimp and Fresh Vegetable Pasta

1½ quarts water
2 pounds unpeeled medium-
   size fresh shrimp
6 Italian-style tomatoes, cut
   into ½-inch pieces
2 medium-size sweet yellow
   peppers, diced
2 medium-size sweet red
   peppers, diced
1 cup olive oil
½ cup fresh lemon juice
¼ teaspoon chili oil (optional)

½ cup chopped fresh dillweed
2 tablespoons chopped shallot
2 tablespoons chopped fresh
   tarragon
2 tablespoons crushed red
   pepper
1 teaspoon salt
1 teaspoon freshly ground
   pepper
1½ cups frozen English peas
3 cups broccoli flowerets
1 (16-ounce) package linguine

Bring water to a boil; add shrimp, and cook 3 to 5 minutes. Drain well; rinse with cold water. Chill. Peel and devein shrimp.

Place shrimp in a large bowl. Add tomato and next 11 ingredients; toss gently to combine. Cover and chill.

Cook peas according to package directions; drain well, and set peas aside.

Cook broccoli in a small amount of boiling water 1 minute. Drain well, and rinse with cold water. Add broccoli to cooked peas; toss gently. Add reserved shrimp mixture, tossing gently to combine.

Cook linguine according to package directions; drain well. Add shrimp mixture, and toss gently to combine. Serve immediately. Yield: 12 to 14 servings.

Cardinal Cuisine
The Mount Vernon Hospital Auxiliary
Alexandria, Virginia

Seafood Tetrazzini

1 (16-ounce) package thin
  spaghetti, broken
4 cups water
1 pound unpeeled fresh
  shrimp
1 (6-ounce) jar sliced
  mushrooms, undrained
¾ cup chopped onion
¾ cup chopped green pepper
½ cup butter or margarine,
  melted
½ cup all-purpose flour
2 teaspoons salt

¼ teaspoon pepper
4 cups milk
1½ cups (6 ounces) shredded
  Cheddar cheese
1 teaspoon lemon juice
1 teaspoon prepared mustard
½ teaspoon Worcestershire
  sauce
1 pound cooked lobster meat,
  cut into ½-inch pieces
1 pound fresh crabmeat,
  drained and flaked
½ cup grated Parmesan cheese

Cook spaghetti according to package directions. Drain well, and set aside.

Bring water to a boil; add shrimp, and cook 3 to 5 minutes. Drain well; rinse with cold water. Chill. Peel and devein shrimp, and set aside.

Drain sliced mushrooms, reserving liquid. Set mushrooms and liquid aside.

Sauté onion and green pepper in melted butter in a Dutch oven until tender. Add reserved mushrooms, flour, salt, and pepper; cook 1 minute, stirring constantly. Gradually add reserved mushroom liquid and milk; cook over medium heat, stirring constantly, until mixture is thickened and bubbly. Add Cheddar cheese and next 3 ingredients; stir until cheese melts. Add reserved spaghetti, lobster, crabmeat, and reserved shrimp; cook over low heat until thoroughly heated.

Pour mixture into a greased 13- x 9- x 2-inch baking pan. Sprinkle with Parmesan cheese; broil 6 inches from heat 3 minutes or until lightly browned. Yield: 10 servings.   Sandy Lasch

Udderly Delicious
The Junior League of Racine, Wisconsin

Popeye's Lasagna

1 cup chopped onion
2 cloves garlic, minced
2 tablespoons olive oil
1 (28-ounce) can whole
tomatoes, undrained and
chopped
1 (6-ounce) can tomato paste
¼ cup minced fresh parsley
1 bay leaf
½ teaspoon dried whole
oregano
1 (8-ounce) package lasagna
noodles

1 (15-ounce) carton ricotta
cheese
1 (10-ounce) package frozen
chopped spinach, thawed and
drained
¾ cup grated Parmesan cheese,
divided
1 egg, beaten
1 teaspoon salt
½ teaspoon pepper
2 cups (8 ounces) shredded
mozzarella cheese

Sauté onion and garlic in oil in a large skillet until tender. Add tomatoes and next 4 ingredients; stir well. Bring to a boil; reduce heat, and simmer, uncovered, 20 minutes. Remove and discard bay leaf. Set aside.

Cook lasagna noodles according to package directions. Drain well, and set aside.

Combine ricotta cheese, spinach, ¼ cup Parmesan cheese, egg, salt, and pepper; stir well, and set aside.

Spread 1⅓ cups reserved tomato mixture in a lightly greased 13- x 9- x 2-inch baking dish. Layer one-third of lasagna noodles, half of spinach mixture, 1 cup mozzarella cheese, and ¼ cup Parmesan cheese in order listed. Top with 1⅓ cups of tomato mixture, one-third of lasagna noodles, and remaining half of spinach mixture. Top with remaining one-third lasagna noodles, 1⅓ cups tomato mixture, ¼ cup Parmesan cheese, and 1 cup mozzarella. Cover and bake at 350° for 45 minutes. Let stand 10 minutes before serving. Yield: 6 to 8 servings.   Bob Curran

Kona Kitchens
Kona Outdoor Circle
Kailua-Kona, Hawaii

Rich White Cheese Lasagna

1 (8-ounce) package lasagna
  noodles
1 teaspoon olive oil
1 pound ground beef
1 cup finely chopped onion
1 cup finely chopped celery
1 clove garlic, crushed
1 cup half-and-half
1 (3-ounce) package cream
  cheese, cubed
2 teaspoons dried whole basil
1 teaspoon dried whole oregano
¾ teaspoon salt

½ teaspoon dried Italian
  seasoning
½ cup Chablis or other dry
  white wine
2 cups (8 ounces) shredded
  Cheddar cheese
1½ cups (6 ounces) shredded
  Gouda cheese
1½ cups small-curd cottage
  cheese
1 egg, lightly beaten
12 (1-ounce) slices mozzarella
  cheese

Cook lasagna noodles according to package directions; drain well. Sprinkle with olive oil; toss gently, and set aside.

Cook ground beef, onion, celery, and garlic in a large skillet until meat is browned, stirring to crumble meat. Drain mixture, and return to skillet. Add half-and-half and next 5 ingredients; cook over low heat, stirring constantly, until cream cheese melts. Add wine, Cheddar cheese, and Gouda cheese; cook, stirring constantly, until cheeses melt. Remove from heat; set aside.

Combine cottage cheese and egg in a small bowl, stirring well. Set aside.

Layer half of the reserved noodles in a greased 13- x 9- x 2-inch baking pan. Top with half the reserved meat mixture, half the cottage cheese mixture, and half the mozzarella cheese slices. Repeat layers, omitting the mozzarella. Bake, uncovered, at 375° for 20 minutes. Top with remaining mozzarella, and bake an additional 15 minutes. Let stand 10 minutes before serving. Yield: 8 to 10 servings.   Fran Doughty

Return Engagement
The Junior Board of the Quad City Symphony Orchestra Association
Davenport, Iowa

Baked Ziti and Italian Sausage

8 ounces ziti macaroni,
  uncooked
1 pound mild or hot link Italian
  sausage
2 tablespoons vegetable oil
¼ cup butter or margarine
¼ cup all-purpose flour
2 cups milk
½ cup grated Parmesan cheese,
  divided
1 teaspoon salt

½ teaspoon pepper
1 (16-ounce) carton small-curd
  cottage cheese
1 egg, lightly beaten
1 tablespoon chopped fresh
  parsley
1 teaspoon salt
⅛ teaspoon pepper
1 cup (4 ounces) shredded
  mozzarella cheese
Paprika

Cook macaroni according to package directions. Drain well, and set aside.

Cook sausage in oil in a large skillet 15 minutes or until browned; drain well. Slice sausage diagonally, and set aside.

Melt butter in a heavy saucepan over low heat; add flour, stirring until smooth. Cook 1 minute, stirring constantly. Gradually add milk; cook over medium heat, stirring constantly, until mixture is thickened and bubbly. Stir in ¼ cup Parmesan cheese, 1 teaspoon salt, and ½ teaspoon pepper. Add reserved macaroni; stir well, and set aside.

Combine remaining ¼ cup Parmesan cheese, cottage cheese, and next 4 ingredients; stir well.

Place half of macaroni mixture in a lightly greased 13- x 9- x 2-inch baking dish. Top with cottage cheese mixture and half of sausage. Top with remaining half of macaroni mixture and sausage. Sprinkle with mozzarella and paprika. Cover and bake at 350° for 1 hour. Yield: 8 to 10 servings.

Gracious Goodness
Penn Laurel Girl Scout Council
York, Pennsylvania

Macaroni and Cheese Stir-Fry

2 cups elbow macaroni, uncooked
½ cup frozen English peas, thawed
¼ cup butter or margarine, divided
1 pound chicken breast halves, skinned, boned, and cut into strips
2 cloves garlic, minced
2 teaspoons chicken-flavored bouillon granules
2 cups small broccoli flowerets
1 medium onion, coarsely chopped
1 medium-size sweet red pepper, cut into julienne strips
1 cup scraped, sliced carrots
¼ teaspoon dried whole tarragon
¼ teaspoon lemon-pepper seasoning
1 tablespoon all-purpose flour
1 cup milk
1½ cups (6 ounces) shredded American cheese

Cook macaroni according to package directions. Drain well, and set aside.

Cook peas according to package directions. Drain well, and set peas aside.

Melt 2 tablespoons butter in a large Dutch oven or wok. Add chicken, garlic, and bouillon granules; stir-fry 5 to 7 minutes or until chicken is lightly browned. Remove chicken, and set aside. Add remaining 2 tablespoons butter, broccoli, and next 5 ingredients; stir-fry 1 minute. Cover and cook until broccoli is tender. Stir in reserved macaroni, peas, and chicken, and cook until thoroughly heated.

Combine flour and 1 tablespoon milk; stir until smooth. Gradually add remaining milk, stirring until blended. Add milk mixture to macaroni mixture; cook 1 minute, stirring constantly. Add cheese; cook, stirring constantly, until cheese melts. Serve immediately. Yield: 8 servings.   Colleen McGraw

Bakers' Secrets
Edison Women's Club
Akron, Ohio

Noodles Parmesan

1 (8-ounce) package cream
   cheese, softened
¼ cup butter or margarine,
   softened
2 to 4 tablespoons minced
   fresh parsley
1 teaspoon dried whole basil
¼ teaspoon salt
¼ teaspoon pepper

⅔ cup boiling water
1 (8-ounce) package fine egg
   noodles
1 large clove garlic, minced
¼ cup butter or margarine,
   melted
1 cup grated Parmesan cheese,
   divided
Garnish: fresh parsley sprigs

Combine first 6 ingredients. Add boiling water, stirring until
cream cheese and butter melt. Set aside, and keep warm.

Cook noodles according to package directions. Drain well, and
set aside.

Sauté garlic in ¼ cup butter in a skillet 2 minutes. Pour over
reserved noodles, tossing gently to combine. Sprinkle with ½ cup
Parmesan cheese; toss gently to combine.

Transfer noodle mixture to a warm serving platter; top with warm
cream cheese sauce. Sprinkle with remaining ½ cup Parmesan cheese.
Garnish, if desired. Yield: 8 servings.   Sonny Gilmore

Plug in to Good Cooking
The National Management Association Corporate Headquarters
Chapter of Alabama Power Company
Birmingham, Alabama

*The Edison Women's Club channels its support to organizations
that take care of homeless women and children in the Akron,
Ohio, area. Proceeds from the sale of the cookbook,* Bakers'
Secrets, *will help support the Shelter for Battered Women and
Toys for Tots.*

Spicy Sesame Noodles

1 (16-ounce) package linguine
  or spaghetti
2 tablespoons sesame oil
¼ cup creamy peanut butter or
  tahini
¼ cup soy sauce
2 tablespoons white wine
  vinegar

1 tablespoon minced fresh
  gingerroot
3 drops of chili oil
4 to 6 green onions, cut into
  2-inch pieces

Cook linguine according to package directions; drain well. Toss linguine with sesame oil, and set aside.

Combine peanut butter and next 4 ingredients in a small bowl; stir well. Add peanut butter mixture to linguine mixture, and toss gently to combine. Add green onions, and toss gently to combine. Serve immediately. Yield: 6 servings.

Marblehead Cooks
Tower School Associates
Marblehead, Massachusetts

Basic Risotto

1 small onion, chopped
2 tablespoons butter or
  margarine, melted
1 cup Arborio or other short-
  grain rice, uncooked
⅓ cup Chablis or other dry
  white wine
1 teaspoon dried parsley
  flakes
½ teaspoon dried whole basil

½ teaspoon paprika
¼ teaspoon onion powder
4½ cups canned diluted
  chicken or beef broth
2 tablespoons grated Parmesan
  cheese
Salt and pepper to taste
Additional grated Parmesan
  cheese (optional)

Sauté onion in melted butter in a large saucepan until tender. Add rice and next 5 ingredients; cook over medium-high heat, stirring constantly, until most of the liquid has been absorbed. Add ½ cup chicken broth, stirring constantly, until most of the liquid has been absorbed. Continue adding broth, ½ cup at a time, stirring until mixture is creamy and rice is tender. Remove from heat; stir in 2 tablespoons Parmesan cheese, and salt and pepper to taste. Sprinkle with additional Parmesan cheese, if desired. Serve immediately. Yield: 4 to 6 servings.   Judy Johnson

Extraordinary Cuisine for Sea & Shore
Seattle Yacht Club
Seattle, Washington

Thai Fried Rice

1 tablespoon minced fresh gingerroot
2 tablespoons vegetable oil
1½ cups long-grain rice, uncooked
2¼ cups canned diluted chicken broth
¼ cup unsweetened coconut milk
¼ cup raisins
2 tablespoons light soy sauce

1 tablespoon lime juice
1 tablespoon curry powder
½ teaspoon Chinese chili sauce
½ teaspoon salt
½ teaspoon grated lemon rind
1 cup seeded, diced tomatoes
½ cup minced green onions
½ cup diced fresh pineapple
⅓ cup slivered almonds, toasted
2 tablespoons lime juice

Sauté gingerroot in oil in a large skillet until tender. Add rice, stirring well; cook 5 minutes. Stir in broth and next 8 ingredients; bring to a boil. Cover, reduce heat, and simmer 20 minutes or until rice is tender and liquid is absorbed. Stir in tomato, green onions, pineapple, almonds, and lime juice. Serve immediately. Yield: 10 to 12 servings.

Capital Classics
The Junior League of Washington, DC

Sour Cream Pilaf

½ cup slivered almonds
1 tablespoon butter or
  margarine, melted
1½ cups long-grain rice,
  uncooked
3 cups canned diluted chicken
  broth
⅓ cup butter or margarine
1 tablespoon grated onion

1 tablespoon fresh lemon juice
1 to 1½ teaspoons salt
¼ teaspoon pepper
1 small bay leaf
1 cup sour cream
1 (4-ounce) can button
  mushrooms, drained
¼ cup minced fresh parsley

Sauté almonds in 1 tablespoon butter in a small skillet until lightly browned; remove from heat, and set aside.

Combine rice and next 7 ingredients in a large saucepan. Bring mixture to a boil; cover, reduce heat, and simmer 20 to 25 minutes or until rice is tender and liquid is absorbed. Remove from heat. Remove and discard bay leaf.

Add sour cream and mushrooms to rice mixture; stir well. Transfer rice mixture to a serving dish; sprinkle with almonds and parsley. Serve immediately. Yield: 6 to 8 servings.   Vernita Bryant

Cohasset Entertains, Encore
The Community Garden Club of Cohasset, Massachusetts

Wild Rice and Walnuts

1½ cups canned diluted
  chicken broth
1½ teaspoons soy sauce
½ teaspoon dried whole thyme
¾ cup wild rice, uncooked
1 medium onion, chopped

1 stalk celery, chopped
1 tablespoon margarine,
  melted
½ cup chopped walnuts,
  toasted

Combine chicken broth, soy sauce, and thyme in a heavy saucepan; bring mixture to a boil. Gradually add rice, stirring constantly. Cover, reduce heat, and simmer 35 to 40 minutes or until rice is tender and liquid is absorbed. Set rice aside.

Sauté onion and celery in margarine in a large skillet until tender. Add reserved rice and walnuts; stir well. Yield: 6 to 8 servings.

To Your Health!
The Junior Woman's Club of West Haven, Connecticut

Toasted Barley and Mushrooms

⅔ cup barley, uncooked
4 cups water
2 beef-flavored bouillon cubes
¼ pound sliced fresh
  mushrooms
2 tablespoons sliced green
  onions

1 clove garlic, minced
3 tablespoons margarine,
  melted
½ teaspoon salt
¼ teaspoon dried whole thyme,
  crushed
Dash of pepper

Place barley on an ungreased baking sheet; bake at 350° for 20 minutes until lightly browned, stirring occasionally. Set toasted barley aside.

Bring water to a boil in a large heavy saucepan; stir in toasted barley. Add bouillon cubes; cover, reduce heat, and simmer 1 hour or until barley is tender, stirring occasionally. Drain well, and set aside.

Sauté mushrooms, green onions, and garlic in margarine in a large skillet until vegetables are tender. Stir in cooked barley, salt, thyme, and pepper. Cook over medium heat 2 to 3 minutes or until thoroughly heated. Serve immediately. Yield: 6 servings.

Spice and Spirit: The Complete Kosher Jewish Cookbook
Lubavitch Women's Organization
Brooklyn, New York

Golden Couscous

1 large sweet yellow pepper, diced	½ teaspoon salt
1 medium onion, finely chopped	¼ teaspoon pepper
3 tablespoons extra virgin olive oil, divided	1½ cups canned diluted chicken broth
2¼ cups fresh whole kernel corn	1 cup couscous, uncooked
	2 teaspoons ground turmeric
	1 teaspoon ground cumin

Sauté sweet yellow pepper and onion in 1 tablespoon olive oil in a large skillet until vegetables are tender. Add corn, and sauté 4 minutes. Stir in salt and pepper; remove from heat, and set sweet yellow pepper mixture aside.

Bring chicken broth to a boil in a large saucepan over medium heat. Stir in remaining 2 tablespoons olive oil, couscous, turmeric, and cumin. Remove from heat; cover and let stand 5 minutes or until liquid is absorbed.

Gently stir in reserved sweet yellow pepper mixture. Serve couscous mixture warm or at room temperature. Yield: 6 servings.

Watch Hill Cooks
The Watch Hill Improvement Society
Watch Hill, Rhode Island

Pies & Pastries

Freshly harvested pumpkins on a Rhode Island farm signal the arrival of autumn and invoke thoughts of homemade pumpkin pies.

Butterscotch Crumb Apple Pie

4 cups peeled, sliced Granny
   Smith apples
1½ teaspoons lemon juice
½ cup sugar
¼ cup all-purpose flour

1 teaspoon ground cinnamon
⅛ teaspoon salt
1 unbaked 9-inch pastry shell
Topping (recipe follows)
Whipped cream (optional)

Combine apple slices and lemon juice in a medium bowl; toss well. Combine sugar, flour, cinnamon, and salt; stir well. Add sugar mixture to apple mixture, stirring gently to combine.

Spoon apple mixture into pastry shell. Cover edges of pastry with strips of aluminum foil to prevent excessive browning. Bake at 375° for 20 minutes. Remove foil, and sprinkle topping over apple mixture; bake an additional 25 minutes. Serve with whipped cream, if desired. Yield: one 9-inch pie.

Topping

1 (6-ounce) package
   butterscotch morsels
¼ cup butter or margarine

¾ cup all-purpose flour
⅛ teaspoon salt

Combine butterscotch morsels and butter in top of a double boiler; bring water to a boil. Reduce heat to low; cook until morsels and butter melt, stirring occasionally. Remove from heat; add flour and salt, stirring well. Let stand 10 minutes or until crumbly. Yield: 1⅓ cups.   Lynn Moss

Greetings from Atlantic City
The Ruth Newman Shapiro Cancer and Heart Fund
Atlantic City, New Jersey

Harvest Moon Fruit Pie

Pastry for double-crust 9-inch
  pie
4 cups peeled, sliced cooking
  apples
1¼ cups sugar
1 cup ground fresh cranberries
1 cup finely chopped dried
  apricots
2 tablespoons all-purpose flour

1 teaspoon grated orange rind
½ teaspoon ground cinnamon
¼ teaspoon salt
¼ teaspoon ground nutmeg
1 tablespoon butter or
  margarine
Chopped pecans, walnuts, or
  thin lemon slices (optional)

Roll half of pastry to ⅛-inch thickness on a lightly floured surface. Place in a 9-inch pieplate; set aside.

Combine apple slices and next 8 ingredients in a medium bowl, and stir gently to combine. Spoon apple mixture into prepared pastry shell. Dot apple mixture evenly with butter. If desired, top apple mixture with chopped pecans, walnuts, or thin lemon slices.

Roll remaining half of pastry to ⅛-inch thickness; transfer pastry to top of pie. Trim off excess pastry along edges. Fold edges under and flute. Cut slits in top crust to allow steam to escape. Bake at 425° for 50 minutes. (Cover edges of pastry with strips of aluminum foil to prevent excessive browning, if necessary.) Yield: one 9-inch pie.

Virginia Hentschel

He Shall Feed His Flock
Church of the Good Shepherd
Acton, Massachusetts

Orange Meringue Pie

¾ cup sugar
¼ cup cornstarch
¼ teaspoon salt
1 tablespoon grated orange
  rind
2 cups fresh orange juice

3 eggs, separated
2 tablespoons lemon juice
1 tablespoon butter or
  margarine
Orange Pastry
¼ cup plus 2 tablespoons sugar

Combine ¾ cup sugar, cornstarch, salt, and orange rind in a heavy saucepan. Gradually add orange juice, stirring until blended. Cook over medium heat, stirring constantly, until mixture thickens and comes to a boil. Boil 1 minute, stirring constantly. Remove from heat.

Beat egg yolks at high speed of an electric mixer until thick and lemon colored. Gradually stir about one-fourth of hot mixture into beaten egg yolks; add to remaining hot mixture, stirring constantly. Cook over medium heat, stirring constantly, 2 to 3 minutes. Remove from heat. Add lemon juice and butter, stirring until butter melts. Spoon hot filling into prepared pastry shell.

Beat egg whites at high speed until foamy. Gradually add ¼ cup plus 2 tablspoons sugar, 1 tablespoon at a time, beating until stiff peaks form and sugar dissolves (2 to 4 minutes). Immediately spread meringue over filling, sealing to edge of pastry. Bake at 350° for 20 minutes or until golden. Let cool completely before serving. Yield: one 9-inch pie.

Orange Pastry

1½ cups all-purpose flour
1 tablespoon sugar
1 teaspoon grated orange rind
½ teaspoon salt

½ cup shortening
¼ cup fresh orange juice, chilled

Combine flour, sugar, orange rind, and salt; cut in shortening with a pastry blender until mixture resembles coarse meal. Sprinkle orange juice (1 tablespoon at a time) evenly over surface; stir with a fork until dry ingredients are moistened. Shape mixture into a ball; cover and chill.

Roll chilled pastry to ⅛-inch thickness on a lightly floured surface; place pastry in a 9-inch pieplate. Prick bottom of pastry with a fork. Bake at 450° for 10 to 12 minutes or until pastry is lightly browned. (Cover edges of pastry with strips of aluminum foil to prevent excessive browning, if necessary.) Yield: one 9-inch pastry shell.   Mrs. J.G. McCormick, Jr.

Break Bread with the Black Belt
Black Belt Ministries
Demopolis, Alabama

Chocolate Chess Pie or Thursday's Sin

½ cup butter or margarine
2 (1-ounce) squares
  unsweetened chocolate
2 eggs
1¼ cups sugar

¼ cup milk
1 teaspoon vanilla extract
1 unbaked 9-inch pastry shell
Whipped cream (optional)

Combine butter and chocolate in top of a double boiler; bring water to a boil. Reduce heat to low; cook until chocolate and butter melt, stirring occasionally. Set aside.

Combine eggs, sugar, milk, and vanilla in a large mixing bowl; beat at medium speed of an electric mixer 3 to 4 minutes. Add melted chocolate mixture, and beat well. Pour chocolate mixture into pastry shell. Bake at 350° for 35 to 40 minutes or until set. Let cool completely. Serve with whipped cream, if desired. Yield: one 9-inch pie.   Nancy Brown

Historic Lexington Cooks: Rockbridge Regional Recipes
Historic Lexington Foundation
Lexington, Virginia

Amish Vanilla Pie

1 cup firmly packed brown
  sugar, divided
1 cup plus 1 tablespoon
  all-purpose flour, divided
1 egg, beaten
1 cup water
¼ cup dark corn syrup

1½ teaspoons vanilla extract
1 unbaked 9-inch pastry shell
½ teaspoon cream of tartar
½ teaspoon baking soda
⅛ teaspoon salt
¼ cup butter or margarine

Combine ½ cup brown sugar, 1 tablespoon flour, and next 4 ingredients in a medium saucepan; stir well. Bring to a boil, stirring constantly. Remove from heat, and let cool. Pour into pastry shell.

Combine remaining ½ cup brown sugar, remaining 1 cup flour, cream of tartar, soda, and salt in a small bowl; stir well. Cut in butter with a pastry blender until mixture resembles coarse meal.

Sprinkle crumb mixture over pie. Bake at 350° for 40 minutes or until lightly browned. Yield: one 9-inch pie.   Betty Rogers

Treasured Recipes from Mason, Ohio
Mason Historical Society
Mason, Ohio

Banana Pie Supreme with Shaved White Chocolate

⅔ cup sugar
¼ cup plus 2 tablespoons
   sifted cake flour
¼ teaspoon salt
1¾ cups milk
2 egg yolks
1¼ teaspoons vanilla extract

½ cup whipping cream, whipped
1 baked 9-inch pastry shell
3 bananas
1½ teaspoons fresh lemon juice
Garnishes: whipped cream and
   shaved white chocolate

Combine first 3 ingredients in top of a double boiler; gradually add milk, stirring well. Bring water to a boil; reduce heat to low, and cook until mixture thickens, stirring constantly.

Beat egg yolks until thick and lemon colored. Gradually stir about one-fourth of hot mixture into yolks; add to remaining hot mixture, stirring constantly. Cook over low heat, stirring constantly, 1 to 2 minutes or until mixture thickens. Remove from heat; stir in vanilla. Let custard cool to room temperature. Cover and chill thoroughly. Stir about one-third whipped cream into custard; fold in remaining whipped cream.

Spoon one-third custard into pastry shell. Slice bananas, and dip in lemon juice to prevent browning. Layer half of banana slices over custard in pastry shell. Repeat layers with remaining custard and banana slices, ending with custard. Cover and chill. Garnish, if desired. Yield: one 9-inch pie.   Sharon Oliver

cook and love it more
Lovett Parent Association, The Lovett School
Atlanta, Georgia

Pumpkin-Lemon Cream Pie

1 (16-ounce) can cooked,
  mashed pumpkin
1⅓ cups half-and-half
⅔ cup sugar
2 eggs, lightly beaten
1 teaspoon ground cinnamon
½ teaspoon salt
½ teaspoon ground ginger

1 unbaked 9-inch pastry shell
1 (8-ounce) carton sour cream
2 tablespoons brown sugar
2 teaspoons grated lemon rind
1 tablespoon lemon juice
¼ cup chopped pecans or
  walnuts

Combine first 7 ingredients; stir well. Pour into pastry shell. Bake at 425° for 15 minutes. Reduce heat to 350°, and bake an additional 45 to 55 minutes or until set. Let cool 20 minutes.

Combine sour cream, brown sugar, lemon rind, and lemon juice in a small bowl; spread sour cream mixture over pie. Bake at 350° for 10 minutes. Sprinkle with pecans. Let cool slightly. Cover and chill. Yield: one 9-inch pie.   Dorothy Mummey

Montana 1889-1989 Centennial Cookbook
The Inter-Denominational Christian Fellowship
Noxon, Montana

Refrigerated Chocolate Pie

6 (1.55-ounce) milk chocolate
  candy bars
18 large marshmallows
½ cup milk

¼ cup whipping cream,
  whipped
½ cup chopped pecans
1 baked 9-inch pastry shell

Combine first 3 ingredients in top of a double boiler; bring water to a boil. Reduce heat to low; cook until chocolate and marshmallows melt, stirring occasionally. Let cool. Fold whipped cream and pecans into cooled chocolate mixture. Pour chocolate mixture into prepared crust. Cover and chill at least 8 hours. Yield: one 9-inch pie.   Sammye Dewoody

Feeding Your Neighbor
Neighbor to Neighbor
Pine Bluff, Arkansas

Sombrero Pie East Chop

1½ cups chocolate wafer
  crumbs
¼ cup plus 2 tablespoons
  butter or margarine, melted
36 large marshmallows (about
  ½ pound)
½ cup milk
½ cup Kahlúa or other coffee-
  flavored liqueur

1 cup whipping cream,
  whipped
1 cup whipping cream
¼ cup sugar
2 tablespoons cocoa
Garnish: shaved semisweet
  chocolate

Combine chocolate wafer crumbs and butter; stir well. Firmly press crumb mixture evenly in bottom and up the sides of a 9-inch pieplate. Freeze 30 minutes.

Combine marshmallows and milk in top of a double boiler; bring water to a boil. Reduce heat to low; cook until marshmallows melt, stirring frequently. Remove from heat; stir in Kahlúa. Cover and chill 30 minutes. Fold 1 cup whipped cream into marshmallow mixture. Pour into prepared crust. Cover and chill 3 hours or until firm.

Beat 1 cup whipping cream until foamy; gradually add sugar and cocoa, 1 tablespoon at a time, beating until soft peaks form. Spread whipped cream mixture over chilled pie. Garnish, if desired. Yield: one 9-inch pie.   Susan P. Snow

Summer Magic
The East Chop Association
Martha's Vineyard, Massachusetts

Proceeds generated from the sale of Summer Magic *will benefit the East Chop Association, a small land trust in Martha's Vineyard, Massachusetts, which supports the small island's conservation efforts.*

Grasshopper Pie

1½ cups chocolate wafer
   crumbs
¼ cup butter or margarine,
   melted
4 cups miniature marshmallows
½ cup milk

¼ cup white crème de cacao
¼ cup green crème de menthe
2 cups whipping cream,
   whipped and divided
Garnish: semisweet chocolate
   curls

Combine chocolate wafer crumbs and melted butter; stir well. Firmly press crumb mixture evenly in bottom and up the sides of a 9-inch pieplate. Chill 1 hour.

Combine marshmallows and milk in top of a double boiler; bring water to a boil. Reduce heat to low; cook until marshmallows melt, stirring frequently. Remove from heat, and let mixture cool slightly.

Stir in crème de cacao and crème de menthe, and let mixture cool completely. Fold in 3½ cups whipped cream. Pour marshmallow mixture into prepared crust. Chill until firm. Top with remaining ½ cup whipped cream. Garnish, if desired. Yield: one 9-inch pie.   Louise Brendlinger

If All the World Were Apple Pie
Athens Mothers' Center
Athens, Georgia

Ice Cream Pie

20 cream-filled chocolate
   sandwich cookies, finely
   crushed
⅓ cup butter or margarine,
   melted
2 (1-ounce) squares
   unsweetened chocolate
½ cup sugar

1 tablespoon butter or
   margarine
1 (5-ounce) can evaporated
   milk
1 quart coffee ice cream,
   softened
Whipped cream

Combine crumbs and ⅓ cup melted butter; stir well. Firmly press crumb mixture evenly in bottom and up the sides of a buttered 10-inch pieplate. Bake at 350° for 8 minutes. Let cool completely.

Combine chocolate, sugar, and 1 tablespoon butter in a small saucepan. Cook over low heat until chocolate, sugar, and butter melt, stirring constantly. Gradually add milk; cook, stirring constantly, until mixture is thickened. Cover and chill.

Spread ice cream evenly over prepared crust, spreading to edge. Spread cooled chocolate mixture over ice cream layer. Freeze until ice cream is firm. To serve, top pie with whipped cream. Yield: one 10-inch pie.   Arlene Krieger

The Best Specialties of the House . . . and More
North Suburban Guild of Children's Memorial Medical Center
Chicago, Illinois

Peanut Butter Ice Cream Pie

1⅔ cups graham cracker
  crumbs
¼ cup plus 2 tablespoons
  butter or margarine, melted
1 tablespoon honey
1 teaspoon sugar
2 quarts vanilla ice cream,
  softened

1 cup creamy peanut butter
¼ cup honey
½ cup whipping cream,
  whipped
1½ cups chopped peanuts,
  divided

Combine first 4 ingredients in a medium bowl; stir well. Firmly press crumb mixture evenly in bottom and up the sides of a 9-inch pieplate. Chill 1 hour.

Combine ice cream, peanut butter, and ¼ cup honey in a large bowl; stir well. Add whipped cream and 1 cup chopped peanuts, stirring until well blended.

Spoon ice cream mixture into prepared crust; sprinkle with remaining ½ cup chopped peanuts. Freeze until firm. Let pie stand at room temperature 5 minutes before serving. Yield: one 9-inch pie.   Matthew Brown

Livre de Cuisine
Pikes Peak Region, American Culinary Federation
Colorado Springs, Colorado

Peach Melba Ice Cream Pie

1 (3½-ounce) can flaked
　coconut
½ cup finely chopped walnuts
2 tablespoons melted butter or
　margarine
1 quart peach ice cream,
　softened
1 pint vanilla ice cream,
　softened

1 (16-ounce) package frozen
　unsweetened raspberries,
　thawed
½ cup sugar
1 tablespoon cornstarch
2 cups sliced fresh peaches
2 tablespoons sugar

Combine coconut, walnuts, and butter, stirring well. Firmly press coconut mixture in bottom and up the sides of a 9-inch pieplate. Bake at 325° for 10 to 15 minutes or until golden. Let cool completely.

Spoon softened peach ice cream into prepared crust, spreading ice cream to edge. Freeze until firm. Spoon softened vanilla ice cream over frozen peach ice cream layer, spreading ice cream to edge. Freeze until firm.

Drain raspberries, reserving juice. Set raspberries aside. Combine juice, ½ cup sugar, and cornstarch in a small saucepan; cook over medium heat, stirring constantly, until mixture comes to a boil. Boil 1 minute, stirring constantly. Gently fold in reserved raspberries. Set aside, and let cool completely.

Combine sliced peaches and 2 tablespoons sugar in a small bowl; stir well.

To serve, let pie stand at room temperature 5 minutes. Arrange sweetened peach slices over pie. Serve with reserved raspberry sauce. Yield: one 9-inch pie.　　　　　　　　　　Silvia Cantwell

For Crying Out Loud . . . Let's Eat!
The Service League of Hammond, Indiana

Chocolate Turtle Tart

2¼ cups pecans
¾ cup firmly packed brown
   sugar
3 tablespoons unsalted butter,
   softened

1 cup whipping cream
¼ cup unsalted butter
1 (8-ounce) package semisweet
   chocolate, chopped
Topping (recipe follows)

Position knife blade in food processor bowl; add pecans, and process until finely ground. Add sugar and 3 tablespoons butter; pulse 3 to 4 times or until blended. Reserve ¼ cup pecan mixture to sprinkle over tart. Firmly press remaining pecan mixture in bottom and up the sides of an 11-inch tart pan with removable sides. Bake at 350° for 12 minutes. Let cool completely in pan on a wire rack.

Combine whipping cream and ¼ cup butter in a small saucepan; bring just to a boil over medium-low heat, stirring until butter melts. Place chopped chocolate in a medium bowl; pour hot cream mixture over chocolate. Cover and let stand 5 minutes; stir until smooth. Let cool to room temperature. Pour chocolate mixture into prepared crust; cover and chill until firm.

Pour topping over chocolate layer; cover and chill until firm. Sprinkle reserved ¼ cup pecan mixture in a circle pattern over tart. Yield: one 11-inch tart.

Topping

¼ cup unsalted butter
¼ cup plus 2 tablespoons
   firmly packed brown sugar
3 tablespoons sugar

½ cup whipping cream
½ teaspoon vanilla extract
1 cup coarsely chopped
   pecans, toasted

Melt butter in a saucepan; add sugars, stirring well. Cook over medium heat 5 minutes, stirring occasionally. Gradually whisk in whipping cream and vanilla; reduce heat to low; cook, stirring constantly, until mixture is smooth. Remove from heat, and stir in pecans. Let cool completely. Yield: 1½ cups.   Ann-Marie Bucceri

Sharing Our Best from Friends of Franklin County
Big Brothers/Big Sisters of Franklin County
Greenfield, Massachusetts

Gingersnap Pear Tart

1½ cups gingersnap crumbs
½ cup finely chopped walnuts
⅓ cup butter or margarine, melted
2 (8-ounce) packages cream cheese, softened
¼ cup sugar

2 tablespoons pear nectar
½ teaspoon vanilla extract
1 (16-ounce) can pear halves in heavy syrup, drained
¼ cup firmly packed brown sugar
¼ teaspoon ground ginger

Combine crumbs, walnuts, and butter, stirring well. Firmly press crumb mixture evenly in bottom and up the sides of a 9-inch pieplate. Bake at 350° for 5 minutes. Let cool.

Beat cream cheese at medium speed of an electric mixer until light and fluffy; gradually add ¼ cup sugar, mixing well. Stir in nectar and vanilla. Spread mixture evenly over prepared crust. Cut pears lengthwise into thin slices. Arrange pear slices on cream cheese mixture. Cover and chill at least 8 hours.

Combine ¼ cup brown sugar and ginger in a small saucepan; cook over medium heat, stirring constantly, until sugar melts. Drizzle mixture over tart. Serve immediately. Yield: one 9-inch tart.

Watch Hill Cooks
The Watch Hill Improvement Society
Watch Hill, Rhode Island

Almond-Apricot Tartlets

1 cup all-purpose flour
3 tablespoons powdered sugar
⅓ cup butter
1 egg yolk, lightly beaten
1 tablespoon cold water

½ cup almond paste
¼ cup butter, softened
1 egg white
¼ teaspoon almond extract
⅓ cup apricot preserves

Combine flour and sugar; cut in ⅓ cup butter with a pastry blender until mixture resembles coarse meal. Combine egg yolk and water; sprinkle over surface of flour mixture, and stir with a fork until dry ingredients are moistened. Shape pastry into 24 balls. Place in ungreased miniature (1¾-inch) muffin pans, shaping each into a shell; chill thoroughly.

Combine almond paste and ¼ cup butter; beat at medium speed of an electric mixer until blended. Add egg white and almond extract; beat well. Spoon mixture into prepared shells, filling three-fourths full. Bake at 350° for 25 minutes or until golden. Spread preserves over tartlets. Let cool in pans on wire racks. Loosen edges from pans using a sharp knife. Yield: 2 dozen.

St. Joseph's Regional School Cookbook
St. Joseph's Regional School
Sea Isle City, New Jersey

Brownie Tassies

¾ cup all-purpose flour	2 tablespoons butter or
⅓ cup sugar	margarine
¼ cup cocoa	⅓ cup sugar
⅛ teaspoon salt	1 egg, beaten
⅓ cup butter or margarine	1 teaspoon vanilla extract
2 to 3 tablespoons cold water	½ teaspoon ground cinnamon
½ cup semisweet chocolate	Additional semisweet chocolate
morsels	morsels

Combine first 4 ingredients in a small bowl; stir well. Cut in ⅓ cup butter with a pastry blender until mixture resembles coarse meal. Sprinkle cold water (1 tablespoon at a time) evenly over surface; stir with a fork just until dry ingredients are moistened. Shape pastry into 24 balls. Place in ungreased miniature (1¾-inch) muffin pans, shaping each into a shell; set aside.

Combine ½ cup morsels and 2 tablespoons butter in top of a double boiler; bring water to a boil. Reduce heat to low; cook until chocolate melts, stirring constantly. Remove from heat; stir in ⅓ cup sugar, egg, vanilla, and cinnamon. Spoon mixture into shells. Bake at 325° for 25 minutes or until set. Top each with a morsel; bake an additional minute. Let cool in pans on wire racks. Loosen edges from pans using a sharp knife. Yield: 2 dozen.   Vickie Morrow

Wish Upon a Star
Mt. Carmel Apparel Employees
Mt. Carmel, Illinois

Michigan Apple Dumplings

3 cups all-purpose flour
2 teaspoons baking powder
1 teaspoon salt
1 cup shortening
¾ cup milk
12 small to medium-size
  cooking apples

2 teaspoons brown sugar
1 teaspoon ground cinnamon,
  divided
½ cup butter or margarine,
  divided
2 cups water
1½ cups sugar

Combine first 3 ingredients; cut in shortening with pastry blender until mixture resembles coarse meal. Gradually add milk, stirring with a fork until dry ingredients are moistened. Roll half of pastry to ¼-inch thickness on a lightly floured surface, shaping pastry into a 21- x 14-inch rectangle. Cut pastry with a fluted pastry wheel into 6 (7-inch) squares. Repeat procedure with remaining half of pastry.

Peel and core apples. Place one apple upright on each pastry square. Combine brown sugar and ½ teaspoon cinnamon. Fill center of each apple evenly with brown sugar mixture; dot apples evenly with ¼ cup butter. Moisten edges of each pastry square with water; bring corners to center, pinching edges to seal. Place in a lightly greased 13- x 9- x 2-inch baking pan.

Combine remaining ½ teaspoon cinnamon, remaining ¼ cup butter, water, and 1½ cups sugar in a medium saucepan. Bring to a boil; reduce heat, and simmer 4 minutes, stirring occasionally, until sugar dissolves and butter melts. Pour hot syrup over dumplings. Bake at 400° for 20 minutes; baste dumplings with syrup. Bake an additional 15 minutes or until lightly browned. Serve warm. Yield: 12 servings.

Thyme & Monet
The Krasl Art Center
St. Joseph, Michigan

Blueberry Bottom Cobbler

2 cups fresh or frozen blueberries, thawed and drained	1 teaspoon baking powder
	¼ teaspoon salt
	½ cup milk
2 tablespoons fresh lemon juice	1 cup sugar
	1 tablespoon cornstarch
3 tablespoons shortening	¼ teaspoon salt
¾ cup sugar	1 cup boiling water
1 cup all-purpose flour	Vanilla ice cream

Place blueberries in bottom of a greased 9-inch square baking pan; sprinkle with lemon juice, and set aside.

Cream shortening; gradually add ¾ cup sugar, beating well at medium speed of an electric mixer. Combine flour, baking powder, and ¼ teaspoon salt; stir well. Add to creamed mixture alternately with milk, beginning and ending with flour mixture. Stir after each addition; spread batter over blueberries.

Combine 1 cup sugar, cornstarch, and ¼ teaspoon salt; stir well, and sprinkle over batter. Pour boiling water over cobbler (do not stir). Bake at 375° for 40 to 50 minutes or until golden. Serve warm with ice cream. Yield: 9 servings.

Hearts & Flour
The Women's Club of Pittsford, New York

In early days, western New York led the nation in the production of wheat, earning the region its nickname "the breadbasket of the nation." Each day, 550 barrels of flour were milled in the town of Pittsford. The Women's Club of Pittsford was founded in 1984 to pursue civic, educational, and charitable goals. Proceeds from the sale of the cookbook, Hearts & Flour, *are returned to the community through the club's philanthropic programs.*

Cherry-Cinnamon Cobbler

1 (16½-ounce) can tart sweet
   cherries in heavy syrup,
   undrained
½ cup sugar
½ cup cold water
2 to 4 tablespoons red
   cinnamon candies
2 tablespoons cornstarch
1½ cups all-purpose flour
2 teaspoons baking powder
½ teaspoon salt
¼ cup plus 2 tablespoons
   firmly packed brown sugar,
   divided

¼ cup shortening
⅓ cup finely chopped pecans
1 egg, beaten
2 tablespoons milk
1 tablespoon butter or
   margarine, melted
¼ teaspoon ground cinnamon
½ cup sifted powdered sugar
1 tablespoon lemon juice

Drain cherries, reserving syrup. Set cherries aside. Combine syrup, ½ cup sugar, water, candies, and cornstarch in a medium saucepan; stir well. Cook over medium heat until mixture is thickened, stirring frequently. Stir in reserved cherries. Pour cherry mixture into an 8-inch square baking dish; set aside.

Combine flour, baking powder, salt, and 3 tablespoons brown sugar in a medium bowl; stir well. Cut in shortening with a pastry blender until mixture resembles coarse meal. Stir in pecans. Combine egg and milk; sprinkle evenly over flour mixture. Stir with a fork just until dry ingredients are moistened.

Roll pastry to a 14- x 12-inch rectangle; brush with melted butter. Combine remaining 3 tablespoons brown sugar and cinnamon; sprinkle over pastry. Roll up jellyroll fashion, starting at short side. Cut into ¾-inch-thick slices. Place slices on top of reserved cherry mixture. Bake at 400° for 25 to 30 minutes or until lightly browned.

Combine powdered sugar and lemon juice; stir well. Drizzle over cobbler. Serve warm. Yield: 6 servings.   Helen Jamison

Favorite Recipes of Edmonds
Edmonds United Methodist Women
Edmonds, Washington

Peach-a-Berry Cobbler

3 cups sliced fresh peaches
¼ cup sugar
½ cup cold water
¼ cup firmly packed brown
   sugar
1 tablespoon cornstarch
1 cup fresh blueberries
1 tablespoon butter or
   margarine
1 tablespoon lemon juice

1 cup all-purpose flour
1½ teaspoons baking powder
½ teaspoon salt
½ cup sugar
½ cup milk
¼ cup butter or margarine,
   softened
2 tablespoons sugar
¼ teaspoon ground nutmeg
Whipping cream

Combine peaches and ¼ cup sugar in a medium bowl; stir well, and set aside.

Combine water, ¼ cup brown sugar, and cornstarch in a large saucepan; stir well. Stir in peach mixture and blueberries; cook over medium heat until mixture is thickened and bubbly, stirring constantly. Remove from heat; add 1 tablespoon butter and lemon juice, stirring until butter melts. Spoon fruit mixture into a greased 2-quart baking dish. Set aside.

Combine flour, baking powder, salt, and ½ cup sugar in a medium mixing bowl; stir well. Add milk and ¼ cup butter; beat at medium speed of an electric mixer until smooth.

Pour batter over reserved fruit mixture. Combine 2 tablespoons sugar and nutmeg; sprinkle mixture evenly over batter. Bake at 350° for 50 minutes or until lightly browned. Serve cobbler warm with whipping cream. Yield: 6 servings.   Jane Stockstill

Methodist Blessings
The United Methodist Women, First United Methodist Church
New Iberia, Louisiana

Baklava

1 (17¼-ounce) package
  commercial frozen phyllo
  pastry, thawed
1 cup butter or margarine,
  melted

1 (16-ounce) package walnuts,
  finely chopped
½ cup sugar
1 teaspoon ground cinnamon
1 (12-ounce) jar honey

Butter a 13- x 9- x 2-inch baking dish. Cut phyllo in half crosswise, and cut each half to fit pan. Discard trimmings. Work with one sheet of phyllo at a time, keeping remaining sheets covered with a slightly damp towel. Layer 6 sheets of phyllo in dish, brushing each sheet with melted butter.

Combine walnuts, sugar, and cinnamon; stir well. Sprinkle 1 cup walnut mixture over phyllo in dish. Top with 6 sheets of phyllo, brushing each sheet with melted butter. Repeat procedure 3 times with remaining walnut mixture, phyllo, and butter, ending with buttered phyllo. Cut into diamond shapes using a sharp knife, cutting to but not through bottom layer of pastry. Bake at 300° for 1 hour and 20 minutes or until browned. Let cool completely in dish on a wire rack.

Heat honey in a small saucepan over medium heat until hot (do not boil). Drizzle hot honey over baklava. Cover baklava, and let cool at least 1 hour. To serve, cut through bottom layer of pastry. Yield: about 3 dozen.   Marie Korsmo

Scotties Present Recipes
Grand Forks Curling Club
Grand Forks, North Dakota

Poultry

The Franciscan Mission of San Carlos Borromeo, located near Carmel, is one of many missions established along the California coast after 1769 by Father Junípero Serra. The Spanish colonial government established missions, military garrisons, and ranches in an effort to maintain control of the territory.

Chicken Rockefeller

1 (7¾-ounce) can chopped
  spinach, undrained
1 cup small-curd cottage cheese
1 egg, beaten
¼ cup grated Parmesan cheese
½ teaspoon garlic salt
Pinch of pepper
1 (2½-pound) broiler-fryer

2 tablespoons olive oil
⅛ teaspoon dried whole
  oregano, crushed
⅛ teaspoon dried whole
  rosemary, crushed
⅛ teaspoon dried whole
  thyme, crushed

Drain spinach; press between paper towels to remove excess moisture. Combine spinach and next 5 ingredients; stir well, and set aside.

Remove giblets and neck from chicken; reserve for other uses. Place chicken on a work surface, breast side up. Cut completely through breast bone. Turn chicken over; flatten chicken back, breaking breast and rib bones.

Turn chicken breast side up. Starting at neck cavity, loosen skin from breast and drumsticks by inserting one hand, palm side down. Gently push hand beneath the skin against the meat to loosen the skin. Spoon reserved spinach mixture into pockets beneath skin.

Place chicken, breast side up, in a roasting pan. Combine olive oil, oregano, rosemary, and thyme; brush over chicken. Bake, uncovered, at 375° for 1 hour or until chicken is done. Yield: 4 servings.

Company's Coming
The Junior League of Kansas City, Missouri

Pucker-Up Chicken

1 (3½-pound) broiler-fryer,
  cut up
½ cup vegetable oil
2 tablespoons grated lemon
  rind
½ cup lemon juice
1 tablespoon soy sauce
1 clove garlic, minced

½ teaspoon salt
½ teaspoon pepper
½ cup all-purpose flour
2 teaspoons paprika
1 teaspoon salt
¼ teaspoon pepper
½ cup butter or margarine,
  melted

Place chicken in a large zip-top heavy-duty plastic bag. Combine oil and next 6 ingredients; pour marinade mixture over chicken. Seal bag securely. Marinate chicken in refrigerator at least 1 hour, and place in a large bowl, turning occasionally.

Combine flour, paprika, 1 teaspoon salt, and ¼ teaspoon pepper; stir well. Remove chicken from marinade; discard marinade. Dredge chicken in flour mixture, and place in a lightly greased 13- x 9- x 2-inch baking pan. Brush butter over chicken. Bake, uncovered, at 400° for 30 minutes. Turn chicken, and baste with pan drippings. Bake an additional 30 minutes. Yield: 4 servings.

Watch Hill Cooks
The Watch Hill Improvement Society
Watch Hill, Rhode Island

★ ★ ★

The Watch Hill Improvement Society was the inspiration of a group of people with a love of Watch Hill, Rhode Island, and an interest in its future. Proceeds from the sale of Watch Hill Cooks *will support the preservation of the historic flying horse carousel, the Watch Hill Lighthouse Keepers Association, and an annual art and photography show.*

Chicken and Artichoke Cacciatore

2 (6-ounce) jars marinated
    artichoke hearts, undrained
1 tablespoon butter
4 pounds assorted chicken
    pieces (breasts, drumsticks,
    and thighs)
1 cup all-purpose flour
1 large onion, chopped
½ pound sliced fresh
    mushrooms
3 cloves garlic, crushed

½ teaspoon dried whole
    oregano
½ teaspoon dried whole basil
½ teaspoon dried whole
    rosemary
1 (28-ounce) can whole
    tomatoes, undrained
Salt and pepper to taste
½ cup Madeira
1 (16-ounce) package linguine

Drain artichoke hearts, reserving marinade. Set artichokes aside. Place marinade and butter in a large skillet; cook over low heat 10 minutes.

Dredge chicken in flour. Brown chicken in butter mixture over medium-high heat. Transfer chicken to a 13- x 9- x 2-inch baking dish, reserving butter mixture in skillet.

Sauté onion next 5 ingredients in reserved butter mixture in large skillet until vegetables are tender. Stir in reserved artichokes, tomatoes, and salt and pepper to taste. Pour tomato mixture over chicken. Cover and bake at 350° for 50 minutes. Remove cover, and pour Madeira over chicken. Cover and bake an additional 10 minutes.

Cook linguine according to package directions; drain well. Serve cacciatore over linguine. Yield: 8 servings.   Vince Kenneally

Our Favorite Recipes
St. Anne's Roman Catholic Church
Rock Hill, South Carolina

Chicken Breasts with Toasted Mustard Seed Sauce

6 whole chicken breasts, boned	2 cups whipping cream
¾ teaspoon salt, divided	¼ cup thinly sliced green
1 teaspoon freshly ground	onions
pepper, divided	3 tablespoons Dijon mustard
1½ tablespoons mustard seeds	2 teaspoons fresh lemon juice

Place chicken breasts, skin side up, on a lightly greased rack in a broiler pan. Sprinkle chicken evenly with ½ teaspoon salt and ½ teaspoon pepper. Bake at 500° for 15 minutes; turn oven to broil, and broil chicken 6 inches from heat 4 to 5 minutes or until browned. Transfer chicken to a large serving platter. Set aside, and keep warm.

Place mustard seeds in a small skillet; cook over medium-high heat 5 minutes or until mustard seeds begin to pop and are lightly browned. Remove skillet from heat. Let mustard cool completely in skillet.

Place whipping cream in a medium saucepan. Bring just to a boil; reduce heat, and simmer 15 to 20 minutes or until reduced to 1½ cups, stirring occasionally.

Stir in reserved mustard seeds, remaining ¼ teaspoon salt, remaining ½ teaspoon pepper, green onions, Dijon mustard, and lemon juice; cook until mixture is thoroughly heated. Pour sauce over reserved chicken. Serve immediately. Yield: 6 servings.

Marblehead Cooks
Tower School Associates
Marblehead, Massachusetts

Chicken Breasts with Asparagus and Artichokes

6 whole chicken breasts, boned
6 large or 12 small fresh
    asparagus spears
6 (1½-ounce) slices mozzarella
    cheese, cut in half and
    divided
6 large fresh mushrooms,
    sliced
1 (14-ounce) can artichoke
    hearts, drained and chopped

1 tablespoon diced pimiento,
    divided
½ teaspoon salt
¼ teaspoon pepper
1 cup all-purpose flour
2 eggs, beaten
1 cup fine, dry breadcrumbs
3 tablespoons butter or
    margarine
3 tablespoons vegetable oil

Place chicken breasts between 2 sheets of wax paper. Flatten to ¼-inch thickness, using a meat mallet or rolling pin. Set aside.

Snap off tough ends of asparagus. Remove scales from stalks with a knife or vegetable peeler, if desired.

Arrange 1 large or 2 small asparagus spears, one cheese slice, and one sliced mushroom on half of each chicken breast. Top each chicken breast evenly with chopped artichoke heart and pimiento. Sprinkle evenly with salt and pepper. Fold remaining half of each chicken breast over vegetable mixture; secure with wooden picks. Dredge chicken in flour; dip in beaten egg, and coat with breadcrumbs.

Combine butter and oil in a large skillet; cook over medium heat until butter melts. Add chicken, and cook 7 to 10 minutes on each side or until browned. Remove chicken from skillet; drain on paper towels.

Place chicken on a baking sheet. Top each with 1 remaining cheese slice. Bake at 350° for 15 minutes or until cheese melts and chicken is done. Yield: 6 servings.   Maria Urbinati

La Cucina Sammarinese
The San Marino Ladies Auxiliary
Troy, Michigan

Lemon-Honey Chicken

½ cup all-purpose flour
1 teaspoon salt
¼ teaspoon pepper
6 chicken breast halves
½ cup butter or margarine,
  melted and divided

¼ cup honey
¼ cup lemon juice
1 tablespoon soy sauce

Combine flour, salt, and pepper; stir well. Dredge chicken in flour mixture. Place chicken breasts, skin side up, in a 13- x 9- x 2-inch baking dish. Drizzle ¼ cup melted butter over chicken. Bake, uncovered, at 350° for 30 minutes.

Combine remaining ¼ cup melted butter, honey, lemon juice, and soy sauce in a small saucepan; cook over medium heat 3 minutes or until mixture is thoroughly heated. Pour sauce over chicken. Bake, uncovered, an additional 20 to 30 minutes or until chicken is done, basting frequently with honey mixture. Yield: 6 servings.   Judy Smith

25 Years of Cooking at Green Valley Baptist Church
Green Valley Baptist Church
Birmingham, Alabama

Chicken Piccata

½ cup all-purpose flour
1 teaspoon salt
½ teaspoon pepper
8 chicken breast halves, boned
2 tablespoons butter or
  margarine
½ cup chopped onion

1 clove garlic, minced
2 tablespoons vegetable oil
1 cup sliced fresh mushrooms
¼ cup lemon juice
¼ cup dry sherry
2 teaspoons capers

Combine flour, salt, and pepper; stir well. Dredge chicken in flour mixture. Melt butter in a large skillet over medium-high heat. Add chicken, and cook 3 minutes on each side or until lightly browned. Remove chicken from skillet. Set chicken aside, and keep warm.

Sauté onion and garlic in oil in skillet until tender. Add mushrooms, and sauté 2 minutes or until tender. Add reserved chicken, lemon juice, sherry, and capers; bring to a boil. Reduce heat, and simmer 1 to 2 minutes or until chicken is done. Yield: 8 servings.   Cissy McCord, Victoria Munn, and Gail Shannon

cook and love it more
Lovett Parent Association, The Lovett School
Atlanta, Georgia

Grilled Chili Chicken

1 tablespoon chili powder
3 tablespoons balsamic vinegar, divided
3½ tablespoons extra virgin olive oil, divided
6 large chicken breast halves (about 2½ pounds), skinned and boned
6 large sweet red peppers, cut in half
1 medium onion, thinly sliced
1 jalapeño pepper, seeded and minced
1 clove garlic, minced
2 tablespoons chopped fresh cilantro

Combine chili powder, 2 tablespoons vinegar, and 2 tablespoons oil; stir well. Brush chili mixture on both sides of chicken breasts. Place in shallow dish; cover and marinate in refrigerator 1 hour.

Grill chicken over hot coals (400° to 500°) 5 to 6 minutes on each side or until chicken is done. Arrange chicken on a serving platter; set aside, and keep warm.

Brush skin of sweet red pepper halves with 1 tablespoon oil. Grill peppers, cut side up, over medium coals (300° to 350°) 6 to 8 minutes or until charred. Cut into thin strips; set aside.

Sauté onion, jalapeño pepper, and garlic in remaining 1½ teaspoons oil in a large skillet until onion is tender. Add reserved sweet red pepper strips; stir well. Add cilantro and remaining 1 tablespoon vinegar; stir well. Remove from heat. Spoon pepper mixture over chicken. Yield: 6 servings.   Joan M. Giampietro

Seasoned with Love
Eastman House, Inc.
Cranston, Rhode Island

Rollatini de Pollo

(Tuscan Chicken Rolls with Pork Stuffing)

6 chicken breast halves,
   skinned and boned
½ pound ground pork
1 small onion, finely chopped
1 clove garlic, minced
½ cup soft breadcrumbs
1 egg, beaten
½ teaspoon salt
¼ teaspoon pepper
¼ teaspoon ground savory

2 tablespoons butter or
   margarine, melted
½ teaspoon salt
½ cup Chablis or other dry
   white wine
2 teaspoons cornstarch
½ cup cold water
½ teaspoon chicken-flavored
   bouillon granules
Chopped fresh parsley

Place chicken between 2 sheets of wax paper. Flatten to ¼-inch thickness, using a meat mallet or rolling pin. Set aside.

Combine ground pork, onion, and garlic in a large skillet. Cook over medium heat until meat is browned, stirring to crumble meat; drain. Combine pork mixture, breadcrumbs, and next 4 ingredients; stir well.

Spoon about ⅓ cup pork mixture over center of each chicken breast half. Roll up chicken jellyroll fashion, starting with short end; secure with wooden picks. Place chicken in a lightly greased 11- x 7- x 1½-inch baking dish; brush chicken with melted butter. Sprinkle ½ teaspoon salt evenly over chicken; pour wine over chicken. Bake, uncovered, at 400° for 40 minutes or until chicken is done.

Transfer chicken to a serving platter, reserving liquid. Set aside, and keep warm. Combine cornstarch and water in a small saucepan; stir in reserved liquid and bouillon. Bring to a boil over medium heat; boil 1 minute, stirring constantly.

Pour sauce over chicken, and sprinkle with chopped parsley. Serve immediately. Yield: 6 servings.   Virginia Tolin

Not So Secret Recipes
4450th Tactical Group, Nellis Air Force Base
Las Vegas, Nevada

The Bride's Chicken

8 chicken breast halves, skinned and boned
½ teaspoon salt
⅛ teaspoon pepper
½ cup butter or margarine, divided
½ pound fresh mushrooms, sliced
1 (14-ounce) can artichoke hearts, drained and halved

1 teaspoon dried whole tarragon, crushed
3 tablespoons all-purpose flour
1½ cups canned diluted chicken broth
⅓ cup dry sherry
1 tablespoon chopped fresh parsley

Sprinkle chicken with salt and pepper. Melt ¼ cup butter in a large skillet over medium-high heat. Add chicken, and cook 4 minutes on each side or until browned. Transfer chicken to a 13- x 9- x 2-inch baking dish, reserving drippings in skillet.

Add remaining ¼ cup butter to skillet. Cook over medium-high heat until butter melts; add mushrooms, and sauté until tender. Remove mushrooms from skillet, reserving drippings in skillet. Place mushrooms and artichoke hearts on top of chicken. Sprinkle with tarragon.

Add flour to drippings in skillet, stirring until smooth. Cook over low heat 1 minute, stirring constantly. Gradually add broth; cook over medium heat, stirring constantly, until mixture is thickened and bubbly. Remove from heat, and stir in sherry.

Pour sauce over chicken. Sprinkle with parsley. Bake, uncovered, at 375° for 45 minutes or until chicken is done. Yield: 8 servings.

Cardinal Cuisine
The Mount Vernon Hospital Auxiliary
Alexandria, Virginia

Chicken Sauté with Oranges and Avocados

6 chicken breast halves,
  skinned and boned
½ cup all-purpose flour
3 tablespoons butter or
  margarine
2 tablespoons vegetable oil
1 teaspoon grated orange rind
¾ cup orange juice
⅓ cup Chablis or other dry
  white wine

⅓ cup sliced fresh mushrooms
2 tablespoons minced fresh
  parsley
⅛ teaspoon dried whole
  rosemary, crushed
3 tablespoons raspberry
  vinegar
2 oranges, peeled and sliced
2 ripe avocados, peeled and
  sliced

Place chicken between 2 sheets of wax paper. Flatten chicken to ¼-inch thickness, using a meat mallet or rolling pin. Dredge chicken in flour.

Combine butter and oil in a large skillet; cook over medium heat until hot. Add chicken, and sauté 3 minutes on each side or until lightly browned. Add orange rind and next 5 ingredients. Bring to a boil; reduce heat, and simmer 5 minutes.

Transfer chicken to a serving platter, reserving liquid in skillet. Set aside, and keep warm.

Add vinegar to skillet; cook, stirring occasionally, until sauce is reduced to ½ cup. Pour sauce over chicken. Top with orange and avocado slices. Yield: 6 servings.   Helen Stoll

Old Capital Cookbook
Monterey History and Art Association
Monterey, California

Chicken-Avocado Melt

4 chicken breast halves,
  skinned and boned
2 tablespoons cornstarch
1 teaspoon ground cumin
1 teaspoon garlic salt
1 egg, lightly beaten
1 tablespoon water
⅓ cup cornmeal
3 tablespoons vegetable oil
1 ripe avocado, peeled and
  sliced

1½ cups (6 ounces) shredded
  Monterey Jack cheese
½ cup sour cream
¼ cup sliced green onions
¼ cup chopped sweet red
  pepper
Garnishes: cherry tomatoes
  and fresh parsley sprigs

Place chicken between 2 sheets of wax paper. Flatten to ¼-inch thickness, using a meat mallet or rolling pin.

Combine cornstarch, cumin, and garlic salt in a small bowl, stirring well.

Combine beaten egg and water in a small bowl, stirring well. Dredge chicken in cornstarch mixture; dip in egg mixture, and dredge in cornmeal.

Sauté chicken in oil in a large skillet 2 minutes on each side or until lightly browned. Transfer chicken to a 13- x 9- x 2-inch baking pan.

Arrange avocado slices over chicken, and sprinkle evenly with shredded cheese. Bake, uncovered, at 350° for 15 minutes or until cheese melts and chicken is done. Top with sour cream, green onions, and sweet red pepper. Garnish, if desired. Yield: 4 servings. Serve immediately.
    Marge Fortier

The Mark Twain Library Cookbook, Volume III
The Mark Twain Library Association
Redding, Connecticut

Sesame Chicken Kabobs

¼ cup soy sauce
¼ cup commercial Russian
   dressing
2 tablespoons lemon juice
1 tablespoon sesame seeds
¼ teaspoon garlic powder
¼ teaspoon ground ginger
6 chicken breast halves,
   skinned, boned, and cut into
   1-inch pieces

2 medium onions
2 cups cherry tomatoes
3 small zucchini, cut into
   ¾-inch pieces
1 large green pepper, cut into
   1-inch pieces

Combine soy sauce, dressing, lemon juice, sesame seeds, garlic powder, and ginger in a small bowl; stir well. Place chicken in a shallow dish. Pour marinade mixture over chicken; cover and marinate in refrigerator 2 hours, turning occasionally.

Remove chicken from marinade, reserving marinade. Place marinade in a small saucepan. Bring to a boil; reduce heat, and simmer 5 minutes. Set aside.

Cut each onion into 8 wedges. Alternate chicken and vegetables on six 15-inch metal skewers. Grill kabobs over medium-hot (350° to 400°) coals 16 to 17 minutes or until chicken is done and vegetables are crisp-tender, turning and basting frequently with reserved marinade. Yield: 6 servings.   Nancy Williford

Not Just Possum
Boy Scout Troop 63
Columbus, Mississippi

Indonesian Peanut Chicken

½ cup cream of coconut
3 tablespoons lime juice
1 tablespoon vegetable oil
2 teaspoons soy sauce
2 cloves garlic, crushed

⅛ teaspoon ground red pepper
4 chicken breast halves,
  skinned and boned
4 (10-inch) wooden skewers
Peanut Sauce

Combine cream of coconut, lime juice, vegetable oil, soy sauce, garlic, and red pepper; stir well. Set marinade mixture aside. Cut each chicken breast half into 4 pieces. Add chicken to marinade; toss gently. Cover and marinate in refrigerator at least 4 hours.

Soak wooden skewers in water for at least 30 minutes. Remove chicken from marinade; discard marinade. Thread chicken onto skewers. Grill over medium-hot coals (350° to 400°) 2 to 3 minutes on each side or until chicken is done. Serve with Peanut Sauce. Yield: 4 servings.

Peanut Sauce

⅓ cup chunky peanut butter
⅓ cup water
2 tablespoons soy sauce

1 tablespoon cider vinegar
2 cloves garlic, crushed
⅛ teaspoon ground red pepper

Combine all ingredients, stirring well. Yield: ¾ cup.

Savor the Flavor of Oregon
The Junior League of Eugene, Oregon

The Junior League of Eugene offers Savor the Flavor of
Oregon *to raise funds to support new projects established for the
betterment of the middle school-aged child. Past community efforts
include refurbishing a classroom, landscaping a park,
conducting an anti-drug campaign, and supporting a local
shelter.*

Almond Chicken

1½ teaspoons soy sauce
1 teaspoon chopped fresh
  gingerroot
½ teaspoon salt
¼ teaspoon sugar
¼ teaspoon dry sherry
2⅓ cups diced uncooked
  chicken breast (about
  1½ pounds)
2½ tablespoons cornstarch
2 tablespoons vegetable oil,
  divided
1 cup chopped celery

½ pound fresh snow pea pods
1 (8-ounce) can bamboo
  shoots, drained and chopped
1 (8-ounce) can water
  chestnuts, drained and
  chopped
1 (4-ounce) can sliced
  mushrooms, drained
½ cup slivered almonds,
  toasted
2 green onions, cut into
  1¼-inch pieces

Combine first 5 ingredients in a large bowl; add chicken, and stir well. Let stand 10 minutes. Sprinkle cornstarch over chicken mixture, stirring well. Set aside.

Pour 1 tablespoon oil around top of preheated wok, coating sides; heat at medium-high (325°) for 1 minute. Add celery, and stir-fry 1 to 2 minutes. Add snow peas, and stir-fry 1 to 2 minutes. Add bamboo shoots, water chestnuts, and mushrooms, and stir-fry 1 to 2 minutes. Remove vegetable mixture; set aside, and keep warm.

Pour remaining 1 tablespoon oil around top of wok, coating sides; heat at medium-high for 1 minute. Add reserved chicken mixture; stir-fry 3 to 4 minutes. Add reserved vegetable mixture, almonds, and green onions, and stir-fry 1 to 2 minutes or until thoroughly heated. Yield: 6 servings.   June Ong

Tea and Chopsticks
The Desert Jade Woman's Club
Phoenix, Arizona

Mediterranean Tart

2 tomatoes, peeled, seeded, and chopped
1 medium onion, chopped
¾ cup plus 3 tablespoons unsalted butter, melted and divided
1 cup sliced fresh mushrooms
½ teaspoon dried whole thyme
2 tablespoons all-purpose flour
1 cup canned diluted chicken broth

1½ cups chopped cooked chicken breast
1½ cups chopped cooked ham
½ teaspoon anchovy paste
⅛ teaspoon salt
¼ teaspoon pepper
16 sheets commercial frozen phyllo pastry, thawed and divided
½ cup (2 ounces) shredded Cheddar cheese

Sauté tomato and onion in 3 tablespoons butter in a large skillet until vegetables are tender. Add mushrooms and thyme, and sauté 3 to 4 minutes or until mushrooms are tender. Stir in flour and broth; bring to a boil. Reduce heat, and simmer 5 minutes or until mixture is thickened, stirring constantly. Add chicken and next 4 ingredients, stirring well. Remove from heat, and set aside.

Lightly brush 1 sheet of phyllo with remaining melted butter (keep remaining phyllo sheets covered with a slightly damp towel). Fold phyllo sheet in half crosswise, and place in a 13- x 9- x 2-inch baking dish; brush phyllo with butter. Repeat procedure, using half of phyllo sheets and butter.

Spoon reserved chicken mixture over phyllo in baking dish; sprinkle with cheese. Top with remaining 8 sheets of phyllo, brushing each sheet with melted butter. Bake, uncovered, at 300° for 1 hour or until lightly browned. Yield: 8 servings.   Marty Hill

Kentucky Kitchens, Volume II
Telephone Pioneers of America, Kentucky Chapter No. 32
Louisville, Kentucky

Fettuccine Enrico Caruso

¼ cup plus 2 tablespoons olive
   oil
2 tablespoons butter
1 medium onion, minced
4 sprigs fresh rosemary
4 chicken livers, finely
   chopped
⅔ cup canned diluted chicken
   broth

2 tablespoons tomato paste
1 (28-ounce) can Italian-style
   tomatoes, drained and
   chopped
½ teaspoon salt
¼ teaspoon pepper
1 (16-ounce) package
   fettuccine
¼ cup grated Parmesan cheese

Combine olive oil and butter in a large skillet; heat over medium heat until hot. Add minced onion and rosemary, and sauté until onion is tender. Add chicken livers, and sauté until livers are browned. Stir in chicken broth and tomato paste; simmer, uncovered, 5 minutes.

Add tomatoes; cover and simmer 20 minutes. Remove cover, and simmer an additional 20 minutes, stirring occasionally. Add salt and pepper; remove and discard rosemary.

Cook fettuccine according to package directions. Drain, and place on a large serving platter. Top with sauce, and sprinkle with Parmesan cheese. Yield: 4 servings.   Nella DeVitto Neeck

The TV-10 Big Brothers/Big Sisters Cookbook
Big Brothers/Big Sisters of Greater Rochester, New York

Lemon and Herb Cornish Hens

3 (1¼- to 1½-pound) Cornish
   hens, split
½ cup fresh lemon juice
¼ cup olive oil
4 cloves garlic, minced
2 teaspoons dried whole
   thyme, crushed

2 teaspoons dried whole
   oregano, crushed
2 teaspoons dried whole
   rosemary, crushed
1 teaspoon salt

Place hens in a 13- x 9- x 2-inch baking dish. Combine lemon juice and remaining ingredients; stir well with a wire whisk. Pour marinade mixture over hens. Cover and marinate in refrigerator at least 8 hours, turning occasionally.

Drain hens, reserving marinade. Place marinade in a small saucepan. Bring to a boil; reduce heat, and simmer 5 minutes.

Grill hens over medium-hot coals (350° to 400°) 30 minutes or until done, turning and basting occasionally with marinade. Yield: 6 servings.

Celebrate
Missouri Bankers Association
Jefferson City, Missouri

Turkey Breast Chinoise

1 (4- to 6-pound) turkey breast
1 to 2 tablespoons butter or
   margarine, melted
3 cloves garlic, crushed
1 teaspoon salt
½ cup lemon juice

½ cup olive oil
¼ cup soy sauce
1 tablespoon molasses
1- to 1½-inch piece fresh
   gingerroot, peeled and sliced

Rinse turkey breast with cold water; pat dry. Combine butter, garlic, and salt; stir well. Brush butter mixture over turkey breast, and set aside.

Combine lemon juice and remaining ingredients in container of an electric blender or food processor, and process until smooth.

Place turkey in a large zip-top heavy-duty plastic bag. Pour marinade mixture over turkey. Seal bag securely. Place turkey in a large bowl; marinate in refrigerator 8 hours, turning occasionally.

Remove turkey from marinade, reserving marinade. Place marinade in a small saucepan. Bring to a boil; reduce heat, and simmer 5 minutes. Place turkey, breast side up, on a rack in a shallow roasting pan. Insert meat thermometer, making sure it does not touch bone. Bake at 350° for 2 hours or until meat thermometer registers 170°, basting occasionally with marinade. Let turkey stand 15 minutes before carving. Yield: 8 to 10 servings.

Vermont Kitchens Revisited
The Women of the Cathedral Church of St. Paul
Burlington, Vermont

Roast Turkey Breast with Apple-Onion Stuffing

1 (5-pound) turkey breast
½ lemon
½ teaspoon salt
¼ teaspoon freshly ground
  pepper

Apple-Onion Stuffing
¼ cup butter or margarine,
  melted

Rinse turkey with cold water; pat dry. Rub skin and cavity with cut side of lemon; sprinkle with salt and pepper. Lightly pack Apple-Onion Stuffing into cavity of turkey. Close cavity with skewers and truss.

Place turkey breast, skin side up, on a rack in a roasting pan; brush with butter. Insert meat thermometer, making sure it does not touch bone. Bake at 325° for 2½ to 3 hours or until meat thermometer registers 170°. Baste occasionally with any remaining butter. Let stand 15 minutes before carving. Yield: 8 servings.

Apple-Onion Stuffing

1 cup diced onion
2 tablespoons butter or
  margarine, melted
2 cups unseasoned cube or
  cornbread stuffing mix
3 tablespoons butter or
  margarine
2 Golden Delicious apples,
  unpeeled and chopped

½ cup plus 1 tablespoon apple
  cider, divided
¼ cup currants
2 tablespoons lemon juice
½ teaspoon salt
¼ teaspoon ground nutmeg
¼ teaspoon ground allspice

Sauté onion in 2 tablespoons butter over medium-high heat until tender. Combine sautéed onion and stuffing mix in a medium bowl; set aside.

Melt 3 tablespoons butter in skillet over low heat; add apple and 1 tablespoon cider. Cover and cook 5 to 7 minutes or until apple is tender, stirring occasionally. Add apple mixture to reserved stuffing mixture, tossing gently to combine. Set aside.

Combine ½ cup apple cider and currants in a saucepan. Bring to a boil; cover, reduce heat, and simmer 3 to 5 minutes or until currants plump. Add currants and liquid to stuffing mixture. Add lemon juice and remaining ingredients, tossing gently to combine. Yield: 3 cups.

Gateways
Auxiliary-Twigs . . . Friends of St. Louis Children's Hospital
St. Louis, Missouri

Turkey Enchiladas with Sour Cream

2 (4-ounce) cans chopped green chiles, drained
2 tablespoons olive oil or vegetable oil
4 small tomatoes, peeled and chopped
2 cups chopped onion
½ cup water
1 large clove garlic, minced
2 teaspoons salt, divided

½ teaspoon dried whole oregano
3 cups shredded cooked turkey
2 cups (8 ounces) shredded Cheddar or Monterey Jack cheese
1 (16-ounce) carton sour cream
⅓ cup vegetable oil
12 (6-inch) corn tortillas

Sauté green chiles in 2 tablespoons oil in a large skillet 1 minute. Add tomato, onion, water, garlic, 1 teaspoon salt, and oregano; stir well. Bring to a boil; reduce heat, and simmer, uncovered, 30 minutes. Set aside.

Combine turkey, cheese, sour cream, and remaining 1 teaspoon salt; stir well, and set aside.

Fry tortillas, one at a time, in ⅓ cup oil in a medium skillet 5 seconds on each side or just until tortillas are softened. Drain well on paper towels.

Place about ⅓ cup reserved turkey mixture on each tortilla. Roll up tortillas; place tortillas, seam side down, in a 13- x 9- x 2-inch baking pan. Spoon reserved tomato mixture over tortillas. Bake, uncovered, at 350° for 30 minutes or until thoroughly heated. Yield: 6 servings.   Rich Escobedo

The Western Gentlemen's Cookbook
The Men's Culinary Cup
Cheyenne, Wyoming

Braised Goose

1 (8- to 10-pound) dressed
   goose
1 cooking apple, peeled and
   sliced
1 medium onion, sliced
1½ cups canned diluted
   chicken broth
2 carrots, scraped and sliced
2 to 3 shallots, chopped
1 tablespoon lemon juice
1 tablespoon canned
   mushroom sauce
1 tablespoon Worcestershire
   sauce

2 whole cloves
½ teaspoon ground mace
½ teaspoon dried whole
   marjoram
½ teaspoon dried whole
   rosemary
⅛ teaspoon ground red pepper
¾ cup port or other sweet red
   wine
4 to 5 slices bacon
1 tablespoon butter or
   margarine
1 tablespoon all-purpose flour

Remove giblets and neck from goose; set aside. Rinse goose thoroughly with cold water; pat dry. Stuff cavity of goose with apple and onion; close cavity with skewers and truss.

Combine reserved giblets, neck, chicken broth, and next 10 ingredients in a large saucepan. Bring to a boil; reduce heat, and simmer, uncovered, 10 minutes. Remove from heat; stir in wine, and set aside.

Place bacon in bottom of a large roasting pan. Place goose, breast side up, on a rack in roasting pan. Insert meat thermometer in thigh, making sure it does not touch bone. Bake, uncovered, at 400° for 15 minutes. Pour reserved broth mixture into roasting pan. Cover and bake an additional 2 hours or until meat thermometer registers 185°. Transfer goose to a serving platter. Let stand 15 minutes before carving.

Strain drippings in roasting pan. Skim off and discard fat. Set drippings aside. Melt butter in a heavy saucepan over low heat; add flour, stirring until smooth. Cook 1 minute, stirring constantly. Gradually add reserved drippings; cook over medium heat, stirring constantly, until mixture is thickened and bubbly. Serve goose with gravy. Yield: 6 to 8 servings.   Wanda Gardner

For Crying Out Loud . . . Let's Eat!
The Service League of Hammond, Indiana

Salads & Salad Dressings

Fresh summer vegetables harvested from the vegetable and herb garden at the Mordecai House in Raleigh, North Carolina, are gathered on a bench in front of the old kitchen.

Harvest Apple Salad

9½ cups unpeeled, diced Red
    Delicious apples (about 8
    medium)
2 tablespoons lemon juice
1 cup chopped celery
1 cup seedless green grapes,
    halved
1 cup chopped walnuts

½ cup raisins
1 cup salad dressing
2 tablespoons sugar
1 teaspoon lemon juice
1 cup whipping cream
1 cup flaked coconut
1 cup miniature marshmallows

Combine apple and 2 tablespoons lemon juice in a large bowl; toss gently. Add celery, grapes, walnuts, and raisins; toss gently to combine. Set aside.

Combine salad dressing, sugar, and 1 teaspoon lemon juice in a medium bowl; stir well. Set aside.

Beat whipping cream at high speed of an electric mixer until soft peaks form. Gently fold whipped cream into reserved salad dressing mixture. Add whipped cream mixture to reserved apple mixture, stirring gently to combine. Stir in flaked coconut and marshmallows. Cover salad, and chill thoroughly. Yield: 22 servings. Teri Kramer

Harrington Cooks
Harrington Homemakers
Harrington, Washington

Citrus Marinated Fruit

1 cup fresh cantaloupe balls
1 cup fresh blueberries
1 cup fresh strawberries,
    halved
1 cup seedless green grapes,
    halved
¾ cup orange juice

¼ cup Chablis or other dry
    white wine or white grape
    juice
2 tablespoons lemon juice
1 tablespoon sugar
Garnish: fresh mint sprigs

Place cantaloupe balls, blueberries, strawberries, and grapes in a large bowl; toss gently to combine. Set fruit mixture aside.

Combine orange juice, wine, lemon juice, and sugar; stir well. Pour orange juice mixture over fruit mixture; toss gently. Cover and chill 2 to 3 hours, stirring occasionally. Garnish, if desired. Yield: 8 servings.   Chris Hodge

Quick 'N Natural No Salt Low Cholesterol Cooking
San Fernando Valley Association for the Retarded
Sepulveda, California

Sweet-and-Sour Fruit Slaw

1 cup cottage cheese
¼ cup milk
3 tablespoons lemon juice
2 tablespoons vegetable oil
2 tablespoons honey
1 small cabbage, coarsely
    shredded
1 medium-size Red Delicious
    apple, unpeeled and
    chopped

1 cup seedless red or green
    grapes, halved
1 (11-ounce) can mandarin
    oranges, drained
¼ cup raisins
Garnish: Red Delicious apple
    wedges

Combine cottage cheese, milk, lemon juice, vegetable oil, and honey in container of an electric blender or food processor, and process until smooth. Set cottage cheese mixture aside.

Place cabbage, chopped apple, grapes, oranges, and raisins in a large bowl; toss gently to combine. Pour reserved cottage cheese mixture over cabbage mixture; toss gently to combine. Cover and chill thoroughly. Garnish, if desired. Yield: 12 servings.   Margaret Crotty

The Cookbook
East Lake United Methodist Church
Birmingham, Alabama

Millie's Frozen Cranberry Salad

2 (3-ounce) packages cream
  cheese, softened
2 tablespoons mayonnaise
2 tablespoons sugar
1 (16-ounce) can whole-berry
  cranberry sauce

1 (8-ounce) can unsweetened
  crushed pineapple, undrained
½ cup chopped pecans
1 cup whipping cream
½ cup sifted powdered sugar
1 teaspoon vanilla extract

Combine cream cheese and mayonnaise in a medium mixing bowl; beat at medium speed of an electric mixer until smooth. Gradually add 2 tablespoons sugar, beating well. Add cranberry sauce, pineapple, and pecans, stirring well to combine. Set cream cheese mixture aside.

Beat whipping cream at high speed until foamy; gradually add ½ cup powdered sugar, beating until soft peaks form. Fold in vanilla. Gently fold whipped cream mixture into cream cheese mixture. Pour mixture into a lightly oiled 5-cup mold, and freeze until firm. Remove salad from freezer 15 to 20 minutes before serving. Yield: 10 servings.   Betty Fairbrother

North Dakota Family Favorites . . . a Collection of Recipes
The Division of Continuing Studies, North Dakota State University
Fargo, North Dakota

Jellied Ambrosia

1 envelope unflavored gelatin
½ cup cold water
¼ cup sugar
1¼ cups orange juice
1 tablespoon lemon juice
3 oranges, peeled, seeded, and
  sectioned

1½ cups sliced bananas
½ cup maraschino cherries,
  halved
¼ cup flaked coconut

Sprinkle gelatin over cold water in a small saucepan; let stand 1 minute. Add sugar to gelatin mixture, stirring with a wire whisk until blended. Cook over low heat, stirring constantly, until gelatin and sugar dissolve.

Stir in orange juice and lemon juice; cover and chill until the consistency of unbeaten egg white. Stir in orange sections and remaining ingredients.

Pour gelatin mixture into a lightly oiled 4-cup mold; chill until firm. Unmold onto a serving plate. Yield: 6 servings.

Favorite Recipes from Union Baptist Church Cooks
Union Baptist Church
Tylertown, Mississippi

Overnight Tossed Green Salad

1 head iceberg lettuce, torn
1 (10-ounce) package fresh
  spinach, torn
½ cup sliced green onions
1 (10-ounce) package frozen
  English peas, thawed and
  drained

1 pound bacon, cooked and
  crumbled
2 cups cherry tomatoes, halved
Dressing (recipe follows)

Place torn lettuce in a large serving bowl; top with torn spinach. Layer green onions, peas, bacon, and cherry tomato in order listed over spinach layer. Spread dressing over cherry tomato layer. Cover and chill 8 hours. Toss salad gently to combine just before serving. Yield: 12 servings.

Dressing

1 cup mayonnaise
1 cup sour cream
2 tablespoons lemon juice
1 teaspoon dried whole basil,
  crushed

1 teaspoon dried whole
  oregano, crushed
¼ teaspoon salt
⅛ teaspoon pepper

Place all ingredients in a small bowl; stir until well blended.
Yield: 2 cups.   Norma Rauch

Wolf Point, Montana, 75th Jubilee Cookbook
Wolf Point Chamber of Commerce & Agriculture
Wolf Point, Montana

Carrot Salad

1 (2-pound) package carrots,
  scraped and sliced
1 medium-size green pepper,
  chopped
1 (7¾-ounce) jar cocktail
  onions, drained

1 cup sugar
½ cup white vinegar
½ cup vegetable oil
1 teaspoon dry mustard

Cook carrot in boiling water 15 minutes or until crisp-tender;
drain well. Place carrot in a large bowl, and set aside.

Combine green pepper and remaining ingredients in a medium
saucepan; bring to a boil over medium heat, stirring frequently.
Pour hot vinegar mixture over carrot. Cover and marinate in
refrigerator at least 8 hours. Serve salad with a slotted spoon.
Yield: 12 servings.   Marilyn M. Blackwelder

Cooking with Vinson Memorial Christian Church
Vinson Memorial Christian Church
Huntington, West Virginia

Gorgonzola-Tomato Salad

4 ounces Gorgonzola cheese
¼ cup minced fresh parsley
3 tablespoons minced shallot
2 tablespoons minced fresh basil
6 medium tomatoes, thinly sliced

⅓ cup olive oil
2 tablespoons fresh lemon juice
2 teaspoons Dijon mustard
Salt and freshly ground pepper to taste

Freeze cheese 30 minutes or until firm. Grate cheese into a small bowl; add parsley, shallot, and basil, stirring gently to combine. Arrange tomato slices on a large serving platter. Sprinkle cheese mixture over tomato slices.

Combine olive oil, lemon juice, mustard, and salt and pepper to taste, beating well with a wire whisk. Drizzle dressing mixture over salad. Yield: 6 servings.

More Than a Tea Party
The Junior League of Boston, Massachusetts

Vegetable Strata

4 to 5 medium potatoes
½ cup red wine vinegar
¼ cup vegetable oil
1 clove garlic, minced
1 teaspoon dried whole basil
½ teaspoon salt
¼ teaspoon dried whole oregano

¼ teaspoon pepper
3 tablespoons sliced green onions
2 tablespoons chopped fresh parsley
2 large tomatoes, sliced
1½ cups shredded zucchini

Cook potatoes in boiling water 30 minutes or just until tender; drain. Set aside, and let cool.

Combine vinegar and next 6 ingredients in a small bowl, beating well with a wire whisk. Stir in green onions and parsley; set aside.

Peel and slice potatoes into ¼-inch slices. Arrange half the potato slices in a 2-quart casserole; top with half the tomato slices. Sprinkle with half the zucchini. Pour half the reserved dressing over layered vegetables. Repeat layers once. Cover and marinate in refrigerator at least 2 hours. Yield: 6 servings.

Simply Colorado
Colorado Dietetic Association
Littleton, Colorado

Caesar-Style Potato Salad

5 pounds potatoes
1 medium onion, chopped
8 slices bacon, cooked and
   crumbled
2 hard-cooked eggs, sliced
¼ cup chopped fresh parsley
½ cup vegetable oil

¼ cup lemon juice
¼ cup grated Parmesan cheese
1 tablespoon salt
1 tablespoon Worcestershire
   sauce
¼ teaspoon pepper

Cook potatoes in boiling water to cover 20 to 30 minutes or until tender; drain. Peel and cube potatoes. Combine potato, onion, bacon, eggs, and parsley; toss gently.

Combine oil and remaining ingredients, beating with a wire whisk until blended. Pour dressing over potato mixture, and toss gently to combine. Yield: 12 servings.   Joan Haller

Cookbook to benefit the Homeless
Lutheran Social Services of Southern California
Riverside, California

The Junior League of Boston focuses its attention on community assistance in the areas of education, children, and the arts. Proceeds from the sale of More Than a Tea Party, *a collection of regional recipes, will benefit more than thirty league projects in the community.*

Panzanella

¾ cup olive oil
8 anchovy fillets
1 clove garlic
2 tablespoons capers
2 tablespoons white vinegar
1 teaspoon salt
1 (16-ounce) loaf French bread
2 tablespoons olive oil
1 clove garlic, sliced

1 medium-size green pepper,
    cut into julienne strips
1 medium-size sweet yellow
    pepper, cut into julienne
    strips
2 medium tomatoes, diced
1 medium-size purple onion,
    thinly sliced

Position knife blade in food processor bowl; add first 6 ingredients, and process until smooth. Set dressing aside.

Trim crust from bread; cut bread into 1-inch cubes. Place cubes on a baking sheet; bake at 350° for 15 minutes or until dry.

Heat 2 tablespoons oil in a large skillet; add sliced garlic, and sauté 1 minute. Remove and discard garlic; add bread cubes, and sauté 2 minutes.

Combine bread cubes, pepper strips, tomato, and onion in a large bowl. Pour reserved dressing over vegetable mixture; toss gently. Serve immediately. Yield: 12 servings.   Susan Pomerantz

Literally Delicious
Abington Friends School Parents' Association
Jenkintown, Pennsylvania

Greek Rotini Salad

3 cups rotini, uncooked
1½ cups crumbled feta cheese
2 medium tomatoes, seeded
    and chopped
1 small cucumber, chopped
1 small green pepper, chopped
8 radishes, sliced
¼ cup chopped green onions
¼ cup small ripe olives
¼ cup pimiento-stuffed olives

2 tablespoons chopped fresh
    parsley
½ cup olive oil
1 clove garlic, crushed
2 tablespoons lemon juice
½ teaspoon salt
¼ teaspoon pepper
¼ teaspoon dried whole
    oregano

Cook rotini according to package directions; drain. Rinse with cold water; drain well. Combine rotini and next 9 ingredients in a large bowl; toss gently.

Combine olive oil, garlic, lemon juice, salt, pepper, and oregano in a jar. Cover tightly, and shake vigorously. Pour dressing over rotini mixture; toss gently to combine. Cover and chill thoroughly. Yield: 10 servings.   Cindy Bodnar

RSVP: Fortress Monroe
The Officers' and Civilians' Wives' Club
Fort Monroe, Virginia

Crab Luigi

8 ounces small seashell
  macaroni, uncooked
1 tablespoon vegetable oil
1 cup mayonnaise
⅓ cup chili sauce
¼ cup sour cream
1 tablespoon lemon juice
1 teaspoon Worcestershire
  sauce

4 hard-cooked eggs
1 pound fresh lump crabmeat
⅓ cup sliced celery
⅓ cup chopped green pepper
¼ cup chopped green onions
2 tomatoes, cut into wedges
½ medium avocado, sliced

Cook macaroni according to package directions; drain well, and place in a medium bowl. Add vegetable oil to macaroni, tossing gently to combine. Cover and chill thoroughly.

Combine mayonnaise, chili sauce, sour cream, lemon juice, and Worcestershire sauce in small bowl; stir well. Set aside.

Chop 2 eggs and 2 egg whites, reserving 2 egg yolks for garnish. Combine chopped egg, crabmeat, celery, green pepper, and green onions. Add reserved mayonnaise mixture and macaroni; toss gently to combine. Cover and chill at least 3 hours. To serve, sieve reserved egg yolks over salad. Arrange tomato wedges and avocado slices on top of salad. Yield: 10 servings.   Snooky Caldwell

100th Anniversary Cookbook
Auxiliary of Harrisburg Hospital
Harrisburg, Pennsylvania

Oriental Beef Salad

1 (2-pound) beef tenderloin
¾ cup Chablis or other dry
  white wine
½ cup soy sauce
¼ cup honey
3 tablespoons minced fresh
  gingerroot
2 cloves garlic, crushed
1½ pounds fresh asparagus
  spears

¾ pound fresh snow pea pods,
  trimmed
¾ pound sliced fresh
  mushrooms
1 tablespoon sesame seeds,
  toasted
2 tablespoons dark sesame oil
1 tablespoon minced fresh
  gingerroot

Cut tenderloin into 1-inch-thick steaks. Place steaks in a large shallow dish. Combine wine and next 4 ingredients; pour marinade mixture over steaks. Cover and marinate in refrigerator at least 2 hours, turning occasionally.

Remove steaks from marinade, reserving marinade. Grill steaks over medium coals (300° to 350°), or broil 6 inches from heat 5 to 7 minutes on each side or until medium rare. Let steaks cool, and cut into thin slices. Cover and chill.

Strain reserved marinade into a small saucepan; cook over medium heat 20 minutes or until reduced by one-half. Transfer marinade to a small bowl; cover and chill.

Snap off tough ends of asparagus. Remove scales from stalks with a knife or vegetable peeler, if desired. Cut asparagus diagonally into 1-inch pieces. Blanch asparagus in boiling water 2 minutes or until crisp-tender; drain. Rinse with cold water, and drain. Cover and chill.

Blanch snow peas in boiling water 1 minute or until crisp-tender; drain. Rinse with cold water, and drain. Cover and chill.

Combine reserved steaks, asparagus, snow peas, mushrooms, and sesame seeds in a large bowl. Combine reserved marinade, sesame oil, and 1 tablespoon gingerroot; stir well. Pour dressing over steak mixture, tossing gently to combine. Serve immediately. Yield: 8 servings.   Ingrid Hyman

Greetings from Atlantic City
The Ruth Newman Shapiro Cancer and Heart Fund
Atlantic City, New Jersey

Watermelon-Poppy Seed Dressing

1¾ cups cubed, seeded
   watermelon
½ teaspoon unflavored gelatin
2 tablespoons honey

1½ teaspoons white wine
   vinegar
2 teaspoons poppy seeds
½ teaspoon dry mustard

Place watermelon in container of an electric blender or food processor, and process until smooth. Pour watermelon puree into a small saucepan; sprinkle gelatin over puree, and let stand 1 minute. Cook over low heat, stirring until gelatin dissolves.

Combine gelatin mixture, honey, and remaining ingredients, stirring until well blended. Cover and chill at least 8 hours. Stir dressing before serving. Serve dressing over salad greens or fresh fruit. Yield: 1 cup.   Debra Petersen

Udderly Delicous
The Junior League of Racine, Wisconsin

Driftwood Dressing

¾ cup sugar
½ cup white vinegar
1 tablespoon grated onion
1½ teaspoons salt

1½ teaspoons dry mustard
1½ cups vegetable oil
2 tablespoons celery seeds

Combine first 5 ingredients in container of an electric blender, and process on low speed 30 seconds. With blender on high speed, gradually add oil in a slow steady stream; blend 30 seconds or until mixture is thickened. Stir in celery seeds. Cover and chill thoroughly. Serve dressing over fresh fruit or shredded cabbage. Yield: 2 cups.   Daphne Kay, Mona Vanek

Montana 1889-1989 Centennial Cookbook
The Inter-Denominational Christian Fellowship
Noxon, Montana

Terrace Hill Vinaigrette

2 tablespoons balsamic or red
    wine vinegar
1½ teaspoons Dijon mustard
¾ teaspoon salt
¼ teaspoon freshly ground
    pepper

1 clove garlic, crushed
½ cup olive oil
3 tablespoons chopped fresh
    tarragon

Combine first 5 ingredients in a small bowl. Gradually add oil, beating with a wire whisk until blended. Stir in tarragon. Serve dressing over salad greens. Yield: ¾ cup.

Recipes & Recollections from Terrace Hill
The Terrace Hill Society
Des Moines, Iowa

Roquefort Salad Dressing

6 ounces crumbled Roquefort
    cheese
1 (3-ounce) package cream
    cheese, softened
1½ cups mayonnaise

¾ cup evaporated milk
1½ tablespoons coarsely
    ground pepper
¼ teaspoon garlic powder

Combine all ingredients in a medium mixing bowl; beat at medium speed of an electric mixer until blended. Serve dressing over salad greens. Yield: 3½ cups.   Kathy Herold

Favorite Recipes of the Episcopal Churches on the Kenai
The Episcopal Churches on the Kenai
Nikiski, Alaska

Sauces & Condiments

Vermont, a state famous for maple sugar and maple syrup, is home to this sugarhouse. Sugar and syrup are extracted from the sap of the maple–Vermont's state tree. The maple-sugar season begins in March when the winter snow starts to melt.

Cinnamon Cream Syrup

1 cup sugar
½ cup light corn syrup
¼ cup water

¾ teaspoon ground cinnamon
½ cup evaporated milk

Combine first 4 ingredients in a small saucepan, stirring well. Bring to a boil over medium heat, stirring constantly; boil 2 minutes, stirring constantly. Remove from heat, and let cool 5 minutes. Stir in evaporated milk. Serve syrup with apple pie, ice cream, pancakes, or waffles. Yield: 1⅔ cups.   Judy Amundsen

Udderly Delicious
The Junior League of Racine, Wisconsin

Grand Marnier Sauce for Fruit

4 egg yolks
¾ cup sugar
1 teaspoon lemon juice
⅛ teaspoon salt
2 tablespoons all-purpose flour

¾ cup Grand Marnier or other
   orange-flavored liqueur,
   divided
2 cups whipping cream,
   whipped

Place egg yolks in top of a double boiler; bring water to a boil. Reduce heat to low; cook, beating at medium speed of an electric mixer, until thick and lemon colored. Gradually add sugar, beating well. Stir in lemon juice and salt.

Combine flour and 2 tablespoons Grand Marnier; stir until smooth. Add flour mixture to egg mixture, stirring well with a wire whisk. Add remaining ½ cup plus 2 tablespoons Grand Marnier; cook over low heat until mixture is thickened, stirring constantly. Remove from heat, and let cool completely. Gently fold in whipped cream. Cover and chill thoroughly. Serve sauce over fresh fruit. Yield: 4½ cups.   Lynn Aquadro

Cooks and Company
The Muscle Shoals District Service League
Sheffield, Alabama

Caramel Butter Sauce

1¼ cups sugar
⅓ cup water
⅛ teaspoon salt
⅛ teaspoon cream of tartar

⅓ cup whipping cream
½ cup unsalted butter, cut into
   pieces

Combine sugar, water, salt, and cream of tartar in a heavy 2-quart saucepan; cook over medium heat, stirring constantly, until sugar dissolves. Cover and cook 2 to 3 minutes to wash down sugar crystals from sides of pan.

Remove cover, and cook, without stirring, to soft crack stage (270°). Remove from heat; add cream and butter, stirring until blended. Serve sauce warm over ice cream, fresh fruit, or cake. Yield: 1⅓ cups.   Nancy Fox

Fellowship Favorites from First Presbyterian
First Presbyterian Church
Downers Grove, Illinois

Raisin Sauce

1¾ cups water
1 cup raisins
⅓ cup firmly packed brown
   sugar
1½ tablespoons cornstarch
2 tablespoons cold water

¼ teaspoon salt
¼ teaspoon dry mustard
¼ teaspoon ground cinnamon
¼ teaspoon ground cloves
1 tablespoon white vinegar

Bring 1¾ cups water to a boil; add raisins, and boil 5 minutes. Stir in sugar; reduce heat to medium. Combine cornstarch and 2 tablespoons water; stir well. Gradually stir cornstarch mixture into raisin mixture. Stir in salt and next 3 ingredients; cook until thickened and bubbly. Stir in vinegar. Serve sauce warm over cooked ham. Yield: 1¾ cups.   Trudy Calef

The Family Affair
Lincolnshire Community Nursery School
Lincolnshire, Illinois

Coney Island Hot Dog Sauce

¼ pound ground round
1½ cups water
1 (6-ounce) can tomato paste
¼ cup sweet pickle relish
1 tablespoon chopped onion
1 tablespoon prepared mustard

1 tablespoon Worcestershire
  sauce
2 to 3 teaspoons chili powder
1 teaspoon salt
1 teaspoon sugar

Cook meat in a large skillet over medium heat until browned, stirring to crumble meat; drain. Add water and remaining ingredients to skillet; stir well. Bring to a boil; reduce heat, and simmer mixture, uncovered, 30 minutes, stirring occasionally. Yield: about 3 cups.   June Rice, Terri McManus

A Taste of Neoucom
Northeastern Ohio Universities College of Medicine
Rootstown, Ohio

Relish for Hamburgers

1 (16-ounce) can chopped
  sauerkraut, undrained
1¼ cups sugar

1 cup chopped onion
1 cup chopped celery
¾ cup chopped green pepper

Combine all ingredients in a medium bowl, stirring well. Cover and chill at least 24 hours. Serve relish with a slotted spoon. Yield: 4 cups.   Anna Kiser

Home Cookin' "AT&T's Right Choices"
Western Electric Council Telephone Pioneers of America
Ballwin, Missouri

Apple Relish

3 Red Delicious apples,
   unpeeled and finely chopped
½ cup chopped onion

½ cup chopped dill pickle
½ cup sugar
¼ cup cider vinegar

Combine first 3 ingredients in a medium bowl; stir well. Combine sugar and vinegar, stirring well. Pour vinegar mixture over apple mixture, and toss gently to combine. Cover and chill at least 1 hour. Serve relish with cooked meats. Yield: 4 cups.

Prairie Potpourri
North Iowa Girl Scout Council
Mason City, Iowa

Salsa Gruda (Fresh Tomato Salsa)

4 medium tomatoes, peeled,
   seeded, and chopped
½ cup finely chopped onion
½ cup finely chopped celery
¼ cup finely chopped green
   pepper
¼ cup olive oil or vegetable oil
2 to 3 tablespoons finely
   chopped canned green chiles

2 tablespoons red wine vinegar
1 teaspoon salt
1 teaspoon coriander seeds,
   crushed
1 teaspoon mustard seeds
Dash of pepper

Combine all ingredients in a medium bowl; stir well. Cover and chill at least 4 hours, stirring occasionally. Serve salsa with grilled chicken or fish. Yield: 3½ cups.   Gloria Weston

Seasoned with Love
Priest Lake Community Church
Nordman, Idaho

Grape and Green Tomato Chutney

2 pounds green tomatoes,
sliced
4 medium Granny Smith
apples, peeled and diced
2¾ cups firmly packed dark
brown sugar
2 cups cider vinegar
1 cup raisins

⅔ cup chopped onion
½ teaspoon salt
3 cups green seedless grapes
1 tablespoon mustard seeds
2 teaspoons ground ginger
1 teaspoon dry mustard
½ teaspoon crushed red
pepper

Combine first 7 ingredients in a large Dutch oven; stir well. Bring to a boil; reduce heat, and simmer, uncovered, 30 minutes. Add grapes and seasonings; stir well. Cook, uncovered, over medium heat 1 hour or until mixture is thickened.

Spoon chutney into hot sterilized jars, leaving ¼-inch headspace; wipe jar rims. Cover at once with metal lids, and screw on bands. Process in boiling-water bath 15 minutes. Serve chutney with curried dishes or cheese. Yield: 2½ pints.

Ocean County Fare and Bounty, Cookbook of the Jersey Shore
Ocean County Girl Scout Council
Toms River, New Jersey

Ocean County Fare and Bounty, Cookbook of the Jersey Shore, *is comprised of recipes collected by members of the Ocean County Girl Scout Council. The girls participated in the cookbook project by submitting their family's favorite recipes that reflected their heritage and traditions. The Girl Scouts shared their recipes at food fairs, troop dinners, and cook offs.*

Cranberries Amaretto

¼ cup butter or margarine
1 (12-ounce) package fresh
  cranberries
2 cups sugar
2 tablespoons lemon juice

⅓ cup amaretto
2 tablespoons orange
  marmalade
2 teaspoons grated lemon rind

Melt butter in a large saucepan over medium heat. Add cranberries, sugar, and lemon juice; stir well to combine. Bring to a boil; reduce heat, and simmer, uncovered, 10 to 15 minutes or until cranberries begin to pop. Remove from heat; stir in amaretto, marmalade, and lemon rind. Serve with pork or turkey. Yield: 3⅔ cups.

Bena Hill

Camellia Delights
The Altrusa Club of Gulfport, Mississippi

Baked Cranberries

4 cups fresh cranberries
1 medium naval orange, peeled
  and sectioned
1½ cups sugar

½ cup fresh orange juice
½ teaspoon ground ginger
½ teaspoon ground cinnamon
½ teaspoon ground nutmeg

Combine all ingredients in a medium bowl; stir well. Spoon cranberry mixture into a 1½-quart casserole. Cover and bake at 350° for 1 hour. Serve warm or chilled with chicken, beef, or pork. Yield: 2½ cups.

Judie Schleifer

Greetings from Atlantic City
The Ruth Newman Shapiro Cancer and Heart Fund
Atlantic City, New Jersey

Cranberry-Pecan Butter

2 cups fresh cranberries
½ cup sugar
2 tablespoons grated orange
  rind
½ cup orange juice
¾ cup butter or margarine,
  softened
½ cup finely chopped pecans

Combine first 4 ingredients in a small saucepan; stir well. Bring to a boil; reduce heat, and simmer, uncovered, 15 minutes, stirring occasionally. Remove from heat, and let cool.

Transfer cranberry mixture to container of an electric blender or food processor, and process until smooth. Set aside.

Cream butter; add reserved cranberry puree, beating well at medium speed of an electric mixer. Stir in pecans.

Spoon cranberry mixture into a dish. Cover and chill thoroughly. Serve butter at room temperature with sweet potatoes or turkey. Yield: 2½ cups.   Joan Alvaro

Our Favorite Recipes
St. Stephen Catholic Community
Winter Springs, Florida

Baked Apple Butter

2 (16-ounce) jars applesauce
2½ cups firmly packed brown
  sugar
½ cup white vinegar
½ teaspoon ground cinnamon
¼ teaspoon ground cloves

Combine all ingredients in a 2-quart casserole; stir well. Bake, uncovered, at 350° for 2½ hours or until thick and almost transparent, stirring occasionally. Spoon hot apple butter into jars; cover and store in refrigerator. Yield: 2 pints.   Barbara Parker

The Secret Ingredient
The Cheer Guild of Indiana University Hospitals
Indianapolis, Indiana

Cinnamon-Apple Jelly

4 cups unsweetened apple
  juice
½ cup red cinnamon candies

1 (1¾-ounce) package
  powdered pectin
5 cups sugar

Combine first 3 ingredients in a Dutch oven; stir well. Bring to a boil; stirring constantly. Add sugar, and bring mixture to a full, rolling boil. Boil 1 minute, stirring constantly. Remove from heat; skim off foam with a metal spoon.

Pour hot jelly into hot sterilized jars, leaving ¼-inch headspace; carefully wipe jar rims. Cover jars at once with metal lids, and screw on bands. Process jelly in boiling-water bath 5 minutes. Yield: 7 half pints.   Pauline C. Godfrey

Delaware DAR Historical Cookbook
The Delaware State Society of the Daughters of the American
Revolution
Newark, Delaware

Tomato-Ginger Jam

1 (28-ounce) can whole
  tomatoes, undrained and
  chopped
1¼ cups sugar

½ cup chopped crystallized
  ginger
½ medium lemon, quartered
  and thinly sliced

Combine all ingredients in a large saucepan; stir well. Cook, uncovered, over low heat 45 to 50 minutes or until thickened, stirring frequently. Quickly pour hot jam into jars. Cover and store in refrigerator. Yield: 2 half pints.

10,000 Tastes of Minnesota
The Woman's Club of Minneapolis, Minnesota

Mustard–Sweet and Hot

¾ cup sugar
¾ cup dry mustard
½ cup Chablis or other dry
  white wine

½ cup cider vinegar
3 eggs, lightly beaten

Combine all ingredients in top of a double boiler; bring water to a boil. Reduce heat to low; cook 15 minutes or until mixture is thickened, stirring constantly with a wire whisk.

Quickly pour hot mustard into jars. Cover and store in refrigerator. Serve mustard as a spread for sandwiches. Yield: about 3 half pints. Dorothy Baker

Favorite Recipes of Edmonds
Edmonds United Methodist Women
Edmonds, Washington

Garlic Olives

1 (7-ounce) jar large pitted
  green olives
4 dried red chiles
2 large cloves garlic, sliced

1½ tablespoons white wine
  vinegar
1 teaspoon dried whole
  dillweed

Drain olives, reserving liquid. Place olives in a small bowl, and set aside.

Place olive liquid in a small saucepan. Add chiles and remaining ingredients; stir well. Bring to a boil; reduce heat, and simmer, uncovered, 5 minutes. Pour hot vinegar mixture over reserved olives; let cool. Cover and chill thoroughly. Drain before serving. Serve with cooked meats. Yield: 1½ cups. Edna Chadburn

Kona Kitchens
Kona Outdoor Circle
Kailua-Kona, Hawaii

Dilly Onion Rings

½ cup white vinegar
⅓ cup sugar
¼ cup water
2 teaspoons salt

1 teaspoon dried whole
   dillweed
1 large onion, thinly sliced and
   separated into rings

Combine first 5 ingredients in a small bowl; stir well. Add sliced onion, and toss gently to combine. Cover and chill at least 5 hours. Serve with cooked meats. Yield: 2 cups.   Phil Shaffer

The Western Gentlemen's Cookbook
The Men's Culinary Cup
Cheyenne, Wyoming

Chive and Garlic Croutons

2 tablespoons minced fresh
   garlic
2 tablespoons minced fresh
   chives
2 tablespoons minced fresh
   parsley

½ teaspoon salt
3 tablespoons olive oil
3 tablespoons butter or
   margarine, melted
10 cups cubed French, Italian,
   or sourdough bread

Sauté first 4 ingredients in oil and butter in a large skillet 1 minute. Add bread cubes, and toss gently until liquid is absorbed.

Spread bread cubes in a single layer on a baking sheet. Bake at 350° for 15 minutes or until crisp and golden, stirring occasionally. Store croutons in an airtight container. Serve over tossed green salads. Yield: 7 cups.

Gateways
Auxiliary-Twigs . . . Friends of St. Louis Children's Hospital
St. Louis, Missouri

Soups & Stews

Whether families gather for warmth or hearty meals, the hearth has always been the focal point of home life. This restored 1750s living room fireplace is located in the John Goddard house in Newport, Rhode Island, where the renowned cabinetmaker once lived with his wife and nine children.

Cold Strawberry Soup

1 quart fresh strawberries,
  hulled
1 quart strawberry or vanilla
  ice cream, softened

½ cup whipping cream
1 tablespoon lemon juice

Combine all ingredients in a large bowl, stirring well. Transfer half of strawberry mixture to container of electric blender, and process until almost smooth. Repeat procedure with remaining half of strawberry mixture. Ladle soup into individual soup bowls. Serve immediately. Yield: 5½ cups.   Elizabeth G. Smith

Friends Come in All Flavors
Buckingham Friends School
Lahaska, Pennsylvania

Chilled Orange-Carrot Soup

1 pound carrots, scraped and
  sliced
1 small onion, sliced
2 cups water
1 (3-inch) strip orange rind
½ teaspoon salt
1 cup orange juice

1 (8-ounce) carton low-fat
  lemon yogurt
¼ teaspoon ground ginger
¼ teaspoon ground cinnamon
Salt and pepper to taste
Garnish: shredded carrot

Combine first 5 ingredients in a medium saucepan. Bring to a boil; reduce heat, and simmer 30 minutes or until carrots are very tender. Transfer carrot mixture to container of an electric blender or food processor, and process until smooth.

Transfer pureed mixture to a bowl. Stir in orange juice, yogurt, ginger, and cinnamon. Cover and chill 4 hours. Add salt and pepper to taste. Ladle soup into individual soup bowls. Garnish, if desired. Yield: 4½ cups.   Charles E. Sutherland

Livre de Cuisine
Pikes Peak Region, American Culinary Federation
Colorado Springs, Colorado

Green Soup

3 large onions, thinly sliced
5 to 6 tablespoons butter or
  margarine, melted
2 large baking potatoes, peeled
  and thinly sliced
1 (10½-ounce) can chicken
  broth, diluted
2½ cups milk
2 teaspoons soy sauce

1 small bay leaf
½ teaspoon dried whole
  tarragon
¼ teaspoon curry powder
Salt to taste
1 (10-ounce) package frozen
  chopped spinach, thawed
1 cup whipping cream
Garnish: fresh mint sprigs

Sauté onion in butter in a large Dutch oven until tender. Add potato and next 7 ingredients; stir well. Bring to a boil; cover, reduce heat, and simmer 15 minutes or until potato is tender. Remove and discard bay leaf. Add spinach; stir well.

Transfer one-third of spinach mixture to container of an electric blender or food processor, and process until smooth. Repeat procedure twice with remaining spinach mixture. Cover and chill thoroughly.

Gently stir whipping cream into chilled spinach mixture. To serve, ladle soup evenly into individual soup bowls. Garnish, if desired. Yield: 3 quarts.   Libby Hopkins

A Century of Good Cooking
The Woman's Club of Waldoboro, Maine

Broccoli Soup

1 cup diced onion
¼ cup vegetable oil
1 large baking potato, peeled
  and diced
⅔ cup diced celery
1 clove garlic, minced
½ teaspoon salt

½ teaspoon pepper
5 cups canned diluted chicken
  broth
1 (10-ounce) package frozen
  chopped broccoli
1 tablespoon dried whole basil

Sauté onion in oil in a Dutch oven until tender. Add potato, celery, garlic, salt, and pepper, and sauté 10 minutes. Add broth, broccoli, and basil; stir well. Bring mixture to a boil; cover, reduce heat, and simmer 20 minutes or until vegetables are tender.

Transfer half of broccoli mixture to container of an electric blender or food processor, and process until smooth. Repeat procedure with remaining half of broccoli mixture. Ladle soup into individual soup bowls. Yield: 8 cups.   Katherine M. Brnjac

What the Winners Eat
Sugar Creek Swim Club
St. Louis, Missouri

Squash, Leek, and Watercress Soup

6 medium leeks
¼ cup unsalted butter, melted
3 pounds yellow squash, chopped
8 cups canned diluted chicken broth
2 cups watercress leaves

Dash of hot sauce
Salt and freshly ground pepper to taste
Garnishes: sour cream, thinly sliced yellow squash, and watercress sprigs

Remove and discard root, tough outer leaves, and tops of leeks to where dark green begins to pale. Chop leeks, and sauté in butter in a large Dutch oven 5 minutes or until tender. Add squash, and sauté 4 minutes. Stir in chicken broth. Bring to a boil; cover, reduce heat, and simmer 15 minutes or until squash is tender. Add watercress, hot sauce, and salt and pepper to taste, and simmer 2 minutes.

Transfer mixture in batches to container of an electric blender or food processor, and process until smooth. Ladle soup into individual soup bowls. Garnish, if desired. Yield: 3½ quarts.

More Than a Tea Party
The Junior League of Boston, Massachusetts

Lentil Soup

5 cups canned diluted chicken
  broth
4 cups water
3 cups dried lentils
2 cups chopped tomatoes
1 cup chopped onion
1 cup chopped celery
1 cup scraped, chopped carrots
3 tablespoons chopped garlic

1 tablespoon olive oil
1 (6-ounce) can tomato paste
2 tablespoons red wine vinegar
1½ tablespoons brown sugar
¼ teaspoon dried whole
  oregano
¼ teaspoon ground sage
¼ teaspoon pepper
⅛ teaspoon ground red pepper

Combine broth, water, lentils, and tomato in a large Dutch oven; stir well. Bring to a boil; reduce heat, and simmer, uncovered, 30 minutes.

Sauté onion, celery, carrot, and garlic in oil in a large skillet until vegetables are tender. Add sautéed vegetables to lentil mixture; stir well. Add tomato paste and remaining ingredients; stir well. Bring to a boil; cover, reduce heat, and simmer 30 minutes or until lentils are tender. Ladle soup into individual soup bowls. Yield: 3¼ quarts.
                                       John Kovac

Palate Pleasers II
Redeemer Women's Guild
Elmhurst, Illinois

Pasta Fagiola (Bean Soup with Pasta)

1 cup dried navy beans
4 cups water
2 (8-ounce) cans tomato sauce
1 medium onion, chopped
1 medium carrot, scraped and
  chopped
½ cup chopped celery
5 to 6 slices bacon
1 bay leaf

¾ teaspoon salt
½ teaspoon dried whole basil
½ teaspoon dried whole
  oregano
½ teaspoon minced garlic
¼ teaspoon pepper
½ cup elbow macaroni,
  uncooked
Grated Parmesan cheese

Sort and wash beans; place beans in a large Dutch oven. Cover with water 2 inches above beans, and let soak 24 hours. Drain beans, and return to Dutch oven. Add 4 cups water and next 11 ingredients; stir well. Bring to a boil; cover, reduce heat, and simmer 1 hour and 35 minutes or until beans are tender. Remove and discard bay leaf. Add macaroni, and cook 10 minutes or until macaroni is tender. Ladle soup into individual soup bowls. Sprinkle with Parmesan cheese. Yield: 9 cups.   Virginia Fazzari

The Walla Walla Italian Heritage Association Cookbook
Walla Walla Italian Heritage Association
Walla Walla, Washington

Luisa's Zuppa

½ **pound sweet Italian sausage**
1 **large onion, chopped**
2 **cloves garlic, minced**
2 **to 3 tablespoons olive oil**
8 **cups canned diluted chicken broth**
3 **cups shredded cabbage**
2 **baking potatoes, peeled and chopped**
2 **carrots, scraped and chopped**
2 **turnips, peeled and chopped**

2 **tomatoes, chopped**
1 **cup frozen English peas**
1 **(15-ounce) can cannellini beans, drained**
1 **teaspoon dried whole basil**
½ **teaspoon ground allspice**
Salt and pepper to taste
2 **cups small seashell macaroni, uncooked**
Freshly grated Parmesan cheese

Remove and discard casing from sausage. Cook sausage in a large skillet over medium heat until sausage is browned, stirring to crumble meat. Drain well, and set aside.

Sauté onion and garlic in oil in large Dutch oven until tender. Add reserved sausage and broth; stir well. Bring to a boil; stir in cabbage and next 9 ingredients. Return mixture to a boil; cover, reduce heat, and simmer 10 minutes. Add macaroni; simmer, uncovered, 15 minutes or until macaroni is tender. Ladle soup into individual soup bowls. Sprinkle each serving with Parmesan cheese. Yield: 3¾ quarts.   Luisa Musso

Culinary Briefs
The San Francisco Lawyers' Wives
San Francisco, California

Onion and Potato Soup

2 large sweet onions, cut into
 ¼-inch-thick slices
3 tablespoons butter or
 margarine, melted
1 pound lean ground beef
4 cups water
2 medium-size red potatoes,
 unpeeled and cut into ⅛-inch-
 thick slices
2 tablespoons red wine vinegar
1 beef-flavored bouillon cube

2 teaspoons salt
½ teaspoon pepper
1 cup (4 ounces) shredded
 Swiss cheese
1 tablespoon plus 1 teaspoon
 butter or margarine
4 (1-inch-thick) slices French
 bread
2 tablespoons grated Parmesan
 cheese

Sauté onion in 3 tablespoons melted butter in a Dutch oven until tender and lightly browned. Remove onions from Dutch oven; set aside, and keep warm.

Add ground beef to Dutch oven; cook over medium heat until meat is browned, stirring to crumble meat. Drain well. Add water and next 5 ingredients to meat in Dutch oven; stir well to combine. Bring mixture to a boil; reduce heat to low, and simmer, uncovered, 25 minutes or until potato is tender.

Ladle soup evenly into four 16-ounce ovenproof soup bowls, and set aside.

Spread 1 teaspoon butter on one side of each slice of French bread; sprinkle evenly with Parmesan cheese. Place one slice of bread on top of each serving of soup. Bake at 375° for 10 minutes or until cheese melts and soup is thoroughly heated. Serve immediately. Yield: 8 cups.   Margy Wilbourn

Sunnyside Stars Sumptuous Savories
Sunnyside PTA
Pullman, Washington

Mulligatawny Soup

½ cup diced onion
1 cup diced celery
½ cup scraped, diced carrots
3 to 4 tablespoons butter or
  margarine, melted
1½ tablespoons all-purpose
  flour
2 teaspoons curry powder
4 cups canned diluted chicken
  broth
½ cup diced cooked chicken

½ cup cooked long-grain rice
½ cup raisins
¼ cup peeled, diced Granny
  Smith apples
1 teaspoon salt
½ teaspoon grated lemon rind
¼ teaspoon pepper
⅛ teaspoon dried whole thyme
1 bay leaf
½ cup warm half-and-half

Sauté onion, celery, and carrot in butter in a Dutch oven until tender. Add flour and curry powder; cook over medium heat 3 minutes, stirring constantly. Gradually add broth; bring to a boil. Reduce heat; simmer, uncovered, 15 minutes. Add chicken and next 8 ingredients; simmer 15 minutes. Remove and discard bay leaf. Stir in warm half-and-half. Ladle soup into individual soup bowls. Serve immediately. Yield: 5½ cups.   William R. Dodge

Cooking by Male
The Greater Pittsburgh Commission for Women
Pittsburgh, Pennsylvania

*The Sunnyside PTA in Pullman, Washington, uses proceeds
from the sale of* Sunnyside Stars Sumptuous Savories *to
support self-esteem programs like Superstar, Teacher Appreciation
Day, and Musical Productions. In addition, the PTA offers a
Fun Run for Kids, visits by a variety of resource people who
provide hands-on learning activities, and programs through
which children can learn coping techniques in order to remain
drug free.*

Celery and Almond Soup

1 large leek
1 bunch celery, quartered
1 large carrot, scraped and
    quartered
1 large onion, quartered
2 tablespoons butter or
    margarine, melted
4 cups canned diluted chicken
    broth
1 teaspoon salt

3 sprigs fresh parsley
1 sprig fresh thyme
1 bay leaf
2 cups half-and-half
¼ cup ground blanched
    almonds
Garnishes: toasted sliced
    natural almonds and whipped
    cream

Remove and discard root, tough outer leaves, and tops of leeks to where dark green begins to pale. Chop leeks. Position knife blade in food processor bowl; add leek, celery, carrot, and onion, and process until coarsely chopped. Sauté chopped vegetables in butter in a Dutch oven until tender. Add broth and salt; stir well.

Place parsley, thyme, and bay leaf on a piece of cheesecloth; tie ends of cheesecloth securely. Add to celery mixture in Dutch oven. Bring to a boil; reduce heat, and simmer, uncovered, 1 hour. Remove and discard cheesecloth bag.

Transfer celery mixture to processor bowl, and process until smooth. Let cool slightly. Add half-and-half and almonds, stirring well to combine. Ladle soup into individual soup bowls. Garnish, if desired. Yield: 6 cups.

Barbara Brodie

Literally Delicious
Abington Friends School Parents' Association
Jenkintown, Pennsylvania

Cream of Zucchini Soup, Andelin Style

2 medium onions, chopped
2 tablespoons butter or
    margarine, melted
6 medium zucchini, sliced
    (about 1½ pounds)
3 cups canned diluted chicken
    broth

½ cup half-and-half
⅛ teaspoon salt
⅛ teaspoon ground nutmeg
Pinch of ground red pepper
Shredded Cheddar cheese

Sauté onion in butter in a large saucepan until tender. Add zucchini and broth; stir well. Bring to a boil; cover, reduce heat, and simmer 15 minutes or until zucchini is tender.

Transfer half of zucchini mixture to container of an electric blender, and process until smooth. Repeat procedure with remaining half of zucchini mixture.

Return pureed mixture to saucepan. Stir in half-and-half and seasonings. Cook zucchini mixture over medium heat, stirring constantly, until mixture is thoroughly heated. Ladle soup into individual soup bowls. Sprinkle evenly with shredded Cheddar cheese. Yield: 7½ cups.   Olive Poor, Jeanne Forsberg

Holladay 7th Ward Cookbook
The Holladay 7th Ward Relief Society
Salt Lake City, Utah

Isle of Wight Stilton Soup

1 cup finely chopped onion
⅓ cup scraped, finely chopped
  carrots
⅓ cup finely chopped celery
1 small bay leaf, crushed
¼ cup butter or margarine,
  melted
¼ cup all-purpose flour

3 cups canned diluted chicken
  broth
3 cups milk
½ pound Stilton or other blue
  cheese, crumbled
1 teaspoon English mustard
Freshly ground pepper to taste
Croutons

Sauté onion, carrot, celery, and bay leaf in butter in a Dutch oven until vegetables are tender. Add flour, stirring well. Cook 1 minute, stirring constantly. Gradually add chicken broth and milk; cook over medium heat, stirring constantly, until mixture is thickened and bubbly.

Add cheese, mustard, and pepper to taste, stirring well to combine. Reduce heat to low; cook, stirring constantly, until cheese melts. Ladle soup into individual soup bowls. Sprinkle with croutons. Yield: 7 cups.   Robert Arnold

Extraordinary Cuisine for Sea & Shore
Seattle Yacht Club
Seattle, Washington

Wild Rice and Corn Chowder

½ pound bacon, diced
2 small onions, diced
1 large sweet red pepper, diced
4 stalks celery, diced
3 cloves garlic, minced
6 cups canned diluted chicken
  broth
1 cup wild rice, uncooked
1 tablespoon chopped fresh
  thyme

1 tablespoon chopped fresh
  basil
½ to 1 teaspoon sweet red
  pepper flakes
2 cups frozen whole kernel
  corn
2 cups whipping cream
Salt to taste

Cook bacon in a large skillet until almost crisp. Add onion, sweet red pepper, celery, and garlic, and sauté 5 minutes. Drain well, and set aside.

Bring chicken broth to a boil in a large Dutch oven; stir in rice. Add reserved vegetable mixture, thyme, basil, and red pepper flakes; stir well. Return mixture to a boil; reduce heat, and simmer, uncovered, 45 minutes.

Cook corn according to package directions; drain. Add corn, cream, and salt to taste to mixture in Dutch oven; simmer 15 minutes. Ladle chowder into individual soup bowls. Yield: 9 cups.

A Taste of San Francisco
The Symphony of San Francisco, California

★ ★ ★

The Black Belt Ministries is a cluster of nine small Episcopal Churches in Alabama. It began in an effort to keep the area's historic churches open and viable through the sharing of expenses, ministers, and other resources. Funds from the sale of Break Bread with the Black Belt *benefit their Outreach Program.*

Christmas on the River Seafood Gumbo

1 gallon water
2 lemons, sliced
1 (3-ounce) package crab boil
1 teaspoon salt
2 pounds unpeeled medium-
size fresh shrimp
1 (16-ounce) package bacon
1 cup all-purpose flour
2 onions, finely chopped
2 medium-size green peppers,
finely chopped
1 pound cooked ham, cubed

2 pounds fresh crabmeat,
drained and flaked
3 pounds fresh okra, sliced
1 (28-ounce) can whole
tomatoes, undrained
½ cup Worcestershire sauce
2 teaspoons garlic powder
2 teaspoons salt
1 teaspoon pepper
3 bay leaves
Hot cooked rice

Combine water, lemon, crab boil, and 1 teaspoon salt in a large
Dutch oven; bring to a boil. Add shrimp, and cook 3 to 5 minutes.
Remove and discard lemon and crab boil. Remove shrimp,
reserving water. Peel and devein shrimp; chill.

Cook bacon in a large skillet until crisp; remove bacon, reserving
drippings in skillet. Crumble bacon, and set aside.

Add flour to drippings in skillet; cook over medium heat, stirring
constantly, until roux is caramel-colored (about 5 minutes). Stir in
onion and green pepper; cook over low heat 10 minutes or until
vegetables are tender.

Add roux mixture, ham, and remaining ingredients except rice
to reserved water in Dutch oven. Bring to a boil; reduce heat, and
simmer 1 hour and 50 minutes. Stir in reserved chilled shrimp
and bacon, and cook 10 minutes. Remove and discard bay leaves.
Serve gumbo over rice. Yield: 7½ quarts.   Charles B. Roberts

Break Bread with the Black Belt
Black Belt Ministries
Demopolis, Alabama

Chicken and Sausage Gumbo

1 pound smoked sausage, cut
  into ¼-inch-thick slices
⅓ cup vegetable oil
1 (3-pound) broiler-fryer, cut
  up and skinned
½ teaspoon salt
¼ teaspoon pepper
½ cup all-purpose flour
1½ cups chopped onion
1 cup chopped green peppers
¾ cup chopped celery
2 cloves garlic, minced
1 quart water

2 cups canned diluted chicken
  broth
Salt and pepper to taste
1 (12-ounce) container fresh
  Standard oysters, undrained
¾ cup frozen sliced okra,
  thawed
¾ cup chopped green onion
  tops
¼ cup chopped fresh parsley
Hot cooked rice
Gumbo filé

Brown sausage in a Dutch oven in oil over medium heat. Remove sausage to paper towels, leaving drippings in Dutch oven. Sprinkle chicken with ½ teaspoon salt and ¼ teaspoon pepper. Brown chicken in drippings; transfer chicken to paper towels, reserving drippings in Dutch oven.

Add flour to drippings in Dutch oven; cook over medium heat, stirring constantly, until roux is caramel-colored (about 5 minutes). Add onion, green pepper, celery, and garlic; sauté 10 minutes or until vegetables are tender. Add reserved sausage, chicken, water, chicken broth, and salt and pepper to taste. Bring to a boil; cover, reduce heat, and simmer 1½ hours or until chicken is tender.

Remove chicken; set aside, and let cool. Add oysters, okra, green onions, and parsley to Dutch oven; cover and simmer 10 minutes or until edges of oysters begin to curl.

Bone chicken, and coarsely chop meat; add to gumbo. Remove from heat, and let stand 10 minutes. Serve gumbo over rice in individual soup bowls. Sprinkle each serving with gumbo filé. Yield: 3½ quarts.   Carolyn Stringer

Family Secrets . . . the Best of the Delta
Lee Academy
Clarksdale, Mississippi

Veal Stew Marsala

½ pound fresh mushrooms, sliced
3 tablespoons minced shallot
2 cloves garlic, crushed
¼ cup margarine, melted
1 cup Marsala wine
2 pounds boneless veal, cubed
¼ cup all-purpose flour
2 tablespoons margarine, melted
3 tomatoes, peeled and quartered

2 medium-size green peppers, cubed
2 large red potatoes, peeled and cubed
1 large onion, chopped
2 tablespoons all-purpose flour
1 teaspoon grated orange rind
1½ cups canned diluted beef broth
1 bay leaf

Sauté sliced mushrooms, shallot, and garlic in ¼ cup melted margarine in a large Dutch oven until vegetables are tender. Add wine, and cook over high heat until mixture is reduced by one-half. Remove mushroom mixture from Dutch oven; set aside, and keep warm.

Dredge veal in ¼ cup flour. Brown veal in 2 tablespoons margarine in Dutch oven over medium heat. Add tomato and next 3 ingredients, and cook 5 minutes. Add 2 tablespoons flour and orange rind, stirring until blended. Cook 1 minute, stirring constantly. Gradually add broth; cook over medium heat, stirring constantly, until mixture is thickened and bubbly.

Add reserved mushroom mixture and bay leaf to veal mixture. Cover and bake at 350° for 1 hour and 15 minutes. Remove and discard bay leaf. Yield: 2¾ quarts.

To Your Health!
The Junior Woman's Club of West Haven, Connecticut

Lamb Ragoût

3½ pounds lean boneless lamb, cut into ¾-inch pieces
¼ cup olive oil, divided
1 medium onion, chopped
4 cloves garlic, minced
1 (14½-ounce) can Italian-style tomatoes, drained and finely chopped
1 teaspoon salt
1 teaspoon dried whole rosemary, crushed
½ teaspoon sugar
½ teaspoon dried whole thyme, crushed
1 cup Chablis or other dry white wine
1¼ cups canned diluted beef broth
¾ pound baby carrots, scraped
¾ pound small turnips, peeled and quartered
¾ pound fresh green beans, halved crosswise
½ pound pearl onions, peeled
¼ pound baby zucchini, halved lengthwise
3 tablespoons cold water
1 tablespoon cornstarch
Salt and pepper to taste
Hot cooked medium egg noodles

Brown half of lamb in 2 tablespoons oil in a large Dutch oven over medium-high heat. Remove browned lamb to a platter with a slotted spoon; set aside, and keep warm. Repeat procedure with remaining 2 tablespoons oil and lamb, reserving drippings in Dutch oven.

Sauté onion and garlic in drippings in Dutch oven until tender. Add tomatoes, salt, rosemary, sugar, and thyme; stir well. Add wine, and bring to a boil. Stir in reserved lamb and beef broth. Bring to a boil; cover and bake at 325° for 1 hour and 20 minutes or until lamb is tender.

Arrange carrots in a vegetable steamer over boiling water; cover and steam 10 minutes or until crisp-tender. Set aside. Repeat procedure with remaining vegetables.

Combine water and cornstarch; add to lamb mixture, stirring well. Cook over medium heat 2 minutes, stirring constantly. Add reserved steamed vegetables, and salt and pepper to taste. Cook over medium-high heat until thoroughly heated. Serve ragoût over noodles. Yield: 3 quarts.

Cardinal Cuisine
The Mount Vernon Hospital Auxiliary
Alexandria, Virginia

San Antonio Stew

2 pounds beef stew meat, cut
in 1-inch pieces
2 tablespoons vegetable oil
1 (10½-ounce) can beef broth,
diluted
1 cup water
1 (8-ounce) jar picante sauce
1 medium onion, cut into
wedges
¼ cup chopped fresh parsley
2 cloves garlic, minced
1 teaspoon salt

1 teaspoon ground cumin
1 (16-ounce) can whole
tomatoes, undrained and
chopped
3 large carrots, scraped and cut
into 1-inch pieces
3 ears fresh corn, cut into 1-
inch pieces
2 zucchini, cut into 1-inch
pieces
½ cup water
2 tablespoons all-purpose flour

Brown beef in oil in a large Dutch oven. Stir in broth and next 7
ingredients. Bring to a boil; cover, reduce heat, and simmer 1
hour, stirring occasionally. Add tomatoes, carrot, corn, and
zucchini; cover and simmer 25 minutes or until vegetables are
tender. Combine ½ cup water and flour; stir until smooth. Add
flour mixture to meat mixture; cook over medium heat until
thickened, stirring occasionally. Yield: 3½ quarts.   Sharon Traina

Best Friends
Terranova West Women's Club
Spring, Texas

Cardinal Cuisine, *a cookbook by the Mount Vernon Hospital
Auxiliary, is named in honor of Virginia's state bird—the
cardinal. Mount Vernon Hospital is located in southern Fairfax
County and stands on a portion of land once included in George
Washington's estate. Auxiliary members support the hospital
through funds raised from the sale of the cookbook, as well as
voluntary service in its gift and thrift shops.*

Okra Goulash

2 pounds ground beef
2 (28-ounce) cans whole
  tomatoes, undrained and
  chopped
6 cups water
1 (16-ounce) package frozen
  cut okra

2½ cups chopped onion
1 teaspoon Worcestershire
  sauce
1 teaspoon salt
¼ teaspoon pepper
Hot cooked rice (optional)

Cook ground beef in a large Dutch oven until meat is browned, stirring to crumble meat; drain well. Add tomatoes and next 6 ingredients; stir well. Bring to a boil; reduce heat, and simmer, uncovered, 3 hours or until thickened. Serve over rice, if desired. Yield: 4 quarts.   Mary P. Quinn

Crossroads Cuisine
The Winona Manor Christmas Fund
Kimichael, Mississippi

Gringo Chili

1 pound ground turkey
1 cup chopped onion
2 teaspoons minced garlic
1 (28-ounce) can whole
  tomatoes, undrained and
  chopped

1 (16-ounce) can pinto or
  kidney beans, drained
1 (6-ounce) can tomato paste
½ cup green chile salsa
1 tablespoon chili powder

Combine first 3 ingredients in a large nonstick skillet. Cook over medium heat until turkey is browned, stirring to crumble turkey; drain. Add tomatoes and remaining ingredients; stir well. Bring mixture to a boil; cover, reduce heat, and simmer 15 to 20 minutes. Yield: 7 cups.

Simply Colorado
Colorado Dietetic Association
Littleton, Colorado

Vegetables

A dutiful scarecrow peers through stalks of corn hoping to frighten would-be predators from the garden crop as the plants begin to tassel.

Stir-Fried Fresh Asparagus

1 pound fresh asparagus
  spears
1 clove garlic, minced
2 tablespoons margarine,
  melted
½ cup canned diluted chicken
  broth

½ teaspoon salt
½ teaspoon sugar
1 tablespoon sliced natural
  almonds or sesame seeds,
  toasted

Snap off tough ends of asparagus. Remove scales from stalks with a knife or vegetable peeler, if desired. Cut asparagus diagonally into 1-inch pieces. Set aside.

Sauté minced garlic in melted margarine in a large skillet 1 minute. Add asparagus pieces, stirring well to combine. Add chicken broth, salt, and sugar, stirring well to combine. Cook over high heat 3 to 4 minutes or until asparagus is crisp-tender, stirring frequently.

Transfer asparagus mixture to a serving platter with a slotted spoon. Sprinkle asparagus mixture with sliced almonds. Serve immediately. Yield: 4 servings.   Marlene Hertz

The When You Live in Hawaii You Get Very Creative During Passover
Cookbook
Congregation of Sof Ma'arav
Honolulu, Hawaii

Asparagus Tomato Stir-Fry

1 tablespoon cold water
2 teaspoons soy sauce
1 teaspoon cornstarch
¼ teaspoon salt
1 pound fresh asparagus spears
1 tablespoon vegetable oil

4 green onions, sliced
  diagonally into 1-inch pieces
1½ cups sliced fresh
  mushrooms
2 small tomatoes, cut into thin
  wedges

Combine first 4 ingredients in a small bowl, stirring until blended. Set aside.

Snap off tough ends of asparagus. Remove scales from stalks with a knife or vegetable peeler, if desired. Cut asparagus diagonally into 1½-inch pieces. Set aside.

Pour oil around top of preheated wok, coating sides; heat at medium-high (325°) for 2 minutes. Add asparagus and green onions; stir-fry 3 to 4 minutes. Add mushrooms; stir-fry 1 minute. Add reserved cornstarch mixture to vegetable mixture in wok; cook until thickened and bubbly. Add tomato, and cook just until heated. Serve immediately. Yield: 6 servings.   Belinda Cronin

Udderly Delicious
The Junior League of Racine, Wisconsin

Green Beans Parmesan

1½ pounds fresh green beans,
  cut in 1-inch pieces
¼ cup vegetable oil
1 cup diced sweet yellow
  pepper
¾ cup diced sweet red pepper
¼ cup chopped onion
1 clove garlic, minced

1 teaspoon dried whole basil
⅛ teaspoon dried whole
  oregano
⅛ teaspoon dried whole thyme
⅛ teaspoon pepper
¾ cup grated Parmesan cheese,
  divided

Cook green beans in boiling water to cover 3 minutes; drain, and plunge into cold water. Drain well, and set aside.

Pour oil into a large skillet; place over medium heat until hot. Add sweet peppers, onion, and garlic, and sauté 3 minutes. Add reserved green beans, basil, and next 3 ingredients; cover, reduce heat, and simmer 7 minutes or until vegetables are tender. Remove from heat; stir in ½ cup cheese. Transfer bean mixture to a serving dish; sprinkle with remaining ¼ cup cheese. Yield: 8 servings.   Cathryn DuBow

The Broker's Cookbook, Second Edition
The Robinson-Humphrey Company, Inc.
Atlanta, Georgia

Three Bean Hotdish

½ pound bacon, cut into
   1-inch pieces
½ pound ground beef
1 cup chopped onion
½ teaspoon salt
¼ teaspoon pepper
1 (16-ounce) can pork and
   beans, undrained

1 (16-ounce) can red kidney
   beans, drained
1 (15-ounce) can butter beans,
   drained
¾ cup firmly packed brown
   sugar
½ cup catsup
1 teaspoon dry mustard

Cook bacon in a large skillet until crisp; remove bacon, and discard drippings. Set bacon aside.

Cook ground beef, onion, salt, and pepper in drippings in skillet over medium heat until meat is browned, stirring to crumble meat. Drain well.

Combine bacon, ground beef mixture, and remaining ingredients. Spoon mixture into an ungreased 2-quart casserole. Cover and bake at 350° for 1 hour or until thoroughly heated. Yield: 10 servings.   Mary Jean Burkhart, Verlee Heinze

North Dakota Family Favorites . . . a Collection of Recipes
The Division of Continuing Studies, North Dakota State University
Fargo, North Dakota

Sublima Limas

1 pound dried Fordhook lima beans	¼ cup dark molasses
1 medium onion, chopped	2 tablespoons brown sugar
1 cup catsup	2 tablespoons prepared mustard

Sort and wash beans; place in a large Dutch oven. Cover with water 2 inches above beans; let soak 8 hours. Drain beans, and return to Dutch oven. Add enough water to cover. Bring to a boil; cover, reduce heat, and simmer 30 minutes.

Drain beans; add onion and remaining ingredients, stirring gently to combine. Pour bean mixture into a lightly greased 3-quart casserole. Cover and bake at 250° for 3 to 4 hours. Yield: 8 servings.

Gracious Goodness
Penn Laurel Girl Scout Council
York, Pennsylvania

Broccoli and Cheese to Please

2 (10-ounce) packages frozen chopped broccoli	¼ cup all-purpose flour
½ cup chopped onion	2 cups milk
½ cup chopped celery	1 (8-ounce) package cream cheese, cubed and softened
¼ cup butter or margarine, melted	½ teaspoon salt
1 (4-ounce) can sliced mushrooms, drained	⅛ teaspoon pepper
¼ cup butter or margarine	1 cup (4 ounces) shredded sharp Cheddar cheese
	½ cup soft breadcrumbs

Cook broccoli according to package directions; drain. Transfer broccoli to a large bowl, and set aside.

Sauté onion and celery in ¼ cup melted butter in a large skillet until vegetables are tender. Add sautéed vegetables and mushrooms to broccoli; set aside.

Melt ¼ cup butter in a heavy saucepan over low heat; add flour, stirring until smooth. Cook 1 minute, stirring constantly.

Gradually add milk; cook over medium heat, stirring constantly, until mixture is thickened and bubbly. Reduce heat to low; add cream cheese, salt, and pepper, stirring until smooth.

Add one-half of cream cheese mixture to broccoli mixture; stir well. Spoon broccoli mixture into a greased 2-quart casserole. Pour remaining one-half of cream cheese mixture over broccoli mixture. Sprinkle evenly with Cheddar cheese and breadcrumbs. Cover and bake at 350° for 30 minutes or until hot and bubbly. Yield: 8 to 10 servings.   Doreen Durand

The Cajun Connection Cookbook
Trintiy Catholic School Booster Club
St. Martinville, Louisiana

Sweet 'n' Sour Red Cabbage

1 medium onion, chopped
2 tablespoons butter or
   margarine, melted
1 medium-size red cabbage,
   shredded
2 small Granny Smith apples,
   peeled and diced

⅔ cup wine vinegar
¼ cup firmly packed dark
   brown sugar
2 tablespoons lemon juice
½ teaspoon salt
½ teaspoon caraway seeds
¼ teaspoon pepper

Sauté onion in melted butter in a large Dutch oven until tender. Add cabbage and remaining ingredients, stirring well to combine. Bring mixture to a boil; cover, reduce heat, and simmer 45 minutes or until cabbage is tender, stirring occasionally. Yield: 10 to 12 servings.   Carol Pence Taylor

What the Winners Eat
Sugar Creek Swim Club
St. Louis, Missouri

Braised Cabbage

4 green onions, chopped
3 tablespoons butter or
  margarine, melted
9 cups shredded cabbage
  (about 1½ pounds)

3 carrots, scraped and grated
½ teaspoon salt
⅛ teaspoon pepper

Sauté green onions in melted butter in a large skillet until tender. Add cabbage and carrot; sauté 4 minutes or until crisp-tender. Stir in salt and pepper. Yield: 6 to 8 servings.   Sue Bell

Family Secrets . . . the Best of the Delta
Lee Academy
Clarksdale, Mississippi

Zesty Carrots

6 to 8 carrots, scraped and cut
  into julienne strips
½ cup mayonnaise
2 tablespoons prepared
  horseradish
2 tablespoons grated onion
½ teaspoon salt

¼ teaspoon pepper
¼ cup fine, dry breadcrumbs
  or buttery cracker crumbs
1 tablespoon butter or
  margarine, melted
Dash of paprika

Place carrot in a medium saucepan; add water to cover. Bring to a boil over medium heat; reduce heat, and simmer 8 minutes or until tender. Drain, reserving ¼ cup liquid.

Arrange carrot in an 11- x 7- x 1½-inch baking dish. Combine reserved liquid, mayonnaise, and next 4 ingredients, stirring well. Pour mayonnaise mixture over carrot. Combine breadcrumbs, butter, and paprika; sprinkle mixture evenly over carrot. Bake at 375° for 15 to 20 minutes or until hot and bubbly. Yield: 6 to 8 servings.   Dennis and Charlyne Berens

First Gentleman's Cookbook
Governor's Mansion Restoration Foundation
Lincoln, Nebraska

Carrot and Cauliflower Casserole

8 carrots, scraped and cut into
  2-inch pieces
1 large cauliflower, broken into
  flowerets
2 tablespoons butter or
  margarine
2 tablespoons all-purpose flour

1 cup canned diluted chicken
  broth
½ cup whipping cream
1¼ cups (5 ounces) shredded
  Swiss cheese, divided
4 green onions, chopped
¼ teaspoon dry mustard

Cook carrot in a small amount of boiling water 8 to 10 minutes or until tender. Drain; place in a lightly greased 2-quart casserole. Cook cauliflower in a small amount of boiling water 6 to 8 minutes or until tender; drain. Add cauliflower to carrot, and set aside.

Melt butter in a heavy saucepan over low heat; add flour, stirring until smooth. Cook 1 minute, stirring constantly. Gradually add broth and cream; cook over medium heat, stirring constantly, until mixture is thickened and bubbly. Add 1 cup shredded cheese, green onions, and mustard, stirring until cheese melts. Pour sauce over reserved vegetables, stirring gently to coat well. Cover and bake at 350° for 20 to 25 minutes or until mixture is thoroughly heated. Remove cover, and sprinkle with remaining ¼ cup shredded cheese; bake an additional 5 minutes or until cheese melts. Yield: 10 servings.
           Jeanne Forsberg

Holladay 7th Ward Cookbook
The Holladay 7th Ward Relief Society
Salt Lake City, Utah

Lee Academy is a college preparatory school which provides an environment of educational excellence for its students. Monies raised from the sale of the cookbook, Family Secrets . . . the Best of the Delta, *will be placed in an endowment fund for special educational projects.*

Celebrated Cauliflower

1 medium cauliflower
1½ cups sliced fresh
  mushrooms
2 tablespoons butter or
  margarine, melted
2 tablespoons all-purpose flour
1 cup milk

1 cup (4 ounces) shredded
  sharp Cheddar cheese
1 teaspoon Dijon mustard
¼ teaspoon salt
Dash of ground white pepper
1 tablespoon minced fresh
  parsley

Remove outer leaves and stalk of cauliflower, leaving head whole. Wash cauliflower. Place in a vegetable steamer over boiling water. Cover and steam 15 to 20 minutes or until crisp-tender. Place cauliflower on a serving plate, and keep warm.

Sauté mushrooms in butter in a skillet over medium heat until tender. Reduce heat to low. Add flour; cook 1 minute, stirring constantly. Gradually add milk; cook over medium heat, stirring constantly, until mixture is thickened and bubbly. Add cheese, mustard, salt, and pepper, stirring until cheese melts.

Spoon about ½ cup cheese sauce over cauliflower. Sprinkle with minced parsley. Serve cauliflower with remaining cheese sauce. Yield: 6 servings.

Thymes Remembered
The Junior League of Tallahassee, Florida

Sweet-and-Sour Celery

4 cups sliced celery
1 egg, beaten
2 tablespoons all-purpose flour
2 tablespoons sugar
¾ teaspoon salt

⅛ teaspoon pepper
1 cup water
2 tablespoons white vinegar
¼ cup sour cream

Cook celery in boiling salted water to cover 10 to 12 minutes or until tender; drain well, and set aside.

Combine egg, flour, sugar, salt, and pepper in a saucepan; stir until smooth. Add water and vinegar; stir with a wire whisk until blended. Cook over medium heat, stirring constantly, until thickened and bubbly. Remove from heat; gently stir in sour cream. Add sauce to celery, stirring gently to combine. Serve immediately. Yield: 6 servings.   Gail Fowler Middleton

The Longyear Cookbook
The Longyear Historical Society & Museum
Brookline, Massachusetts

Golden Eggplant Casserole

8 cups peeled, cubed eggplant (about 2 pounds)

2½ cups crushed saltine crackers

1½ cups half-and-half

1½ cups (6 ounces) shredded sharp Cheddar cheese

¼ cup chopped celery

1 (4-ounce) jar diced pimiento, drained

3 tablespoons unsalted butter or margarine, melted

1½ teaspoons salt

½ teaspoon freshly ground pepper

Cook eggplant in boiling salted water to cover 10 minutes or until tender. Drain well, and set aside.

Combine cracker crumbs and remaining ingredients in a large bowl; stir well. Add eggplant, and stir gently to combine.

Pour eggplant mixture into a lightly greased 13- x 9- x 2-inch baking dish. Bake, uncovered, at 350° for 45 minutes or until golden. Yield: 8 to 10 servings.

Watch Hill Cooks
The Watch Hill Improvement Society
Watch Hill, Rhode Island

Peas with Prosciutto

1 cup canned diluted chicken
  broth
2 (16-ounce) packages frozen
  English peas
1 medium onion, thinly sliced
  and separated into rings

3 tablespoons olive oil
¼ pound prosciutto, diced
½ teaspoon salt
¼ teaspoon pepper

Bring chicken broth to a boil in a large saucepan over high heat; add peas, and return to a boil. Cover, reduce heat, and simmer 5 to 10 minutes or until peas are tender. Drain well, and set aside.

Sauté onion in oil in a skillet over medium heat until tender. Add prosciutto; sauté 3 minutes. Stir in peas, salt, and pepper. Serve immediately. Yield: 8 servings.   Jackie Locati Pancake

The Walla Walla Italian Heritage Association Cookbook
Walla Walla Italian Heritage Association
Walla Walla, Washington

Cheesy Scalloped Potatoes

5 medium-size baking potatoes,
  peeled and cut into ¼-inch-
  thick slices
12 slices bacon, cooked and
  crumbled
½ cup sliced green onions
3 tablespoons butter or
  margarine
2 tablespoons all-purpose flour

2 cups half-and-half
1 large clove garlic, crushed
1 bay leaf
¼ teaspoon salt
¼ teaspoon celery seeds
¼ teaspoon pepper
1½ cups (6 ounces) shredded
  Cheddar cheese

Cook potato slices, covered, in boiling water to cover 5 minutes; drain well. Place potato slices in a greased 13- x 9- x 2-inch baking dish. Sprinkle with bacon and green onions; set aside.

Melt butter in a heavy saucepan over low heat; add flour, stirring until smooth. Cook 1 minute, stirring constantly. Gradually add half-and-half; cook over medium heat, stirring constantly, until mixture is slightly thickened and bubbly. Add crushed garlic and next 5 ingredients, stirring until cheese melts. Remove and discard bay leaf.

Pour cheese sauce over reserved potato slices. Cover and bake at 350° for 30 minutes. Remove cover, and bake an additional 15 minutes or until potato is tender and mixture is lightly browned. Yield: 6 to 8 servings.   Joanne Edmiston

The Two Billion Dollar Cookbook
Volunteers engaged in the Alaskan oil-spill cleanup
Anchorage, Alaska

Garlic Potatoes

4 cloves garlic, crushed
¼ cup plus 2 tablespoons
  butter or margarine, melted
4 large baking potatoes, peeled
  (about 3 pounds)

¾ cup grated Parmesan cheese,
  divided
½ teaspoon salt
½ teaspoon pepper

Sauté garlic in melted butter in a small skillet over medium heat 1 minute; set aside.

Cut potatoes in half lengthwise; cut into ¼-inch-thick slices. Rinse potato slices; drain well on paper towels. Place potato slices in a large bowl. Add garlic, ¼ cup plus 2 tablespoons cheese, salt, and pepper; stir gently to combine. Spoon mixture into a greased 13- x 9- x 2-inch baking dish. Sprinkle with remaining ¼ cup plus 2 tablespoons cheese. Bake at 400° for 30 to 35 minutes or until golden. Yield: 8 servings.   Kathy Charboneau

Bakers' Secrets
Edison Women's Club
Akron, Ohio

Party Potatoes

8 to 10 medium-size baking
 potatoes, peeled and
 quartered
1 (8-ounce) package cream
 cheese, softened
1 (8-ounce) carton sour cream

Garlic salt to taste
Freeze-dried chives to taste
Dried parsley flakes to taste
Butter or margarine, melted
Paprika

Cook potato, covered, in boiling water to cover 15 minutes or until tender. Drain well; mash potato in a medium mixing bowl. Add cream cheese and next 4 ingredients; beat at medium speed of an electric mixer just until smooth.

Spoon potato mixture into a 1½-quart casserole; brush with melted butter. Sprinkle with paprika. Bake at 350° for 30 minutes. Yield: 6 to 8 servings.   Linda Wintter

25 Years of Cooking at Green Valley Baptist Church
Green Valley Baptist Church
Birmingham, Alabama

Potato Casserole Supreme

9 medium-size baking potatoes,
 peeled and quartered
⅔ cup milk
½ cup butter or margarine,
 softened
1½ to 2 teaspoons salt

¼ teaspoon pepper
1½ cups (6 ounces) shredded
 Cheddar cheese
1 cup whipping cream,
 whipped

Cook potato, covered, in boiling water to cover 15 minutes or until tender. Drain; mash in a mixing bowl. Add milk, butter, salt, and pepper; beat at medium speed of an electric mixer until smooth. Spoon potato mixture into a lightly greased 13- x 9- x 2-inch baking dish. Fold cheese into whipped cream, and spread over potato mixture. Bake at 350° for 25 minutes or until lightly browned. Yield: 10 servings.   Hon. and Mrs. Roger J. Robach

The TV-10 Big Brothers/Big Sisters Cookbook
Big Brothers/Big Sisters of Greater Rochester, New York

Apricot-Glazed Yams

1 (29-ounce) can yams, drained
1 (16-ounce) can apricot
   halves, undrained
3 tablespoons brown sugar
1 tablespoon cornstarch

¼ teaspoon salt
⅛ teaspoon ground cinnamon
⅓ cup golden raisins
3 tablespoons dry sherry
¼ teaspoon grated orange rind

Place yams in an 11- x 7- x 1½-inch baking dish. Drain apricots, reserving syrup. Arrange apricots over yams.

Combine sugar, cornstarch, salt, and cinnamon in a medium saucepan. Add water to reserved syrup to equal 1 cup. Add syrup and raisins to cornstarch mixture, stirring well. Bring to a boil over medium heat; stir in sherry and orange rind. Pour syrup mixture over yams and apricots. Bake, uncovered, at 350° for 20 minutes, basting occasionally. Yield: 4 servings.   Heather Kay

Culinary Briefs
The San Francisco Lawyers' Wives
San Francisco, California

Butterscotch Yams

2 (16-ounce) cans yams,
   drained and quartered
½ cup firmly packed brown
   sugar
½ cup corn syrup

¼ cup whipping cream
2 tablespoons butter or
   margarine
½ teaspoon salt
½ teaspoon ground cinnamon

Arrange yams in a single layer in an 11- x 7- x 1½-inch baking dish. Bake at 325° for 10 minutes.

Combine sugar and remaining ingredients in a saucepan; stir well. Bring to a boil over medium heat; boil 5 minutes, stirring constantly. Pour syrup mixture over yams; bake an additional 20 minutes, basting frequently. Yield: 6 servings.   Estella Tscherter

Batter's Up!
Rembrandt Area Craft Club
Rembrandt, Iowa

Spinach and Artichoke Casserole

1 (14-ounce) can artichoke
  hearts, drained and halved
3 (10-ounce) packages frozen
  chopped spinach
1 (8-ounce) package cream
  cheese
¼ cup butter or margarine
¼ teaspoon garlic salt

¼ teaspoon salt
⅛ teaspoon pepper
2 tablespoons grated Parmesan
  cheese
½ cup soft breadcrumbs
1 tablespoon butter or
  margarine, melted

Arrange artichokes in a greased 1-quart casserole, and set aside.

Cook spinach according to package directions; drain well. Combine spinach and next 5 ingredients, stirring until cream cheese and butter melt. Spoon spinach mixture evenly over artichokes; sprinkle with Parmesan cheese.

Combine breadcrumbs and 1 tablespoon butter; sprinkle evenly over casserole. Bake at 350° for 30 minutes or until lightly browned. Yield: 6 servings.   Romona Shannon

Plug in to Good Cooking
The National Management Association Corporate Headquarters
Chapter of Alabama Power Company
Birmingham, Alabama

Spinach, Chinese Style

4 bunches fresh spinach (about
  2¾ pounds)
3 tablespoons vegetable oil

1 clove garlic, crushed
½ teaspoon soy sauce
¼ teaspoon sugar

Remove stems from spinach; wash leaves thoroughly, and pat dry. Tear spinach into bite-sized pieces. Heat oil in a large Dutch oven or wok over high heat. Add garlic; sauté 1 minute. Add spinach; stir until coated with oil. Add soy sauce and sugar; sauté 2 minutes. Serve immediately. Yield: 6 servings.   Elaine Wong

Tea and Chopsticks
The Desert Jade Woman's Club
Phoenix, Arizona

Tomato-Zucchini Scallop

2 small zucchini, sliced (about 1 pound)
2 small tomatoes, peeled and diced
1 medium onion, thinly sliced
1 cup plain croutons

¾ teaspoon salt
Dash of pepper
1 medium tomato, cut into wedges
1 cup (4 ounces) shredded sharp Cheddar cheese

Place half of zucchini slices in a 1½-quart casserole. Top with half of diced tomato, onion, croutons, salt, and pepper. Repeat layers once; top with tomato wedges. Cover and bake at 350° for 1 hour. Remove cover, and sprinkle with cheese. Bake an additional 5 minutes or until cheese melts. Serve immediately. Yield: 6 servings.   Geneive Kimm

Favorite Recipes of Edmonds
Edmonds United Methodist Women
Edmonds, Washington

Quick Corn and Zucchini Sauté

2 medium zucchini, sliced
1 medium-size sweet red pepper, cut into julienne strips
1 medium-size green pepper, cut into julienne strips

¼ cup vegetable oil
2 cups frozen whole kernel corn, thawed
1 teaspoon garlic salt
½ teaspoon dried Italian seasoning

Sauté zucchini and peppers in oil in a large skillet 5 minutes or until crisp-tender. Add corn, garlic salt, and Italian seasoning, and sauté 3 to 5 minutes or until corn is crisp-tender. Yield: 6 to 8 servings.   Carla Nowag

Grrr-eat Grub
Faith Bible Fellowship
Huston, Alaska

Zucchini Baked in Sour Cream

6 small zucchini, cut into
½-inch-thick slices
1 cup (4 ounces) shredded
Cheddar cheese
⅔ cup sour cream
1 tablespoon butter or
margarine, melted

½ teaspoon salt
3 tablespoons fine, dry
breadcrumbs
2 tablespoons grated Parmesan
cheese

Cook zucchini in small amount of boiling water in a large saucepan 6 minutes or until tender; drain. Place zucchini in a 1½-quart casserole; set aside.

Combine cheese, sour cream, butter, and salt in a small saucepan; cook over medium-low heat until cheese melts, stirring constantly. Pour cheese sauce over reserved zucchini.

Combine breadcrumbs and Parmesan cheese; sprinkle over casserole. Bake, uncovered, at 375° for 10 to 12 minutes or until lightly browned. Yield: 6 servings.   Phyllis Ambrose

Old Capital Cookbook
Monterey History and Art Association
Monterey, California

Steamed Spaghetti Squash
with Fresh Tomatoes

4 large tomatoes, seeded and
chopped
½ cup Niçoise or other small
ripe olives
¼ cup plus 1 tablespoon olive
oil
¼ cup fresh basil leaves, cut
into julienne strips

3 to 4 green onions, chopped
2 cloves garlic, minced
2 tablespoons red wine vinegar
¼ teaspoon pepper
1 (4-pound) spaghetti squash
1½ cups (6 ounces) shredded
mozzarella cheese

Combine first 8 ingredients in a large bowl; stir well. Cover and let stand at room temperature 1 hour.

Wash squash; cut in half lengthwise. Remove and discard seeds and membranes. Place squash, cut side down, in a large Dutch oven. Pour water into Dutch oven to a depth of 2 inches. Bring to a boil; cover, reduce heat, and simmer 20 to 25 minutes or until squash is tender. Drain squash, and let cool 5 minutes. Remove spaghetti-like strands with a fork. Combine squash strands and reserved tomato mixture; toss gently. Sprinkle with cheese, and serve immediately. Yield: 8 servings.

Stirring Performances
The Junior League of Winston-Salem, North Carolina

Baked Butternut Squash

**5 to 6 carrots, scraped and
   sliced**
**1 large butternut squash
   (about 1 pound)**
1 egg, beaten
**½ cup firmly packed brown
   sugar**

**2 tablespoons butter or
   margarine**
½ teaspoon salt
1 tablespoon brown sugar

Cook carrot in a small amount of boiling water until crisp-tender; drain well, and set aside.

Cut squash in half lengthwise; remove and discard seeds and membranes. Place squash, cut side down, in a large Dutch oven. Pour water into Dutch oven to a depth of 2 to 3 inches. Bring to a boil; cover, reduce heat, and simmer until tender. Drain well, and let cool.

Scoop pulp into a large bowl, and discard shells. Mash pulp. Add egg, ½ cup brown sugar, butter, and salt; stir well.

Spoon squash mixture into a buttered 11- x 7- x 1½-inch baking dish. Toss reserved carrot with 1 tablespoon brown sugar. Arrange carrot mixture over squash mixture. Bake, uncovered, at 350° for 30 to 45 minutes. Yield: 4 to 6 servings.   Rosalie Coughenour

Flenniken's Favorites
The Flenniken Public Library
Carmichaels, Pennsylvania

Acknowledgments

The editors salute the three national and six regional winners of the 1991 Tabasco® Community Cookbook Awards competition sponsored by McIlhenny Company, Avery Island, Louisiana. **First Place Winner:** *Come On In!,* Junior League of Jackson, Mississippi; **Second Place Winner:** *Preserving Our Italian Heritage,* Sons of Italy Foundation, Tampa, Florida; **Third Place Winner:** *Cranbrook Reflections,* Cranbrook House & Gardens, Bloomfield Hills, Michigan; **New England:** *Boston Cooks,* Women's Educational and Industrial Union, Boston, Massachusetts; **Mid-Atlantic:** *Settings,* Junior League of Philadelphia, Pennsylvania; **South:** *A Centennial Sampler,* American Association of University Women (Elkins Branch), Elkins, West Virginia; **Midwest:** *German Heritage Recipes Cookbook,* American/Schleswig-Holstein Heritage Society, LeClaire, Iowa; **Southwest:** *Potluck on the Pedernales,* Community Garden Club of Johnson City, Texas; and **West:** *Cooking With All Your Faculties,* Faculty Auxiliary of the University of Washington, Seattle, Washington.

Special thanks to Dot Gibson and Ellen Rolfes for their continuing efforts to promote the sale of community cookbooks throughout America. While each of the cookbooks listed below is represented by recipes appearing in *America's Best Recipes 1992,* the editors also included descriptions of several of these fund-raising volumes to give a sampling of the diverse nature of the books and organizations represented. Unless otherwise noted, the copyright is held by the sponsoring organization whose mailing address is included below.

25 Years of Cooking at Green Valley Baptist Church, Green Valley Baptist Church, 1815 Patton Chapel Rd., Birmingham, AL 35226

100th Anniversary Cookbook, Auxiliary of Harrisburg Hospital, 17 S. Market Sq., P.O. Box 8700, Harrisburg, PA 17105

10,000 Tastes of Minnesota, Woman's Club of Minneapolis, 410 Oak Grove St., Minneapolis, MN 55403

Alaska's Cooking, Volume II, Anchorage Woman's Club, P.O. Box 100273, Anchorage, AK 99510

Angel Fare, Ladies Benevolent Association, Christ Episcopal Church, 407 E. Seneca St., Manlius, NY 13104

Bakers' Secrets, Edison Women's Club, 76 S. Main St., Akron, OH, 44308

Batter's Up!, Rembrandt Area Craft Club, 101 E. Main, Rembrandt, IA 50576

Bergan Family Favorites, Archbishop Bergan Mercy Hospital, 7500 Mercy Rd., Omaha, NE 61824

Best Friends, Terranova West Women's Club, 17806 Asphodel Ln., Spring, TX 77379

The Best Recipes of Green Valley United Methodist Women, Green Valley United Methodist Women, 620 E. Turkeyfoot Rd., Akron, OH 44319

The Best Specialties of the House . . . and More, North Suburban Guild of Children's Memorial Medical Center, 243 Aspen Ln., Highland Park, IL 60035

Birthright Sampler, Birthright of Johnstown, Inc., 607 Main St., Johnstown, PA 15901

Bless This Food, Man Does Not Live by Art Alone, New Mexico Alliance for Arts Education, P.O. Box 870, Los Alamos, NM 87544

Break Bread with the Black Belt, Black Belt Ministries, P.O. Drawer T, Demopolis, AL 36732

The Broker's Cookbook, Second Edition, The Robinson-Humphrey Company, Inc., 3333 Peachtree Rd. NE, Atlanta, GA 30326

The Cajun Connection Cookbook, Trinity Catholic School Booster Club, 201 Gary St., P.O. Box 438, St. Martinville, LA 70582

Camellia Delights, Altrusa Club of Gulfport, Inc., 911 S. Wanda Pl., Gulfport, MS 39501

Capital Classics, Junior League of Washington, DC, 3039 M Street NW, Washington, DC 20007

Cardinal Cuisine, Mount Vernon Hospital Auxiliary, 2501 Parker's Ln., Alexandria, VA 22306

Celebrate, Missouri Bankers Association, P.O. Box 1338, Jefferson City, MO 65102

The Center of Attention Cookbook, Medical Center Foundation, 1000 Dutch Ridge Rd., Beaver, PA 15009
A Century of Good Cooking, Waldoboro Woman's Club, P.O. Box 607, Waldoboro, ME 04572
Chef's EscORT, Women's American ORT, Southeast District, 2101 E. Hallandale Beach Blvd., Ste. 301,
    Hallandale, FL 33009
Cohasset Entertains, Encore, Community Garden Club of Cohasset, P.O. Box 502, Cohasset, MA 02025
Come and Get It!, Junior Welfare League of Talladega, P.O. Box 331, Talladega, AL 35160
Command Performances, Southwest Virginia Opera Society, 111 W. Campbell Ave., Roanoke, VA 24011
Company's Coming, Junior League of Kansas City, 4651 Roanoke Pkwy., Kansas City, MO 64112
Connecticut Cooks III, American Cancer Society, Connecticut Division, Inc., 14 Village Ln., P.O. Box 410,
    Wallingford, CT 06492
cook and love it more, Lovett Parent Association, The Lovett School, 4075 Paces Ferry Rd. NW, Atlanta, GA 30327
The Cookbook, East Lake United Methodist Church, 7753 1st Ave. S, Birmingham, AL 35206
Cookbook to benefit the Homeless, Lutheran Social Services of Southern California, 2882 Arlington Ave.,
    Riverside, CA 92506
Cookin' with the Crusaders, Most Holy Redeemer Inter-Parochial School, 302 E. Linebaugh Ave., Tampa,
    FL 33612
Cooking by Male, Greater Pittsburgh Commission for Women, 428 Forbes Ave., 250 Lawyers Bldg., Pittsburgh,
    PA 15219
Cooking Elementary Style, Ridgedale Elementary School PTA, 2900 Ridgedale Rd., Knoxville, TN 37921
Cooking with Love, For Love of Children Foster Home Management Board, 415 U St. NW, Washington,
    DC 20001
Cooking with Vinson Memorial Christian Church, Vinson Memorial Christian Church, 3800 Piedmont Rd.,
    Huntington, WV 25704
Cooks and Company, Muscle Shoals District Service League, P.O. Box 793, Sheffield, AL 35660
Crossroads Cuisine, Winona Manor Christmas Fund, P.O. Box 158, Kilmichael, MS 39747
Culinary Briefs, San Francisco Lawyers' Wives, 101 St. Francis Blvd., San Francisco, CA 94127
Delaware DAR Historical Cookbook, Delaware State Society, Daughters of the American Revolution, 3205 Falcon
    Ln. #217, Wilmington, DE 19808
Delectable Edibles from the Livable Forest, Kingwood Women's Club, P.O. Box 5411, Kingwood, TX 77325
Dining with the Daughters, Daughters of Hawaii, 2913 Pali Hwy., Honolulu, HI 96817
East Cooper Cuisine, Christ Our King Ladies Club, 1122 Russell Dr., Mt. Pleasant, SC 29464
eating, First Lutheran Church, 6400 State Line Rd., Mission Hills, KS 66208
Evening Shade, Future Homemakers of America, Evening Shade High School, P.O. Box 240, Evening Shade,
    AR 72532
Extraordinary Cuisine for Sea & Shore, Seattle Yacht Club, 1807 E. Hamlin St., Seattle, WA 98112
The Family Affair, Lincolnshire Community Nursery School, 30 Riverwoods Rd., Lincolnshire, IL 60069
Family Secrets . . . the Best of the Delta, Lee Academy , 415 Lee Dr., Clarksdale, MS 38614
Favorite Recipes from Union Baptist Church Cooks, Union Baptist Church, 816 Tyler Ave., Tylertown, MS 39667
Favorite Recipes of Edmonds, Edmonds United Methodist Women, 828 Caspers St., Edmonds, WA 98020
Favorite Recipes of the Episcopal Churches on the Kenai, Episcopal Churches on the Kenai, P.O. Box 7068, Nikiski,
    AK 99635
Feeding Your Neighbor, Neighbor to Neighbor, 1419 Pine St., Pine Bluff, AR 71601
Fellowship Favorites from First Presbyterian, First Presbyterian Church, 4th and Fairview, Downers Grove,
    IL 60515
The Fine Art of Cooking, Women's Committee of the Philadelphia Museum of Art, P.O. Box 7646,
    Philadelphia, PA 19101
First Gentleman's Cookbook, Governor's Mansion Restoration Foundation, 1425 H St., Lincoln, NE 68505
Flenniken's Favorites, Flenniken Public Library, 102 George St., Carmichaels, PA 15901
For Crying Out Loud . . . Let's Eat!, Service League of Hammond, P.O. Box 4442, Hammond, IN 46324
The Fort Leavenworth Recollection, Fort Leavenworth Officers' & Civilians' Wives' Club, P.O. Box 3004,
    Fort Leavenworth, KS 66027

Frantic Elegance, Arendell Parrott Academy, P.O. Box 1314, Kinston, NC 28501

Friends Come in All Flavors, Buckingham Friends School, P.O. Box 158, Lahaska, PA 18931

From a Lighthouse Window, Chesapeake Bay Maritime Museum, P.O. Box 636, St. Michaels, MD 21663

"From the Heart of the Teche," Jeanerette Chamber of Commerce, 500 E. Main St., P.O. Box 31, Jeanerette, LA 70544

The Galloping Chef, Combined Training Equestrian Team Alliance, 750 Whiskey Hill Rd., Woodside, CA 94062

Gateways, Auxiliary-Twigs . . . Friends of St. Louis Children's Hospital, 400 S. Kingshighway, St. Louis, MO 63110

Good Cookin' from Giffin, Giffin Elementary School PTA, Beech St., Knoxville, TN 37920

Gracious Goodness, Penn Laurel Girl Scout Council, 1600 Mt. Zion Rd., York, PA 17402

Gracious Goodness: The Taste of Memphis, Memphis Symphony League, 3100 Walnut Grove Rd., Ste. 402, Memphis, TN 38111

Greetings from Atlantic City, Ruth Newman Shapiro Cancer and Heart Fund, 2024 Pacific Ave., Atlantic City, NJ 08401

Grrr-eat Grub, Faith Bible Fellowship, 3200 Whispering Wood Dr., Wasilla, AK 99654

Harrington Cooks, Harrington Homemakers, Box 447, Harrington, WA 99134

Harvest of Home Cookin', Trailways Girl Scout Council, Inc., 1533 Spencer Rd., Joliet, IL 60433

He Shall Feed His Flock, Church of the Good Shepherd, P.O. Box 25, Acton, MA 01720

Hearts & Flour, Women's Club of Pittsford, P.O. Box 208, Pittsford, NY 14534

Heavenly Delights, St. Mary's Catholic Church Christian Women, 225 S. Hartwell Ave., Waukesha, WI 53186

Historic Lexington Cooks: Rockbridge Regional Recipes, Historic Lexington Foundation, 8 E. Washington St., Lexington, VA 24450

Holiday Recipes, Gulf Pines Girl Scout Council, 500 Hutchison Ave., Hattiesburg, MS 39563

Holladay 7th Ward Cookbook, Holladay 7th Ward Relief Society, 4407 Fortuna Way, Salt Lake City, UT 84124

Home Cookin', "AT&T's Right Choices," Western Electric Council Telephone Pioneers of America, 1111 Woods Mill Rd., Ballwin, MO 63011

Home Cookin' is a Family Affair, New Life Ladies Fellowship, P.O. Box 654, Nashville, IN 47448

Honest to Goodness, Junior League of Springfield, Inc., P.O. Box 1736, Springfield, IL 62705

If All the World Were Apple Pie, Athens Mothers' Center, P.O. Box 7114, Athens, GA 30604

It's Our Serve!, Junior League of Long Island, 1395 Old Northern Blvd., Roslyn, NY 11576

Just Like Mom Used to Make, Northfield Community Nursery School, 285 Maple Row, Northfield, IL 60093

Kentucky Kitchens, Volume II, Telephone Pioneers of America, Kentucky Chapter No. 32, 534 Armory Pl. B-9, P.O. Box 32410, Louisville, KY 40232

Kettle's On, Cooking with Leaders, Burlington County Girl Scout Council, Inc., P.O. Box 438, Rancocas, NJ 08073

Kitchen Keys, Episcopal Church Women Organization of St. Peter's Parish Church, Rt. 1, Box 139A, New Kent, VA 23124

Kona Kitchens, Kona Outdoor Circle, 76-6280 Kuakini Hwy., Kailua-Kona, HI 96740

La Cucina Sammarinese, San Marino Ladies Auxiliary, 1685 E. Big Beaver Rd., Troy, MI 48083

Liberal Portions, Unitarian Universalist Church of Nashua, 58 Lowell St., Nashua, NH 03060

Literally Delicious, Abington Friends School Parents' Association, 575 Washington Ln., Jenkintown, PA 19046

Livre de Cuisine, Pikes Peak Region, American Culinary Federation, 1023 W. Pikes Peak Ave., Colorado Springs, CO 80904

The Longyear Cookbook, Longyear Historical Society & Museum, 120 Seaver St., Brookline, MA 02146

Marblehead Cooks, Tower School Associates, 61 W. Shore Dr., Marblehead, MA 01945

The Mark Twain Library Cookbook, Volume III, Mark Twain Library Association, P.O. Box 9, Redding, CT 06875

Methodist Blessings, United Methodist Women, First United Methodist Church, 119 Jefferson St., New Iberia, LA 70560

Montana 1889-1989 Centennial Cookbook, Inter-Denominational Christian Fellowship, P.O. Box 506, Noxon, MT 59853

More Than a Tea Party, Junior League of Boston, 117 Newbury St., Boston, MA 02116

Musical Tastes, Chancel and Bell Choir, First United Methodist Church , 101 E. Jefferson St., Charlottesville, VA 22901

North Dakota Family Favorites . . . a Collection of Recipes, Division of Continuing Studies, North Dakota State University, Fargo, ND 58105

Not Just Possum, Boy Scout Troop 63, Billups Dr., Columbus, MS 39701

Not So Secret Recipes, 4450th Tactical Group, Nellis Air Force Base, Las Vegas, NV 89115

Note-Worthy Recipes, Iowa Falls High School, 1903 N. Ave., Iowa Falls, IA 50126

Ocean County Fare and Bounty, Cookbook of the Jersey Shore, Ocean County Girl Scout Council of New Jersey, Inc., 1405 Old Freehold Rd., Toms River, NJ 08753

Old Capital Cookbook, Monterey History and Art Association, Ltd., 550 Calle Principal, P.O. Box 805, Monterey, CA 93942

"One Lump or Two?", All Children's Hospital Foundation, 801 5th St. S, P.O. Box 3142, St. Petersburg, FL 33731

Only in California, Children's Home Society of California, 2727 W. 6th St., Los Angeles, CA 90057

Oregon County Cookbook, Milwaukie Elementary School, 11250 SE 27th Ave., Milwaukie, OR 97222

Our Favorite Recipes, Hope Lutheran Church, P.O. Box 422, Moose Lake, MN 55767

Our Favorite Recipes, St. Anne's Roman Catholic Church , 648 S. Jones Ave., Rock Hill, SC 29730

Our Favorite Recipes, St. Stephen Catholic Community, 1603 N. Wind Ct., Winter Springs, FL 32708

Our Pet Recipes, Humane Society Calumet Area, Inc., 6546 Columbia Ave., Hammond, IN 46321

Out of This World, Wood Acres Elementary School, 5800 Cromwell Dr., Bethesda, MD 20816

Palate Pleasers II, Redeemer Women's Guild, 345 S. Kenilworth Ave., Elmhurst, IL 60126

People Food, Animal Rescue League of Southern Rhode Island, P.O. Box 458, Wakefield, RI 02880

Plug in to Good Cooking, National Management Association Corporate Headquarters Chapter of Alabama Power Company, P.O. Box 2641, Birmingham, AL 35291

Prairie Potpourri, North Iowa Girl Scout Council, 307 N. Monroe Ave., Mason City, IA 50401

Quick 'N Natural No Salt Low Cholesterol Cooking, San Fernando Valley Association for the Retarded, 15725 Parthenia St., Sepulveda, CA 91343

"R" Little Red School Cookbook, Cedar Falls Historical Society, 303 Franklin St., Cedar Falls, IA 50613

Recipes & Recollections from Terrace Hill, Terrace Hill Society, 2300 Grand Ave., Des Moines, IA 50212

Recipes to Come Home to, Oologah Area Chamber of Commerce, 105 S. Maple St., P.O. Box 109, Oologah, OK 74053

Return Engagement, Junior Board of the Quad City Symphony Orchestra Association, P.O. Box 1144, Davenport, IA 52805

RiverFeast: Still Celebrating Cincinnati, Junior League of Cincinnati, 3500 Columbia Pkwy., Cincinnati, OH 45208

RSVP: Fortress Monroe, Officers' and Civilians' Wives' Club, P.O. Box 114, Fort Monroe, VA 23651

St. Joseph's Regional School Cookbook, St. Joseph's Regional School, 132 44th St., Sea Isle City, NJ 08243

Savor the Flavor of Oregon, Junior League of Eugene, 2839 Willamette St., Eugene, OR 97405

Scotties Present Recipes, Grand Forks Curling Club, 1124 7 Ave. S, Grand Forks, ND 58201

Seasoned with Love, Eastman House, Inc., 1545 Pontiac Ave., Cranston, RI 02920

Seasoned with Love, Metro Women's Auxiliary, Marcy-Newberry Association, Inc., 1073 W. Maxwell St., Chicago, IL 60608

Seasoned with Love, Priest Lake Community Church, P.O. Box 422, Nordman, ID 83848

Seasoned with Sun, Junior League of El Paso, Inc., 520 Thunderbird, El Paso, TX 79912

Second Round, Tea-Time at the Masters®, Junior League of Augusta, Inc., P.O. Box 3232, Augusta, GA 30904

The Secret Ingredient, Cheer Guild of Indiana University Hospitals, Inc., 702 Barnhill Dr., Rm. 403, Indianapolis, IN 46202

Sharing Our Best from Friends of Franklin County, Big Brothers/Big Sisters of Franklin County, 116 Federal St., Greenfield, MA 01301

Sharing Recipes, St. John's Lutheran Church, 2477 W. Washington, Springfield, IL 62702

Simply Colorado, Colorado Dietetic Association, 6930 S. Bemis St., Littleton, CO 80120

Sound Seasonings, Junior League of Westchester on the Sound, Inc., P.O. Box 765, Larchmont, NY 10538

South Dakota Centennial Cookbook, South Dakota Historical Society, 900 Governor's Dr., Pierre, SD 57501

Spice and Spirit: The Complete Kosher Jewish Cookbook, Lubavitch Women's Organization, 852 Eastern Pkwy., Brooklyn, NY 11213

Spokane Cooks!© Northwest, Spokane Community Centers Foundation, E. 2500 Sprague, Spokane, WA 99202

Stirring Performances, Junior League of Winston-Salem, Inc., 909 S. Main St., Winston-Salem, NC 27101

Summer Magic, East Chop Association, Quality Living Publications, P.O. Box 1, Valle Crucis, NC 28691

Sunnyside Stars Sumptuous Savories, Sunnyside PTA, SW 1430 Wadleigh, Pullman, WA 99163

A Taste of Neoucom, Northeastern Ohio Universities College of Medicine, 4209 St. Rt. 44, Rootstown, OH 44272

A Taste of San Francisco, San Francisco Symphony, Davies Symphony Hall, San Francisco, CA 94102

Tastes in Plaid: Alamance County Entertains, Alamance County Historical Museum, Inc., Rt. 1, Box 71, Burlington, NC 27215

Tea and Chopsticks, Desert Jade Woman's Club, 10426 W. Harmont Dr., Peoria, AZ 85345

Three Rivers Cookbook, Volume III, Child Health Association of Sewickley, 1108 Ohio River Blvd., Sewickley, PA 15143

Thyme & Monet, Krasl Art Center, 707 Lake Blvd., St. Joseph, MI 49065

Thymes Remembered, Junior League of Tallahassee, Inc., 259-B John Knox Rd., Tallahassee, FL 32303

A Touch of Atlanta, Marist School, 3790 Ashford-Dunwoody Rd. NE, Atlanta, GA 30319

To Your Health!, West Haven Junior Woman's Club, Inc., P.O. Box 126, West Haven, CT 06877

Treasured Recipes, Ketchikan Volunteer Fire Department, 319 Main St., Ketchikan, AK 99901

Treasured Recipes from Mason, Ohio, Mason Historical Society, 207 W. Church St., P.O. Box 82, Mason, OH 45040

Treasured Recipes from Wellington Christian School, Parent Teacher Fellowship of Wellington Christian School, 1000 Wellington Tr., West Palm Beach, FL 33414

Treasured Recipes of the Past, Pomeroy Sesquicentennial Committee, 200 E. 2nd St., Pomeroy OH 45769

Trinity Episcopal School, Classroom Classics, Parents and Students of Trinity Episcopal School, 708 W. 2nd, Pine Bluff, AR 71601

The TV-10 Big Brothers/Big Sisters Cookbook, Big Brothers/Big Sisters of Greater Rochester, 12 Mortimer St., Rochester, NY 14604

The Two Billion Dollar Cookbook, Volunteers engaged in the Alaskan oil-spill cleanup, P.O. Box 242944, Anchorage, AK 99524

Udderly Delicious, Junior League of Racine, Inc., P.O. Box 1531, Racine, WI 53401

Vermont Kitchens Revisited, Women of the Cathedral Church of St. Paul, 2 Cherry St., Burlington, VT 05403

View Beyond the Park, Fairview Park Junior Women's Club, P.O. Box 26283, Fairview Park, OH 44126

The Walla Walla Italian Heritage Association Cookbook, Walla Walla Italian Heritage Association, P.O. Box 752, Walla Walla, WA 99362

Watch Hill Cooks, Watch Hill Improvement Society, Everett Ave., Watch Hill, RI 02891

The Western Gentlemen's Cookbook, Men's Culinary Cup, 326 Parsley Blvd., Cheyenne, WY 82007

What's Cooking in Cazenovia, St. James Women's Council, 4 Green St., Cazenovia, NY 13035

What's Cooking in Chagrin Falls, Chagrin Falls Parent Teacher Organization, 45 Heather Ct., Chagrin Falls, OH 44022

What the Winners Eat, Sugar Creek Swim Club, P.O. Box 31427, St. Louis, MO 63131

The When You Live in Hawaii You Get Very Creative During Passover Cookbook, Congregation Sof Ma'arav, P.O. Box 11154, Honolulu, HI 96828

Wish Upon a Star, Mt. Carmel Apparel Employees, RR #3, Box 9, Mt. Carmel, IL 62863

Wolf Point, Montana, 75th Jubilee Cookbook, Wolf Point Chamber of Commerce & Agriculture, 201 4th Ave. S, P.O. Box 237, Wolf Point, MT 59201

World Heritage of Cooking, Friends of the World Heritage Museum, 702 S. Wright St., 484 Lincoln Hall, Urbana, IL 61801

You Make the Best Better, Macoupin County 4-H Foundation, 210 N. Broad St., Carlinville, IL 62626

Index